Ted Williams in his rookie year, 1939.

THE

Ted Williams

READER

EDITED BY
LAWRENCE BALDASSARO

A FIRESIDE BOOK   Published by Simon & Schuster
New York   London   Toronto   Sydney   Tokyo   Singapore

FIRESIDE
Simon & Schuster Building
Rockefeller Center
1230 Avenue of the Americas
New York, New York, 10020

Manufactured in the United States of America

1   3   5   7   9   10   8   6   4   2

Library of Congress Cataloging in Publication Data

The Ted Williams reader / edited by Lawrence Baldassaro.
        p.   cm.
    "A Fireside book."
    ISBN 0-671-73536-5
    1. Williams, Ted, 1918–   . 2. Baseball players—United
States—Biography. 3. Boston Red Sox (Baseball team)—History.
        I. Baldassaro, Lawrence.
        GV865.W5T437   1991
        796.357′092—dc20
[B]   91-27679
                                                         CIP

Photo Credits

Frontispiece: National Baseball Library, Cooperstown, NY
Following acknowledgments: page 10 (top) Wide World Photos; *page 10
(bottom)* Courtesy Bettmann Archive; *page 11 (top and bottom)* Wide
World Photos.

Permissions start on page 296.

To my son,

Jim,

for the baseball memories we have shared,

including the batting lesson he got

from Ted Williams when he was five years old.

As long as he plays baseball, as long as he lives, perhaps as long as baseball itself lives, people will want to read about Ted Williams.

—Al Hirshberg, in "Handsome Bad Boy of the
Boston Red Sox"

CONTENTS

Acknowledgments 9

Preface 13

Introduction by Lawrence Baldassaro 15

Williams Case Grand Lesson by Bill Cunningham 29

As a Soph by Joe Williams 35

Ted Williams Blasts Boston by Austen Lake 38

Theodore Goes Mild by M. J. Brandt 44

Theodore the .400 Thumper by Jack Malaney 51

Williams' Head Start by Bill Bryson 61

The "Why" of Ted Williams by Bob Considine 66

Open Letter to Ted Williams by Grantland Rice 70

Two Guys Named Ted Williams by Ed Fitzgerald 76

Why We Pick on Ted Williams by Harold Kaese 116

Why I Would Trade Ted Williams by Joe Williams 125

Ted Undeserving of Fans' Tribute by Dave Egan 135

Return of the Master by Arthur Daley 139

Handsome Bad Boy of the Boston Red Sox by Al Hirshberg 143

Ted Is Hope by Robert Creamer 160

Ted Williams Spits by Red Smith 166

Sidetracked Again by Arthur Daley 170

The Ted Williams Miracle by Ed Linn 174

CONTENTS

•

How Ted Williams Became Popular by Mike Gillooly   188

Hub Fans Bid Kid Adieu by John Updike   201

The Kid's Last Game by Ed Linn   222

"Saint" Goes Marching In by Bud Collins   256

The Batter by Jimmy Cannon   259

Strictly Personal by Arthur Daley   263

The Kid Comes Back by Robert Lipsyte   267

Islamorada, Miramichi, Bangor, and Winter Haven by Thomas Boswell   270

The Necessary Shape of the Old-Timers' Game by Donald Hall   275

Couplet by Donald Hall   279

Williams: The Slugging Professor by Ira Berkow   280

Ted Williams by John Updike   284

An Evening with The Kid by Ira Berkow   289

Source List   293

ACKNOWLEDGMENTS

What was from the beginning a labor of love was made even less burdensome by the many people who assisted me in a variety of ways. To each of them I express my sincere gratitude.

For their suggestions and encouragement I thank Tom Begner, Dick Johnson, Bob Lindsay, Luke Salisbury, Glenn Stout, John Thorn, and Ed Walton.

The staff at the Hall of Fame Library in Cooperstown was, as always, generous in sharing their resources and expertise. Special thanks go to Tom Heitz, Bill Deane, and Pat Kelly.

I am grateful to my colleagues at the University of Wisconsin—Milwaukee, John Koethe and Ron Snyder, for their helpful comments, and Mel Friedman, for giving me my first opportunity to write about Ted Williams. Thanks also to Darlene Hagopian and Sally Gendron for their invaluable clerical assistance.

A long-standing debt of gratitude is owed to my mother, Olive, and my late father, Gerald, who first nurtured my love for baseball in general and for the Red Sox in particular.

Finally, a special note of thanks to my editor, Ed Walters, and his assistant, Dave Dunton, for their patient and knowledgeable guidance throughout this project.

With Joe DiMaggio, following Williams' game-winning home run
in the 1941 All-Star Game

Williams in 1957 contemplating a third Triple Crown

Williams crossing home plate after hitting a home run
in the final at-bat of his career, 1960

Williams with Carl Yastrzemski at Red Sox spring training, 1983

PREFACE

It has become an unchallenged commonplace that baseball has inspired more good writing than any other sport. The premise of this anthology is that Ted Williams has been the subject of more of that good writing than any other individual in baseball. The wealth of material written about him—in newspapers, magazines, and books—throughout his career, and beyond, attests both to his appeal and his uncommon longevity, both as an athlete and as an American icon. In an era in which the rapid and frequent creation, and disposal, of "superstars" by the media has trivialized the very concept of a hero, Ted Williams stands as a reminder of a time in our recent past when there were more enduring legends.

He has been one of the most colorful and controversial figures in the history of American sports. It follows that not everything written about him has been complimentary or flattering. Far from it. He was knocked down by writers far more often than he ever was by opposing pitchers. This collection attempts to reflect the variety of opinions and sentiments Williams has evoked over the years. In choosing the selections I have also attempted to provide a chronological panorama of Williams' life in baseball, from his early days as a legend in the making to his current status as a revered elder statesman of baseball.

Unlike a biography, this collection does not provide a retrospective summary from a single point of view. Instead, it offers a kaleidoscope of contemporary profiles sketched by many voices over a span of fifty years. No single essay can capture the essence of the half century of Ted Williams' life in baseball, or of his complex personality. Taken as a whole, these essays provide a vivid portrait of a genuine American hero, a rugged frontier individualist, but one with a quick wit and a sharp tongue.

I have compiled this collection as an expression of my abiding passion for baseball, and for the good prose it has inspired, and as a token of gratitude to Williams himself, whose artistry as a player provided some of the great memories of my youth. It is my hope that this work will not only rekindle the same kinds of memories for those who grew up admiring his talent as a hitter, but will also bring him to life for those too young to remember him as a player and who know him only as a legend.

INTRODUCTION

"It was the center of my heart, hitting a baseball."
—Ted Williams, in *My Turn at Bat*

Long before the age of media hype, self-promotion, and television saturation, Ted Williams was a genuine—and controversial—celebrity. From the beginning of his career he attracted the attention of sportswriters, as much for his colorful personality as for his obvious talent as a hitter. A true original, he defied the unwritten code that decreed that American heroes, in the mold of Frank Merriwell, were to be modest, self-effacing, and polite. Instead he was outspoken, brash, and often tempestuous.

An essential element of his complex personality—one which explains in part his appeal, both negative and positive—was his intense desire to be the absolute best at what he did. In his acceptance speech at the Hall of Fame induction ceremonies in 1966, Williams expressed what could be taken as the summation of his uncompromising approach not only to baseball, but to life in general: "Baseball gives every American boy a chance to excel, not just to be as good as someone else, but to be better. This is the nature of man and the name of the game."

Ted Williams took that natural desire to excel to its

logical conclusion. Early in his career he announced, with a brashness that was characteristic of his youth, that his goal was to have people say one day: "There goes Ted Williams, the greatest hitter who ever lived." He would settle for nothing less than being *the* best. And today there are many who willingly acknowledge that he reached that goal. Most baseball experts who have ventured to make a final choice consider only Babe Ruth as a serious contender for the title. In virtually every statistical analysis measuring all-around hitting ability (power and average), including the sophisticated compilations devised in recent years by sabermetricians, Ruth and Williams rank first and second. (At the 1989 induction ceremony at Cooperstown, within 100 yards of the Babe's Hall of Fame plaque, George Grande—a Yankee announcer, no less—unreservedly introduced Ted Williams as the greatest hitter of all time.)

While his status as the greatest hitter ever may be open to debate, the fact remains that he is the only man to hit .400 in the last half century. Since World War II, in fact, only five players have hit .370 or better, one of them being Williams himself with his .388 average in 1957. His lifetime batting average of .344 is the sixth highest ever among players with at least 4000 at bats, his slugging average of .634 is second only to that of Ruth, and his on-base percentage of .483 is the highest in baseball history. Only he and Rogers Hornsby have ever won the Triple Crown twice. He led the league in home runs and runs batted in four times each. He won six batting titles, losing a seventh in 1949 to George Kell by a fraction of a percentage point; in two other years (1954 and 1955) he led the league in hitting, but walks and injuries deprived him of the minimum four hundred at-bats needed to qualify for the title.

It is unfair, and impossible, to judge Williams by statistics alone, since he lost three years to World War II, almost two years to the Korean War, and almost half of two other seasons because of injuries. At the very least he is acknowledged as the greatest hitter of his era, the standard by which all hitters of the postwar period are measured. In 1960, *The Sporting News* named him "Player of the Decade." Even though Williams was forty-two at the time, he was chosen, by acclamation, over such stars as Mantle, Mays, and Banks, young men in the prime of their careers. When *Sports Illustrated* published a story on April 16, 1990, comparing the quality of baseball in 1990 with that of 1950, the magazine put a picture of Williams on the cover and titled the story "Was It a Better Game in Ted's Day?".

There is a kind of ironic justice to the recognition now accorded Williams. While he worked tirelessly to become the greatest hitter ever, he stubbornly refused to curry favor from those who would ultimately have to be the ones to bestow that title on him—the fans and the sportswriters. His career-long refusal to tip his hat to the fans (even after hitting a home run in his last time at bat), his harsh responses (both in word and gesture) to those fans who taunted him from Fenway's left-field stands, and his spitting episodes in 1956 are legendary. In spite of those transgressions the vast majority of Red Sox fans adored him. Williams himself acknowledged as much during the pregame ceremonies of his final game at Fenway in 1960. "If someone should ask me the one place I would like to play if I had to do it all over again," he said, "I would say Boston, for it has the greatest owner in baseball and the greatest fans in America."

His relationship with the press—the very people who decide who gets to be MVP and who gets into the Hall of Fame—was something else. To the end he was unable to make peace with many of them. During those same pregame ceremonies in 1960 he sarcastically dubbed them "the knights of the keyboard." His disdain was strongest for the

Boston writers. In his 1969 autobiography, *My Turn at Bat,* he succinctly summed up his opinion: "I think without question that Boston had the worst bunch of writers who ever came down the pike in baseball." He has, on other occasions, been more generous in his appraisal of the Boston press, claiming that only a handful had been unfair to him.

No one has come up with a conclusive explanation of how the feud between Williams and the press began. Some would attribute it to Williams' volatile temperament, or to his stubborn refusal to cooperate. It has also been suggested that Williams was the victim of a subscription war among Boston's numerous newspapers, whose editors were pressing their writers to come up with as much dirt as possible in order to attract more readers than the competition. Whatever the reason—hungry writers or Williams' own temperament—he would remain throughout his career a favorite subject—and target—of sportswriters. In the category of colorful sources of newsprint, not even Ruth was his equal.

From the moment he first appeared on the major league scene his outspoken, volatile behavior stirred the imagination of sportswriters. He amused, angered, charmed, frustrated, and otherwise fascinated baseball analysts, who have been trying ever since to understand and explain his complex character. Many were more interested in analyzing his psyche than his swing. In 1949 Harold Kaese wrote: "In Boston, a man does not qualify as a baseball writer until he has psychoanalyzed Ted Williams."

Writers were constantly trying to peer behind the Williams mask, a difficult task made even more difficult by the variety of masks he assumed in public. He could be alternately charming or surly, cooperative or reclusive, friendly or belligerent. But he was never dull, and for that the writers devoured him. Great athletes who have little to say may generate impressive statistics for the record books, but they rarely provide good copy. Ted Williams gave sportswriters the best of both worlds: heroic exploits on the field, plus a volatile temperament and a willingness to say what was on his mind, whatever the consequences.

Williams himself understood the ultimate futility of writers' efforts to "explain" him, pointing out in *My Turn at Bat:* "I was and am too complex a personality, too much a confusion of boyish enthusiasm and bitter experience to be completely understood by everybody."

Part of that complex personality was his almost obsessive dedication to becoming the best. The single-minded and unashamed commitment to greatness implicit in that goal would, over the course of his career, earn him the respect and admiration of his fans, as well as the scorn of his detractors. The independent spirit that drove him to be the best at what he did also guaranteed that he would run afoul of at least some of those whose job it was to report on his relentless pursuit of perfection. It was as if his public declaration of his private passion for excellence were an invitation to closer scrutiny. Some writers apparently thought that anyone so dedicated to perfection in his profession deserved to be reprimanded for failing to achieve it in any other aspect of his life. Everything about Williams' professional and private life became fair game. For all his greatness as a player, he was often vilified by the press, who accused him of any number of professional and personal flaws.

It was a curiously symbiotic relationship. On the one hand, some writers exploited Williams' sensitivity to criticism, knowing that his angry response to what they wrote would provide material for yet another column or story. Williams, in turn, seemed to thrive on his own anger. The same rage that vented itself in outbursts of profanity against reporters in the locker room was somehow channeled inside the batter's box into controlled intensity and heightened performance that served as vengeance against his critics.

Ted Williams was many things to those who wrote about him. The points of view expressed by his chroniclers were as varied as the nicknames he spawned: The Kid, The Splendid Splinter, The Thumper, Teddy Ballgame, Terrible Ted. Of all the nicknames, the one that stuck, and the one that appears repeatedly in the articles and columns written about him, is "The Kid." To his detractors it provided a convenient epithet to sum up their perception of him as a petulant adult who never outgrew his adolescence. To others it captured the essence of his endless exuberance for the act of hitting a baseball.

There is no question that Williams paid a price for his refusal to play by the rules of celebrity that were in effect during his playing days. By not adhering to those standards he sacrificed the right to eternal adulation by the press. One need only compare Williams' press coverage with the more benign and respectful treatment given to his more taciturn and cooperative contemporary, Joe DiMaggio, whom the New York writers helped make into the archetypal American hero of his era. A writer of the stature of Jimmy Cannon might go to nightclubs with Joe DiMaggio, but he would not tell his readers about it the next day.

The most obvious example of the discrepancy came in 1947, when Williams, in spite of winning the Triple Crown, lost the Most Valuable Player award to DiMaggio by one vote. Williams hit .343, with 32 home runs and 114 runs batted in; DiMaggio's average was .315, with 20 homers and 97 runs batted in. Even granting that DiMaggio played for the pennant winner, Williams' superior performance would seem to have merited the award. Yet one of the twenty-four voting writers did not even include Williams among the ten candidates he was allowed to list. A tenth-place vote for Williams, worth one point, would have created a tie, and a ninth-place vote would have given him the award. Then, in 1957, in spite of a season that was remarkable for a player of *any* age, Williams again finished second to a Yankee, this time to Mickey Mantle, whose average was twenty-three points lower and who hit four fewer home runs. Even Mantle expressed surprise at the decision. And again, as in 1947, it appeared that personal animosity had prevailed over objective judgment; two of the voting writers (neither one from Boston) had placed Williams ninth and tenth on their ballots.

While Williams did feud with, and was disliked by, a fair number of writers, there were also those he respected and who, in turn, liked and admired him, and who celebrated his greatness as a player without deifying him as a human being. It is from these writers (including such legends as Grantland Rice, Arthur Daley, and Red Smith) that we get some of the best—and most honest—portraits. Then, too, there are those chroniclers of baseball who are not professional sportswriters, writers of the caliber of John Updike and Donald Hall, who have provided a perspective on Williams from outside the locker room.

The filtering lens of nostalgia likes to soften the hard edges of reality. The writing in this collection often brings those hard edges back into focus and reminds even the most loyal of fans that memories of Ted Williams can be bittersweet. He elicited mixed emotions not only from the journalists who were paid to write about him, but also from the fans who paid to see him play.

How or when I became a Red Sox fan is not at all clear to me. It was, I think, pretty much an accident of birth. Just about everybody in Massachusetts (where I was born and raised), and the rest of New England for that matter, who cared about baseball at all was a Red Sox fan. The few

Yankee fans in the area were dismissed as front-runners who rooted for the Yanks because they won the pennant and the World Series every year—or so it seemed.

Roger Kahn summed it up in his book *The Boys of Summer:* "You may glory in a team triumphant, but you fall in love with a team in defeat." He was referring to Brooklyn Dodger fans, but the statement serves equally well to define the dichotomy between Yankee and Red Sox fans of the forties and early fifties. The Yankees were as invincible as the Sox were fallible. Perennial champions versus perennial bridesmaids. The efficient Yankee machine always came through in September, while the Sox, who looked at least as strong on paper, had an annoying habit of fading in the stretch. But their human fallibility created a fierce sense of devotion among the fans in New England. Yankee fans were smug and dispassionate; Wall Street people in pinstriped suits. Red Sox fans were intense, hopeful, and inevitably disappointed.

There were many outstanding players on the Red Sox teams of my youth: Bobby Doerr, Dom DiMaggio, Johnny Pesky, Mel Parnell; later, Frank Malzone and Jackie Jensen. But one alone I chose to idolize: Ted Williams. To me, he *was* the Red Sox. The others were mere mortals; Williams was a legend.

There is, I suppose, a distinctly American irony in the fact that a third generation Italian-American boy from Massachusetts grew up idolizing a WASP baseball player from California named Williams. Why not, after all, Joe DiMaggio, who was at the time *the* American hero, and a fellow Italian-American? The answer, of course, is simple; DiMaggio played for the Yankees, and that made him the enemy, regardless of his ethnic background. I was aware that DiMaggio was Italian, but that certainly was not enough to absolve him of the cardinal sin of playing for New York.

All this may explain why I did not idolize the Yankee Clipper, but why *did* I idolize Ted Williams? Many would argue, in fact, that he was hardly the type of hero you would want your child to emulate. I was aware, even as a child, of the darker side of my idol; the sportswriters made certain of that. Dave Egan, the Boston columnist who rarely missed a chance to berate Williams, once wrote: "The kid has set a sorry example for a generation of kids. He has been a Pied Piper, leading them along a bitter, lonely road." Leaving aside the hyperbole common to Egan's treatment of Williams, it would seem that as a role model Terrible Ted left a lot to be desired.

But my mother, herself one of the true believers, made certain that I was also aware of Williams' off-the-field heroics, particularly his unpublicized visits to children's hospitals. Ed Linn, in his article "The Kid's Last Game" (see p. 222), would later verify my mother's defense by pointing out that Ted had become attached to thousands of sick and dying children, going so far as to charter special planes to bring him to their death beds. Of course, we all knew about his work on behalf of the Jimmy Fund, the fund-raising arm of the Children's Cancer Hospital in Boston. I still remember seeing Ted's face appear on the movie screen during the intermission of a double feature; he would make a brief appeal for the Jimmy Fund, then ushers would pass collection cans among the audience.

Still, if one were asked which of the two, DiMaggio or Williams, Gentleman Joe or Terrible Ted, was more qualified to serve as a childhood idol, DiMaggio would seem to be the obvious choice. At that time Americans expected their sports heroes to be models of behavior fit for emulation by youngsters whose personalities were not yet shaped. Judging by his press coverage, at least, DiMaggio lived up to those ideals; he was the superb yet modest athlete who was always polite and cooperative. Williams, on the other hand, hardly was portrayed as a dime-novel hero; he was, the press told us, abusive of fan and writer alike, given to profanity, quick-tempered, and a selfish ball player.

Williams' greatness as a hitter covered a multitude of sins and made him an object of adoration in spite of himself. But if we must insist on the exemplary nature of our heroes, there was, I think, a valuable lesson for youngsters like myself to learn from Ted Williams, and that was his tireless dedication to the perfection of his skills as a hitter. His natural talent and his legendary 20/10 eyesight (which Williams himself has played down as a significant factor) are not enough to account for his extraordinary achievements, particularly a .388 batting average at the age of thirty-nine.

He was perhaps the most diligent student of hitting ever to play the game, studying every pitcher carefully to learn what kind of pitches he threw in which situations, and perhaps detect some weakness that would give him the edge. "I didn't have to keep a written book on pitchers," Williams wrote in *My Turn at Bat*, "I *lived* a book on pitchers." He liked to do nothing more than hit—"it was the center of my heart"—and he drove himself constantly to achieve that early-set goal of becoming the greatest of all time. If other traits in his personality made him something less than the ideal role model, his constant pursuit of excellence provided for his youthful worshipers a successful example of the Puritan work ethic in action.

With a career that ultimately spanned twenty-two years (1939–60), Ted Williams had a long time to fulfill his pursuit of excellence. Three events in that long career stand out in my mind as hallmarks of the man's relentless drive toward realizing his goal to be the best hitter ever.

The first came on the final day of the 1941 season. Going into that doubleheader at Shibe Park in Philadelphia, Williams was hitting .3995, which rounded out to .400. No one had hit .400 or better since Bill Terry in 1930, and only seven players had reached that magic plateau since 1901. Williams could have chosen to sit out the final day and assure himself that historic achievement, and several teammates encouraged him to do just that. But Williams had to prove, to himself and the world, that he was a .400 hitter for the entire season. In a performance that was both a response to challenge and a measure of his desire, he played both games, went six for eight, and ended up with a .406 average. A player of lesser talent and courage would have been sorely tempted to pass up such a test. Nothing could be more characteristic of Ted Williams than this stubborn defiance of fate that demonstrated not only courage but supreme confidence in his ability.

As if to balance that early one-day act of drama, Williams put on a season-long performance toward the end of his career that Ed Linn would call "The Ted Williams Miracle" (see p. 174). In 1957, Williams hit .388 (which stood as the highest batting average since his own .406 until George Brett hit .390 in 1980), and fell only five hits short of .400. What makes that average truly remarkable, however, is that he was thirty-nine years old at the time, making him the oldest player ever to win a title. (He erased that record the following year when he won his sixth and last batting title at the age of forty, a record that still stands.) Williams' .388 average was twenty-three points higher than that of twenty-five-year-old Mickey Mantle (whose .365 average was the highest of his career) and more than sixty points higher than that of anyone else. Nor had Williams been reduced to a singles hitter in old age; he hit thirty-eight home runs and his slugging percentage of .731 was his highest since 1941. What makes this record all the more impressive is that he maintained his personal desire for perfection while playing on a mediocre team that finished sixteen games behind the Yankees. Throughout his

career, in spite of injuries, military service, and other dis-
tractions, the razor's edge of discipline and dedication never
seemed to dull. If durability is one of the marks of greatness,
Williams endured as few others have.

The final testimony of his intensity and determination
came in the last game of his career, on September 28, 1960,
when Williams was forty-two years old. His dramatic home
run in his last time at bat is the subject of two essays in
this collection and needs no further description here. For
me, that final act of wizardry, so perfect in its timing, was
both climax and summary of an entire career. There had
been thousands of such confrontations with the pitcher
through the years, and more had been lost than won, but
he was not to be denied his final triumph. It was as if all
those years of compulsive dedication to his chosen art had
been in preparation for one final, perfect swing, the moment
of apotheosis, when performance passed forever into memory and myth.

How do we explain the endurance of Ted Williams' need
to excel, even in that last of nearly 10,000 appearances at
the plate in a game that was otherwise meaningless? In a
1990 interview I asked Lou Brock, who then still held the
all-time stolen base record, what had motivated him to sur-
pass those who came before him. His answer was decep-
tively simple: "Passion for the moment, a love affair with
the act." Ted Williams was obviously able to sustain that
passion for the moment, right to the end.

He may have been an avid student of "the science of
hitting," which is what he titled his book on the subject,
but anyone who ever saw Ted Williams hit knows that when
he got to the plate and put all that study and practice into
his swing he turned science into art. Whatever else he did
on or off the field made no difference; it was what he did as
a hitter that made him so wondrous. Statistics may serve
to verify the magnitude of Williams' accomplishments, but

they can tell us nothing about the *experience* of watching him at bat. Just the sight of number 9 stepping out of the dugout to take his place in the on-deck circle was enough to make you tingle in anticipation. There was an unmistakable air of supremacy about this man. Watching him kneel there, twisting the bat in his hands, you could sense *his* anticipation. You knew he couldn't wait to get into the batter's box to begin again the private war between pitcher and hitter, a drama unlike anything else in sports. He was the fussiest of hitters, refusing to swing, with less than two strikes, at any pitch he did not think he could hit well. But when he got a pitch he liked, he unleashed the energy that until then had been stored in eager expectation of this moment; the hands cocking the bat, then the full hip turn, followed by the whiplike swing, ending in a full and smooth follow-through. Such was the beauty of the act itself that its outcome was almost incidental.

Of all the times I saw Williams in person, one game in particular stands out in my mind. It was in the mid-1950s, when he was suffering the effects of one of his numerous injuries. I went to a Red Sox–Yankee game at Fenway with my parents and a friend of the family. I clearly remember this man as a meek, quiet gentleman nearing retirement age, someone who never showed his emotions. An unidentified Yankee player had recently endeared himself to Sox fans by (reportedly) saying that Ted Williams was all washed up. Everyone was anxious to see how Williams would respond to the challenge. Not one to let such an occasion slip by, he responded by hitting one of Don Larsen's fast balls out of the park. It wasn't a classic Williams home run, not a line shot into the right–center field bullpen, but a lofted fly ball that fell into the net atop the Green Monster in left. But that made no difference to the devout. The place went wild. And, much to my surprise, no one yelled louder or longer than our laconic friend. I'll never forget the sight of that stodgy old man suddenly brought to life; there he was, actually jumping up and down, clapping his hands, and screaming with joy. Ovid never imagined a more unlikely metamorphosis. Not that *any* home run would have released that delirium; this was a home run by The Kid, The Splendid Splinter, the greatest hitter who ever lived. Nothing I have witnessed since has so strongly impressed upon me the ability of baseball, in its finest moments, to touch the child that survives in each of us.

The imprint is indelible; the upright stance, the intense concentration, the smooth but lightning-quick swing, the screaming line drives, the loping home run trot with head bowed. While I can remember what it was like to idolize this man, I remain unable to explain why I did, just as our friend could not have explained why he behaved as he did when he saw that home run. Whatever the reasons, I do know that baseball made my childhood a wondrous time, and for that I remain grateful to the game itself, and in particular to Ted Williams, who personified the poetry of the game. More important and demanding loyalties have ruled my adult years, but the memory of that first, innocent devotion remains intact.

Williams Case Grand Lesson

BILL CUNNINGHAM

1939

In his first season in the majors, Ted Williams had a .327 average, hit 31 homers, and drove in 145 runs. In *My Turn at Bat* he wrote: "I can't imagine anyone having a better, happier year in the big leagues."

In fact, 1939 would prove to be his happiest year in terms of relations with the press and the fans, both of whom were generally delighted by the superb hitting and refreshing personality of "The Kid." In the following column published in the Boston *Post* on August 10, Bill Cunningham points out that Williams was "already an idol of the crowds in every American League ballpark."

As successful and happy as he was in that first season, Williams still allowed his impatience with his own lack of perfection to trigger outbursts of anger and moodiness. In the incident discussed in this column, he failed to run out a pop fly and was benched by manager Joe Cronin. Cunningham's coverage of the event is indicative of the favorable attitude of the press toward Williams in his rookie year. He uses the occasion of Williams' benching not to chastise him but to offer friendly advice to a young player of great promise, and to provide an object lesson to his younger readers.

This column also provides a prophetic forecast of what would be a blessing and a curse throughout Williams' career. Whether he liked it or not, his rare combination of talent and personality would make him subject to close scrutiny and thrust him "onto what amounts to a great public stage where the simplest and most understandable mistake is magnified into a major issue."

On an earlier occasion Cunningham proved to be a much less accurate prophet. After watching Williams in spring training in 1938, before the Red Sox prospect was sent back to the minors, Cunningham was not impressed by what he saw and boldly predicted: "I don't believe this kid will ever hit half a Singer midget's weight in a bathing suit."

T he older folk can pass along this morning.

A pleasant Good Morning to you, and all, but what follows is strictly a private discussion with such young gentlemen between the ages of—say 10 and 16—as will step over here for a minute. In plain words, that won't be a strain upon anybody's thinker, let's analyze that incident in the Red Sox ball game Tuesday wherein Joe Cronin benched young Ted Williams because he didn't run as hard as he could after hitting a fly about a thousand miles into the air just back of second base.

Of course, you fellows know that big league baseball differs from the sort you play, not only because it's played by grown men who are real stars, but because it's played for money and for the entertainment of crowds who pay to watch it. That's all the reason it needs for existence. It's entertainment—like the movies, an automobile race, or anything else exciting that people pay to see.

But what you maybe don't know is that one of the several fine things about sport, all sport, even professional sport such as this, is the lessons it can teach a fellow who's smart enough to see them, lessons that will help him in the more important game of living. For living, getting along with people, doing your share, is a game, too. It's the greatest game of all as a matter of fact and, furthermore, it's one we've all got to play whether we want to or not. Strangely enough, too, its rules are almost precisely the same as those of baseball, football, hockey, and other team sports.

• *YOU KNOW THE RULES*

You can sum up most of them yourself. Play fair. Give your
best. Don't take an unfair advantage. Be clean. Remember
the other fellow's rights. Forget self. Remember it's what
the team does that counts. Fit your part in with the others.
Be alert. Be courageous and fight with all you've got, no
matter what the odds may seem, but remember always that,
on the field or on the street, you're only a part of a bigger
whole. Make it the finest part you can, but your cooperation
is the real measure of your value. Neither game, the actual
one of turf or rink or floor, or the figurative one of living,
is rigged up for much of a solo performance.

Now the case of young Williams, and this isn't intended
as any spanking for him either. He's a young fellow, not
much older than many of you as it chances, but fate has
thrust him suddenly onto what amounts to a great public
stage where the simplest and most understandable mistake
is magnified into a major issue.

He made one.

Blessed with every God-given natural talent to become
one of the great stars of a highly paid profession, already
an idol of the crowds in every American league ball park,
destined, if he takes care of himself and has even the average amount of luck, to be rich, famous and perhaps even
immortal in athletic annals before he's really a mature man,
he made the mistake of forgetting his team for a moment
while he felt sorry for himself.

In case you aren't familiar with the whole situation,
here's the way it was.

Young Ted is justifiably proud of his hitting. He has
every right to be. It's amazing for a lad in his first year of
big league competition. For weeks he had led the entire big
league flock in the all-important figure of "Runs Batted In."
So far as any team is concerned, that's the most valuable

figure of all. The fellows who get the most safe hits are the ones with the big personal averages, sometimes, and while those are highly publicized, they may not mean a thing so far as the team's good is concerned. A lot of their safe hits may be made when nobody's on base and unless somebody scores they're just personal figures.

The darling of any ball club, and of the fans who really know baseball, is the fellow who can come through with the safe hit that brings runners home. That's what they call "hitting in the clutch." Maybe such a player's batting average is only .275 instead of .350, but if most of those blows have brought mates safely scampering in from second and third, he's more valuable to the ball club than the fellow who bangs out doubles and triples when nobody is on.

Young Williams held that record and he was justifiably proud of it.

• THEY ALL HAVE SLUMPS

All hitters on ball clubs, for some unaccountable reason, go into batting slumps occasionally, and young Williams has been in a bad one here on his home field of late. Part of the reason unquestionably is because of the way the field is laid out. He's what the ball players call "a pull hitter," meaning he customarily pulls the ball all the way around to the opposite field from the one he is facing. In other words, being a left-handed batter, he customarily drives the ball into right field, and right field at Fenway Park is such a vast open pasture that most of his long hits out there can be caught by the outfielders, whereas they'd be home runs in a lot of other parks.

As the slump hung on, other ball players began to gain on the young man in "Runs Batted In," and the one who gained the fastest was his teammate, the great Jimmy Foxx. Foxx had whacked in around 20 markers during the home stay while Ted was still short of five. And, in this particular contest, James had just poled a mighty clout that took the record away from the youngster by the thin margin of 88 to 87.

But now—it was the sixth inning—the stage was all set for Williams to take it right back, if he could hit the ball at all, for the Red Sox had the bases loaded and even a good clean single to his usual territory would be good for a couple of runs. With that obviously in mind, Williams swung on the pitch with every ounce of his power. Instead of socking it squarely, however, he got only the bottom half of the baseball and it popped high in the air away above second base for what look like a certain out.

So great was his disgust that, instead of running it out with everything he had on the long chance that it wouldn't be caught, he merely took a heads-down, disgusted slow jog toward first as if he didn't care what happened to the ball. And in that moment he didn't. He was in too much of a rage because he hadn't hit a home run. Cronin yelled at him to run, but not even that moved him on.

You know the rest of the story. The high wind caught the ball and did such tricks with it that none of the Philadelphians could catch it. Two of the alert other Red Sockers scored on the play. The other got to third base. Williams himself should have been on second at the finish. A man can score from second on a single, but he'd spent so much time being mad that he'd gone only half way. The law in baseball, and in life, is "run 'em all out." Manager Cronin sent in Finney, removed Williams, and let him sit down to think it over.

Under the circumstances, as the score stood, it wasn't really a crucial nor a serious crime and wasn't so permanently considered by the Red Sox manager, who had Young Ted back in the lineup yesterday, but the wise Red Sox boss knew that removal from the game would impress upon the potential star a lesson that he'd have to learn if he's to live up to the great promise that is in him, the lesson of never putting thoughts of self ahead of thoughts of something bigger—the good of the team, and the good of the game.

As a Soph

JOE WILLIAMS

1940

A prolific and provocative writer, Joe Williams wrote a column six days a week for thirty-four years for the New York *World Telegram and Sun* and its predecessors.

The positive attitude of the press toward Williams in his rookie year remains evident in this piece written at the 1940 spring training camp. Ironically, the same Joe Williams who here writes that "Ted Williams may be a new Ruth in embryo" would write, in 1951, an article entitled "Why I Would Trade Ted Williams" (see p. 125).

March 16, 1940. SARA-SOTA—One of the finest young hitters to come to the big leagues in a number of years is Ted Williams of the Boston Red Sox. We met him down here a year ago when he was fresh out of the bushes. A mutual friend in San Diego had sent us a letter asking that we talk with the youngster and "try to make him feel at home." We don't know yet whether Mr. James Wood Coffroth was ribbing us. Williams is the kind of tangerine who will feel at home any place, any time, including daylight saving.

He was standing near the batting cage swinging three

bats when we introduced ourselves and told him about the letter. He paused briefly to shake hands, patted us cheerfully on the shoulder and said: "Well, the Williamses must stick together." Then he floated two bats in the direction of the dugout, stepped to the plate, and hit the center-field wall on a line.

You couldn't call him a fresh young man, perhaps not cocky, either, but he wasn't shortchanged at the self-reliance counter. He has the abandon, spontaneity and unpredictability of youth. Around the camp here they call him the kid. And that's what he is. But he's no kid when he swings a bat and there's no kidding about his hitting.

He's as natural at the plate as next day's dawn. A free, loose swinger with powerful wrists and forearms, he hits for tremendous distances. It's not entirely silly to toy with the dream that he may be a new Ruth in embryo.

There's nothing Williams would rather do than hit—except, possibly, discourse on the extraordinary virtues of San Diego, his home. Yesterday someone suggested going over to the Ringling Brothers lot, where the famous circus hibernates for the winter, to see Gargantua, the blue-ribbon gorilla.

"Say, if you want to see some really big gorillas go out to San Diego," boasted Williams. "We got the two biggest in the world in our zoo."

Williams rooms with Charlie Wagner, one of the young pitchers. The other morning Wagner came to Phil Troy, the club secretary, and said he wanted another roommate.

"What's the matter?" asked Troy. "I thought you and Williams got along okay."

"We do. But he wakes me up at seven o'clock every morning. He stands in front of a mirror with a hairbrush, holding it like a bat, and he scowls in the mirror, like he's facing a pitcher, and he growls. 'Come on, you big so and so. Put it over the plate and I'll drive it down your throat.' "

That's a good picture of Williams' intensity; his absorption in hitting.

Jimmy Foxx is his idol, or at least one of his very pronounced favorites. Down here he stands behind the batting cage when old Double X is up and studies every move. Foxx likes him, too.

"He gave me a laugh last summer," recalls Foxx. "I hit 10 homers in seven days. When I hit the tenth he came to me, solemn as a sleepy old owl, and shook hands. 'You know,' he said, 'I always suspected you could hit, but now you've convinced me.' "

Williams is starting out with a heap of character and we hope the hurly-burly of baseball leaves him untouched. Because of his great season last year the testimonial people rushed him. One wanted him to endorse a beer product and another wanted him to sing praises to a cigaret. The money he could have picked up was certainly not inconsequential.

"I don't drink beer and I don't smoke cigarets and I'm not going to say I do anything I don't." Needless to add, he didn't sign.

But his main, vital interest is hitting. His curiosity and studiousness are endless. He wants to know how Lajoie hit, how Hornsby stood, how Ruth gripped the bat.

"What kind of a hitter was Pop Anson?" he asked us suddenly yesterday.

We departed quickly, in a gathering gray melancholy. Pop Anson! How old did this kid think we were? Next thing, he'd be asking us about Abner Doubleday.

Ted Williams Blasts Boston

AUSTEN LAKE

1940

The honeymoon between Williams and the press ended in 1940 when a number of Boston writers turned critical of his attitude and performance. For one thing, Williams was not hitting as many home runs as had been expected, especially after the distance to the right field fence had been shortened by the addition of a bullpen. When some of the writers started to criticize his lack of power, Williams fought back. He was only twenty-one years old and, by his own admission, "high strung and prone to tantrums."

It was also in 1940 that Williams, frustrated by what he perceived to be the fickle behavior of fans who would cheer him one minute, then boo him the next, vowed he would never again tip his cap to the fans—a promise he kept for a half-century. (On May 12, 1991, during ceremonies at Fenway Park honoring the fiftieth anniversary of his .406 season, Williams put on a Red Sox cap, then took it off and waved it to the crowd, saying "Today, I tip my hat to all the fans of New England, the greatest sports fans on earth.")

Williams made a bad situation worse when, in August, he expressed to columnist Austen Lake (who would prove to be one of Williams' most severe critics) his distaste for Boston and its fans. The next day (August 13) Lake reported Williams' diatribe in his column in the Boston *Evening American*. As much as any other, this column ignited the feud with the press that was to continue, at varying degrees of intensity, for the rest of Williams' career.

Y

oung Ted Samuel Williams, adolescent Red Sox outfielder, detests Boston!

Theodore wants to be traded to some other major league town.

Ted-kid loathes Boston newspapermen and blames them for inciting the bleacher "wolves."

He said so, frankly and vociferously, in a sit-down before he flew to rejoin his Sox mates in New York today.

"And you can print the whole rotten mess just as I said it," he challenged, as he draped his long frame over a Fenway box pipe rail.

"I've asked Cronin and Yawkey to trade me away from Boston many times this summer," he said. "I don't like the town, I don't like the people, and the newspapermen have been on my back all year. Why?"

His voice was strident, in the key of exasperation, so that several of the ground crew, stirring the infield turf with rakes, paused and cocked an ear.

"Well, why," I asked Ted, "do you think the newsmen have maliciously picked you out to needle? They've hurrahed for you in print, given you more favorable lineage than any other youngster in twenty years."

"Well I earned it, didn't I?" he growled. "What other rookie ever had a better first-year average? Why shouldn't they give me credit?"

"Fine, Ted," I answered, "the town and the newspapers are for you. And you get paid for it proportionately. Twelve thousand five hundred dollars is a . . ."

"Yes," he snorted, "and they're going to pay me more next year—plenty. And I could name some other ball players who got $12,500 in their second year." He spat disgustedly, repeating, "I earned it," and then with emphasis, "I want to get out of the town and I'm praying that they trade me."

"Well look around," I suggested, "where will you find a better ball town or more tolerant fans?"

"Huh," sniffed Ted, his lean, boyish face curled in a pucker, "I suppose Detroit isn't as good a town. Cleveland, Chicago—they need outfielders. And I'll say this too, if they trade me to one of those burgs I'll hold out until they trade me somewhere else."

"New York?" I asked.

Ted stayed ominously silent. New York clearly was the terminus he wished.

Plainly, too, Ted had been nursing his torrent of spleen. The week that he had spent alone in Boston with his sprained sacrum should have purged any superficial sourness in his system. But obviously this was no mere ball player's grouch, a passing black mood, no temporary curdle in his inner chemistry. He felt what he said with a vast conviction. He didn't like Boston's streets, the way the houses were built, the parks, the people, the riverway. Phooie!

But most of all he didn't like the human crows who perch on the rim of the ballpark and write typographical sneers.

"I don't like 'em and I never will," he said.

"We've seen some pretty good ball players come and go in this town, . . ." I began.

"Yeah, and I suppose you're going to say 'a lot better than me,' " he grumbled.

"Yes," I said, "some of them were. Babe Ruth was pretty good, Duffy Lewis, Tris Speaker, Harry Hooper. And all of them had their good days and their bad and took their praise and their criticism with equal good nature. Have you ever thought that maybe you're to blame sometimes?"

Ted cocked a hen's eye, lifting a bitter brow.

"O.K., you tell me?" he invited.

"Well," I said, "you've sat sullen and aloof in the locker rooms and the hotels. Sometimes you've looked lazy and careless on fly balls. Occasionally you've snarled things back at the bleachers. You've taken the attitude, perhaps, that you're bigger than the game. Irritation begets irritation both in the locker room and the field. But Boston, both the fans and the newsmen, like you in spite of the random hoots and critical remarks. They want you to stay."

"Not me," he reiterated, "I want to be traded."

That the months that intervene to October and the end of the season can effect a reconciliation between Ted and his ingrown gripe is improbable. For the boy, now twenty-two, is impregnated with a wish to get away. In the end the club may, in self-defense, have to trade him—unless the combined papa-talking of Joe Cronin and Tom Yawkey can calm him down.

He has, for one thing, a grand illusion about money and the amount that he should be paid, on the premise that despite his junior years he is the equal of any star, both in action and personality, in the league. What he would demand at the close of this season, in the event that he is not bartered elsewhere, he would not say. But he hinted that the figure would be above $15,000. It wouldn't be "peanuts" he said.

The writer has argued with himself the advisability of printing Ted's verbal frothings or, by silence, allowing Ted and the club to work out their problems inside the family. But the situation is such that inevitably the ulcerous condition will have to be lanced publicly. If not now, then in late September or during the mid-autumn. So, to begin with, I had told Ted:

"Whatever you wish to say that is 'off the record,' I'll keep your confidence." But he had thrown his arms wide, palms outward as though wiping the horizon, and said,

"You can print anything, that's how it is and how I feel about it."

"They pay you on your record," he vouchsafed. "The bleachers can boo, the newspapers can sneer, but right out there [he pointed to his outfield acre] is where you get the dough or you don't, and I'm going to get mine."

Young Ted's attitude changed suddenly this summer from the half-artless, calf-like good nature of a year ago. Something had happened to his ego, and his clubhouse attitude toward his mates, the press, and the public, became acid. Yet, as this writer wrote, earlier in the year, the Kid was hitting and hustling, so that his inner nature was between himself, his manager, and his parson just as long as he splashed the outfield and fences with his wooshing drives.

He could wear a nest of robins in his hair, eat schnitzel for breakfast, put his pants on backwards, and blister the whole of the Red Sox fellowship—if he busted up ball games. His private behavior and thoughts were his own business—except where he wants to get away and is saturated with that desire, or where he detests the uniform he wears and abhors the people he represents. That is a public matter.

Between the newsmen and himself there has been an increasing coolness—due to Ted's prolonged funks and his self-segregation. The result has been a mutual avoidance. Still, his treatment by the Boston press has been fair in the opinion of this writer—a preponderance of praise and a minimum of criticism. But such is the youth's supersensitivity that he forgets the cheers and remembers the blurts.

Five or eight years from now, when mature judgment settles in and his adolescent muscle jerks and junior spasms disappear, he may take moral stock of his past and maybe tsk-tsk himself. For the lad is a high-strung nerve victim who thinks whole headfuls of thoughts at a time in a kind of cerebral chop suey instead of single ideas in a sequence like little pig sausages.

Then, like Foxx and Cronin, he may learn to accept the sour with the sweet—maybe in Boston, maybe in Detroit, or New York. Big money, quick fame, mass adulation, a celebrity at twenty-two, have fogged his perspective.

Theodore Goes Mild

M. J. BRANDT

1940

Based on an interview given at the end of the 1940 season, this article acknowledges the rough time Williams had had with the press during his sophomore year. However, impressed by Williams' demeanor during the interview, the author concludes, as the title suggests, that perhaps the young star has grown up as a result of his squabbles with the writers.

As if foreshadowing what was to become a recurring theme in stories written throughout Williams' career, Brandt points out the duality of Ted's personality; the affable young man he describes in this feature is hardly the same "problem child" portrayed by many writers in 1940.

In the early spring of 1939 word came up from Florida that a Red Sox rookie outfielder had dropped a fly ball in an exhibition game; then, in disgust, had seized the ball and heaved it over the grandstand. From that moment Ted Williams was news.

His records alone were fine enough to win him attention: batting cleanup for a heavy hitting club like the Red Sox in his first year as a major leaguer; slamming 31 home runs; leading the American League in runs batted in; and being selected as the outstanding rookie of the year.

But, although he was regarded as a great hitter, writers made him more famous as "the Boston Screwball" and "the kid with the jitterbug soul." Almost daily the stories of Williams' antics appeared in print: how he took batting practice with the pillows in his hotel room, and his habit of grabbing a knife or fork in the dining room to take a cut at an imaginary ball.

Writers watched Ted's sophomore year with even greater interest, and there came a decided change in the tone of their stories. From early March a succession of uncomplimentary articles about Williams were published. He was accused of acting like a baby, wanting the whole show, being jealous of his teammates' accomplishments, denouncing fans and writers, threatening to give up baseball to become a fireman, and finally announcing that he wanted to be traded to the New York Yankees.

All things considered, the prospects of interviewing the Red Sox "problem child" weren't any too promising. The fact that he was late seemed to confirm a preconceived bad impression.

Suddenly he appeared—crossing the lobby of the hotel in a few long, easy strides. He was wearing a white shirt open at the throat, tan trousers, and a green plaid sport coat. He had a package tucked under his arm.

"Hello," he grinned. "I'm sorry I'm late."

He went on to explain as he sat down and crossed his legs. "You see, I'm having a coat made and I had to go down the street to have it fitted. Then on my way back I stopped in and bought this pair of shoes." He held up the package.

Williams admitted that his interest in wearing apparel has been developed only recently. He claims he doesn't wear clothes well, but keeps buying them just the same. During the summer he accumulated three trunks full of clothing and sometimes wonders what he'll do with them.

When with Ted Williams, the conversation just naturally turns to hitting.

Although right-handed in everything else, he has never
been anything but a left-handed hitter. Why? Well, he just
happened to start that way in high school and has never
changed. He doesn't try to be scientific about his batting—
just grabs his favorite club and swings.

"Oh, I study a pitcher and try to figure what he's going
to throw," he explained. "I generally wait for a fast ball.
That's the kind I like to hit. But I don't try experimenting
with my batting stance, grip on the bat, or any of that stuff."

Ted didn't find the pitchers bearing down on him any
more this year than last. He considers Ken Chase of the
Washington Senators the most difficult pitcher to hit and,
after a hasty process of elimination, named Mel Harder of
Cleveland as the second most troublesome.

He finds St. Louis the easiest park in which to hit . . . No,
it's Detroit . . . Cleveland isn't bad either. His final decision:
none are especially tough; Fenway Park in Boston being
the hardest. Even though Tom Yawkey, owner of the Red
Sox, has had the right field stands moved twenty feet closer
to home plate, Williams says he still doesn't get enough
home runs there.

"Home runs?" Ted smiled. He loves to hit them, he admitted. "But I'd rather drive in runs," he added. "That's
what I like to do."

Unlike many others Williams didn't lay all the blame
for the Red Sox troubles during the past year on the pitching
staff.

"Maybe our pitching wasn't good," he said. "I don't know
what was wrong with it. But another one of our big troubles
was that we didn't get our pitching and hitting together."

He reads all the news on the sport pages and enjoys
being a spectator at most any game.

As for the articles that are written about him, he had

this to say: "Sure, I read them, but I don't let them bother me." His reason being that he considers mental attitude a vital factor in a player's record.

Asked how he feels when the fans are down on him, Ted began slowly. "Well, the Boston fans let us know what they want, but—they're all right," he affirmed with a quick nod. He even went so far as to allow that rabid fans are probably a lot better for a team than indifferent ones. Of course, an unsociable reception from fans while on the road is accepted as the natural thing.

Taking a riding from the players doesn't bother him at all. He chuckled about the day when Jimmy Dykes supplied his club with papier maché firemen's hats. That was shortly after Ted let it be known that he wouldn't mind being a fireman.

"Well, being a fireman *is* a good job," Williams argued. "You get $150 a month, they put you on pension, and—" He continued to outline the advantages of working for the fire department.

"But," he concluded, "I have no intention of giving up baseball to become a fireman. I hope my luck and ability hold out for a good many years to come. Sure, I've been lucky. You need ability in baseball, yes, but a large part of the game is luck."

Ted says he hasn't thought seriously yet of what he'll do when his playing days are over.

He classed the story that he doesn't go to see motion pictures in order to take care of his eyes as "bunk." Buying clothes and going to shows keep him busy between ball games. He seldom spends much time in hotels. But he doesn't welcome a day off.

"No," he said seriously. "I like to play every day. I can feel myself stiffen up with just one day's layoff. Although, when I was hurt this season and was out of the lineup for several days, I was sure my hitting would fall off when I went back and instead it picked up. Aw, you're never sure what's going to happen."

Ted surprised his listeners by strongly criticizing the people who aren't gracious about giving autographs. He realizes that all ball players, including himself, find autographing very annoying at times, but says he feels they are under an obligation to the public. He considers it a compliment to a player when someone will stand around just waiting for his signature. He also pointed out that ball players' salaries depend upon popularity as well as ability and, therefore, cannot understand how they can afford to snub the fans.

The mention of autograph hounds led to a discussion of fan mail. Ted doesn't personally answer the letters he receives. He has the Red Sox secretary take care of his mail. Oh, yes, he reads it—that is, he *starts* to read every letter. When they're too gushing he just skips to the last paragraph.

"They most all only want a picture anyway," he said, "so that's what they get. And when the letters are too insulting I skip to the last paragraph again," he laughed, "because there they generally apologize for bawling me out."

Ted didn't disguise the fact that he has a lot of trouble with writers. Perhaps some of that trouble can be traced to Williams himself. He answers questions instantaneously without giving much thought to the fact that his statements can take on different meanings when his facial and vocal expression are lost. In addition, there's little doubt that he has been striving to live up to his former "screwball" publicity.

But there was no maligning nor bitterness about the things that have been printed. Quite calmly Ted told how he has found that you can't tell how people are going to react.

His matter-of-fact attitude didn't belie his concern about the unfavorable publicity he has received; but he is accepting all this as part of a baseball career, because playing baseball has always been the big ambition in Ted's life.

It looks as though Ted Williams has "grown up" as a result of this rough season with the press. If so, it's undoubtedly best for his popularity in the future. Now, it's possible that on this particular day he had been in a pleasant mood, or perhaps he had learned to guard his answers— at any rate, it was a relief to find that the "kid" didn't live up to his "problem child" reputation.

Ted brightened again when the conversation turned to his activities during the winter. He used to be a big California booster, now he finds that he likes the eastern part of the country very much. In fact, he hasn't visited California for two years. But his favorite haunt is Minnesota.

"I'm telling you," he said, "it really gets cold up there in the winter."

He goes there for hunting, the recreation to which he is most partial. Last winter he was also learning to ice skate.

"I wanted to go fast and I cleaned up the ice," he smiled, "so I gave it up."

He used to play football in high school until he decided to devote himself entirely to baseball.

"I went out for basketball too, but, oh, I was lousy," he confided. His first appearance on the court was also his last.

There are no superstitions that trouble this Williams fellow. He just never goes out of his way to let black cats walk in front of him.

He often turns on the radio the first thing in the morning to hear swing music. He likes too many bands to name a particular favorite.

"Well, I hope you'll excuse me, because I must be going," he said, uncrossing his long legs and standing up. He was

THE TED WILLIAMS READER

going to meet three aunts who were coming from New York to see him. He says they are his only relatives in the East.

"And when you have this published," Williams concluded, "I'll read it and say 'So that's what another one of those lousy writers thought of me!' "

He laughed and winked and was gone.

Theodore the .400 Thumper

JACK MALANEY

1941

Jack Malaney, a writer for the Boston *Post* who later became the Red Sox publicity director, was one of the Boston sportswriters who got along well with Williams. In its relentless enthusiasm and praise, this article from *Baseball Magazine* represents the positive end of the spectrum of press opinions of Ted Williams.

Malaney applauds both Williams' courageous decision to jeopardize his .400 average by playing on the last day of the season and his abstinent, All-American life-style. While he does mention the 1940 feud with the press (for which he blames Williams), Malaney is clearly enthralled by "Teddy the Kid Williams," calling him "a most likable youngster."

I want to become such a great hitter that when I walk down the street people will say, 'There goes Ted Williams, the greatest hitter in baseball.' Then I'll be happy. That's all that interests me in this world—to be the greatest hitter in all baseball."

Teddy Williams was finishing a workout during the spring training of the Red Sox in March of 1940 when he made that statement. He had completed his bath, but instead of drying himself with the huge Turkish towel, he was swinging it much as he would a baseball bat. He was swing conscious; but it was not swing music that got his body and his feet into action. The only swing he was interested in was the one he made from a so-called left-handed stance. He was happiest if he made that swing with a 34-ounce, 36-inch-long baseball bat in his hands, but if a bat was not available nor conditions suitable for the swinging of a bat, a towel or even an imaginary bat would suffice.

One year and three-quarters of another have passed since Ted Williams made that statement. At that time he was an immature, overenthusiastic 21-year-old boy. Not only was he keenly imaginative and youthfully confident, but he had some facts and figures to offer in evidence that while he might sound boastful, he had performed feats of batting which offered proof that he might be capable of his boast—becoming the greatest batter in all baseball.

At the conclusion of the 1941 American League season, Ted Williams had made such strides towards the goal he had set for himself as mentioned in that youthful boast in the early spring of 1940 that even the most case hardened baseball veteran volunteered the information that "the greatest batter in their time" had been seen, and they added further that he was only getting into his real stride.

When the official season of 1941 had been concluded and those baseball men, who had seen them all for at least one and, for others, two decades, had made their assertions: Teddy Williams had made history.

He had completed the season with a batting average of better than .400.

Not since 1923 had an American Leaguer been able to complete a season with a batting average which topped the .400 mark. Teddy Williams was a three-year-old toddler in San Diego, Cal., when Harry Heilmann, playing with Detroit's Tigers, had compiled an average of .403, in the 1923 season.

In the near decade which followed Heilmann's feat, some of the greatest batsmen in the history of baseball performed their feats of batting. Babe Ruth, and nobody will deny his skill as one of the all-time great batsmen of baseball, succeeded Heilmann as champion batter, and it was the only time he ever was the leader, but the Babe batted for "only" .378 in becoming the 1924 champion.

Heilmann approached the magic figure again in 1927 when he batted for .398, and Al Simmons, another of the greatest of all batsmen, batted .381 in 1930 to wear the crown, and then improved that mark to hit for .390 in 1931; and Luke Appling, Chicago White Sox shortstop, managed to create enough small hits in 1936 to achieve a mark of .388.

Never again until Teddy "the Kid" Williams swung and connected so happily and successfully during the 1941 season did an American League batter ever complete a season with an average of over .400.

In the interim between Heilmann's 1923 feat and that of Teddy in 1941, there were such champion batters as Heinie Manush, Goose Goslin, Lou Fonseca, Simmons, Dale Alexander, Jimmy Foxx, Lou Gehrig, Buddy Myer, Charley Gehringer and Joe DiMaggio.

Nary a one of those great batters ever had even approached the magic .400 mark which Ted Williams bettered in 1941.

So it must be concluded that Teddy Williams, the Kid, partly had made good his boast of the early spring of 1940. He had performed a batting feat which only six other men had been able to do in the more modern baseball of this century.

Not only did Ted finish with an average of over .400, but he was up in that bracket more than he was under it during the season. For that reason, it was almost heartbreaking to him and his legion of friends and well-wishers when he went into somewhat of a slump in the final week of the season, culminating with a drop to a mark of .3996 on the second last day of the season.

From the rock-bound coast of Maine to the rock-bound coast of California, baseball fans wanted to know only one thing on the evening of September 28, the final day of the American League season.

"What did Ted Williams do?" was the All-America query.

Ted did all right. The Red Sox played a doubleheader that day with Philadelphia's Athletics. Ted got himself six hits in eight times at bat and left no doubt in anybody's mind concerning his average. He made four successive hits his first four times up in the first game that day, the second hit being a tremendous home run over the right-field wall at Shibe Park, his 36th of the year. That cinched matters for him. He could go to bat four times in the second game and still be over .400 if he didn't make a hit. But he made hits his first two times up in that game to delight the people who were watching him and to further please his bosses and mates.

Tom Yawkey, owner of the Red Sox, and Joe Cronin, the manager, were particularly hopeful and anxious for Ted to keep up in the .400 class. Ted had expressed himself several times during the final month of the season as to how desirous he was of staying up there.

There were long faces, therefore, when Ted fell below the mark after the game of Saturday, September 27. Two games were left to be played by Ted. If he managed to get back in the .400 class with a couple of hits in the first game, how about pulling him out of the lineup to preserve the batting average?

His mates on the team all were for that procedure and even promised to trip him up and "sprain his ankle" if necessary to keep him out of action. Joe Cronin was of an open mind. Either way was all right with him and all depended on what Ted wanted to do.

"I'll stay in there and take my regular turn at bat even if I finish with only .390," was Ted's firm answer to the problem. "If I am not capable of holding the mark, I don't deserve the honor. But don't worry, I'll get enough hits in those two games."

Get them he did. There wasn't any serving up of soft pitches, either. The one thing the Athletic pitchers who worked in that doubleheader did was pitch the ball so that it was hittable if he could get a piece of the pitches. In other words, they did not intentionally issue bases on balls nor did they attempt to continually pitch inside and make it impossible for him to connect safely.

There wasn't any question about the six hits Ted got in that final day of the season. The three singles he made in the first game were terrific line drives to right field. The homer would have been a round-tripper in almost any park in the league. He hit another line-drive single his first time up in the second game and then missed another homer only by a couple of feet. The ball he hit that second time up was a line drive that rose as it went on its way. It reached the right center field wall before it got high enough to clear the barrier, and when it crashed, it hit one of the horns of the public address system and cut a hole just big enough for a baseball to get through, finally dropping for a two-bagger.

His batting for that day thrilled not only the people who saw him do it, but the fans of the country who read about it the next day. Thrilling the fans was no new stunt to Teddy.

How about his performance in the 1941 All-Star game?

Two men were out in the ninth inning. Joe Gordon was on third base, Joe DiMaggio on first. The American League team was behind, 5 to 4, when Ted came to bat. A hit would tie up the game, but Teddy Williams had other ideas. He was not playing for a tie.

Detroit's park is Ted's favorite in which to bat. He likes everything about the layout there. So that when Claude Passeau served up the pitch that Ted was waiting for, he swung into it. The hit was a homer from the instant it left his bat. The ball soared and soared until, finally, it met resistance in the form of the front wall of the extreme upper deck which in reality is the continuation of the press stand on the roof.

That game was broadcast nationally so that the fans of the entire country were able to enthuse over that momentous home-run drive. There were 54,674 people watching the game and the scene when it was realized that Teddy had turned the tide with his home run and had brought a last-minute victory to his American League team almost defies description. It was Frank Merriwell stuff of the highest order. Ted was the baseball hero of the country.

When Ted went to Detroit for the All-Star game, his batting average was .405. He had reached the .400 mark on May 25 and had stayed there. He had risen steadily from his low of the season, .308, which was his mark May 2. He got up to .436, which he reached June 6 at Chicago when he hit a homer and a two-bagger off John Rigney in four times at bat.

Ted got a great kick out of reaching .436. That was only two points lower than the mark of .438 made back in 1894 by Hugh Duffy, which mark never has been equalled. Hugh Duffy was manager of the Red Sox in 1921 and 1922 and has been associated with the Sox since. He is one of Ted's firmest friends and admirers and he is one of Ted's idols. Any man who could bat for such a figure is a great man in Ted's book.

The pitchers saw to it that Ted did not stay at that dizzy

mark. The tall, loose-as-a-goose youth had become a distinct menace to all pitchers. Right- or left-handed, they all were alike to Ted. So they adopted the course which prevented him from hitting and breaking up ball games. They walked him. If they did not do so intentionally, it was the next thing to it. They pitched outside or they kept the ball inside and low and almost knicked his left knee with those no-good-to-hit pitches.

So his mark dwindled down to .405 at All-Star game time. The Red Sox resumed championship play at Detroit after the "dream" game. It was not bad enough that Ted went hitless in four times at bat July 11, which dropped his mark to .398. The following day he was walked his first three times at bat, and in one of his jaunts down to second, his foot caught in the dirt and a bone in his right foot which had been broken during spring training had been damaged again.

Although he pinch-hit four times while he was out of the regular line-up, Ted was sidelined for 10 days. When he got back into regular action again, his mark had gone down to .393.

Being out of the game failed to set Ted back in batting. In three days he had regained his .400 mark. Twice from July 25 on he got as high as .414 and he stayed in the select .400 class until the day before the final one of the season.

To his credit it should be brought out that not in any game he played in this past season was Ted physically perfect. Ted had broken that bone in his foot in an exhibition game at the Sox training camp at Sarasota, Fla., in mid-March. It was not a serious break, and the doctors had stated that Ted would be able to play if the foot was properly bandaged.

It was not until April 29 that Ted decided he could withstand pressure on the foot in playing regularly. From that day on, Ted had the foot carefully and tightly bandaged each day before he went on the playing field. That precaution became even more necessary when he injured the foot a second time, and the bandage was on there when he closed the season with that amazing six hits in eight times at bat on September 28.

Ted had a great batting season in 1940, batting for .344. But things happened during that season which will make that year an unpleasant one for him to recall in future years. The youth developed a peculiar quirk that sportswriters were loathesome things. Ted feuded with newspapermen the major portion of the season. He defied them. He vilified them, to their faces and not behind their backs.

The result was not a situation which aided the youngster in the pursuit of baseball honors. It had been an unfortunate decision for him to make that the newspapermen did not like him and were against him. It was quite the opposite from actuality. Writers had liked his boyish frankness, had found him great "copy" and had been thrilled often by his prodigious batting stunts. But he went so far with his feud that it was decided he had to be stopped. He was "set down" many times in many sections of the country during the 1940 season.

The 1941 season started with a new clean slate. What had transpired last year was water over the dam. It was forgotten by Ted and the writers. The 1941 season with his remarkable batting was pleasant and thoroughly enjoyable.

Ted is a most likable youngster. A tall, string-bean youth of six feet, three and a half inches, weighing hardly over 185, he is affable and pleasant to look at and to talk to. Ted does not use tobacco in any form nor has he ever taken liquor of any sort. His smile is infectious and displays a beautiful set of ivory white teeth which would do credit to a tooth paste advertisement.

His habits are normal ones. He loves to hunt in the winter and spends his off months near Minneapolis, where he can shoot to his heart's content, the game wardens being willing. The movies get him during the baseball season and a Buck Jones picture would make him break any engagement.

He wouldn't be natural if he did not like the girls. There isn't any one particular girl yet. Ted declares he has no thoughts of matrimony at present although there was one girl he had been decidedly interested in, but that is all off now.

His one main peculiarity is a thorough dislike for neckties. Ted will not adorn himself with ties. He affects the open neck sport shirt the year round. He runs into difficulties at times because of this strange affectation. There are hotel dining rooms which insist that sportswear is insufficient dress so that Ted often has to eat his meals within the confines of his room. But that doesn't bother him a bit. He persists in refusing to wear neckties.

Ted batted for .327 in 1939, his first season in the majors, for .344 in 1940 and .406 in 1941. Baseball men who have watched him closely and intently say he can continue to improve his mark despite his great campaign in 1941.

Ted agrees with them on that point. He is convinced of his own ability as a batsman. The pitcher does not exist who can fool him consistently, is his firm belief. The best part of that is that he proves his point constantly. You may fool him one day, but look out! He will explode like TNT the next time.

Ted did not pay too much attention to fielding the first two years he was in the majors. He thought that batting was all that was required of him, but as he grew older and more mature, he learned that he had to be efficient defensively as well as potent as a batsman in order to be the great ball player he wanted to be known as. So his fielding this past season left very little to be desired. He has a strong throwing arm, too, as so many base runners have found out.

Ted became 23 years old August 30 last. The record books list his birthday as October 30, but Ted now says that is incorrect. So he has at least 10 years to go in a normal life.

If he continues to improve as he has, baseball records are almost sure to be all cracked and broken before Teddy Williams hangs up his glove for good.

He was batting champion for 1941 and also led the league in home runs. He missed as leader in runs batted in. Perhaps the opposing pitchers with their intentional walks to Ted had much to do with that failure. But that will be taken care of another year.

Teddy Williams and his baseball bat will be back on the job again in a few more months.

Williams' Head Start

BILL BRYSON

1942

Bill Bryson, who wrote for the *Des Moines Register* for almost fifty years and contributed to numerous national magazines, was a highly respected and knowledgeable sportswriter. This piece is of interest not only for its iconoclastic comparison of Williams (who had played in the majors for only three years) with immortals such as Cobb and Hornsby, but also for its comparison of Williams and DiMaggio. It was a comparison, and rivalry, that would be debated throughout the careers of both players.

Bryson's final sentence would prove to be prophetic. Williams would win not only the batting title in 1942, but the first of his two Triple Crowns.

If Ted Williams doesn't eclipse the lifetime batting averages of Ty Cobb, Rogers Hornsby, Tris Speaker, and the other offensive terrors of modern baseball, it won't be because the youthful Red Socker doesn't have a good start.

Fourteen players, beginning in the majors since 1900, have wound up careers of at least ten years with averages over .330. It's a small company and a select one. A half-dozen of the brightest stars of baseball history are there.

Yet Ted Williams, the brash, slim, smiling "kid," can top them all—in the matter of batting percentage anyway.

Sure, there's an "if." Williams can do it if he improves upon his present pace at anywhere near the same rate that Cobb, Hornsby, Speaker, and the rest improved as they matured. With two exceptions—and they are notable ones which will pop up a bit later in this piece—Ted's record for three opening years in the majors is unparalleled.

Williams' trail to modern batting supremacy is as rough and tortuous as the path to a mountain hermit's cave. But already the "Boston Long Boy" has splintered records set by such exalted swatsmiths as Joe Jackson and Ty Cobb.

When, at the age of twenty-two, Ted bombed American League pitching for a .406 average in 1941, he became the youngest .400 hitter since 1900. Cobb was twenty-four before he reached that rarefied height, Joe Jackson was twenty-three, Nap Lajoie twenty-five, Hornsby twenty-six, George Sisler twenty-seven, Harry Heilmann twenty-nine, and Bill Terry thirty-one.

Furthermore, that .406 mark gave Williams the widest batting championship margin in American League annals. Runner-up Cecil Travis finished forty-seven points behind. That surpassed the record thirty-eight point edge compiled by Cobb when he batted .370 to .332 for second-place Eddie Collins in 1915. The National League produced a bigger advantage only in 1921 when Hornsby, reaching the modern peak of .424, led by fifty-nine points.

It is, of course, foolish to compare Williams' current record with the batting achievements of Cobb, Collins, Gehrig, Hornsby, Lajoie, Ruth, Speaker, Sisler, and others whose periods of greatness spanned from seventeen to twenty-four years. But there's one thing we can do to sketch a graphic preliminary comparison. That is to stack Ted's sparkling record for his first three seasons against the composite

marks of the all-time greats for their three starting campaigns. Here they are, as well as their lifetime figures:

	3 Years	Lifetime
Ted Williams	.356	.356
Ty Cobb	.333	.367
Rogers Hornsby	.309	.358
Joe Jackson	.387	.356
Tris Speaker	.325	.344
Babe Ruth	.336	.342
Harry Heilmann	.280	.342
Bill Terry	.317	.341
Lou Gehrig	.330	.340
George Sisler	.332	.340
Paul Waner	.363	.338
Al Simmons	.346	.337
Eddie Collins	.321	.333
Joe Medwick	.327	.332
Jimmy Foxx	.339	.330
Heinie Manush	.307	.330

Which shows that, of all the ten-year veterans who
reached .330, only Paul Waner and Joe Jackson got away
more brilliantly. Until late in his career, the elder Waner
never skidded below .300. But, after his sensational beginning, his peak figures came in spurts—.368 one year, .322
the next; again, a .362 followed by a .321 and, later, a drop
from .354 to .280. He couldn't put together consistent high
runs the way Cobb and Hornsby and Sisler did.

The case of Jackson was a strange one. Never better
than a .358 hitter in three minor league campaigns, Shoeless Joe nudged the nugget to the extent of a .408 average
his first full season in the majors. That mark would have
led the American League in thirty-eight of its forty-one

seasons. Unfortunately for Joe, Ty Cobb did 420 points worth of stick-work the same season.

Jackson followed with noble efforts of .395 and .373, only to have them trumped by Cobb's .410 and .390, respectively. After that, Joe declined sharply. Ironically, it wasn't until the final season before he was barred from organized ball, that Joe again leaped above the .350's, batting .382 in 1920.

Some of the oldsters may think it iconoclasm to be already comparing Williams with Ty Cobb. Probably the oldsters of another generation were skeptical when the then-youthful Cobb was compared with such nineteenth-century greats as Dan Brouthers, Cap Anson, Ed Delahanty, Willie Keeler, and Billy Hamilton. It's not the intention of this screed to paint Williams as Cobb's all-around equal. Impressed by the early comparisons, we merely want to point out that red-stockinged Theodore Francis has a whale of a chance to rank with the most formidable players who ever dug their spikes into a batter's box.

It must be remembered, though, that even Williams' position as the outstanding present-day batsman is not secure. There's that almost legendary Joe DiMaggio to contend with. Despite the disparity of forty-nine points in their 1941 averages, there are plenty of fans and critics who rate DiMaggio a better hitter than Ted. After all, the top flailers among both the old-timers and the moderns couldn't come close to maintaining the consecutive-game hitting streak which Joe ran to fifty-six.

The freshman and sophomore batting records of DiMaggio and Williams were almost identical. Joe hit .323 his first season, .346 his second. Williams' averages were .327 and .344. The third campaigns brought the huge discrepancy. DiMag slumped to .324. Ted soared to .406. At his present rate of improvement, Williams would hit .446 next season. Even Ted's most delirious admirers wouldn't dare dream of such an achievement. They'll be satisfied if the one-time American Legion Junior pitcher can groove himself to the steady gait Ty Cobb struck at the same age. For eleven straight years, Tyrus Raymond never fell below .370.

At first glance, it seems rather amazing that Williams, in batting .406, did it on 185 hits—exactly the same number he collected in his first major league season when he hit only .327. The answer is, of course, that he was officially at bat far fewer times in 1941. Injuries kept him from several games and his "at bat" total was kept down by frequent bases on balls, most of them issued by cautious pitchers who knew what it meant to feed him something good, or because they were protecting narrow leads with men on the sacks.

DiMaggio, twice American League batting champion, is still very much in the running for one of the highest positions in the lifetime batting records. Joe's six-year average of .345 leads all American League players who have had five or more years of service, to date.

It appears that the junior circuit can look forward to a long series of spectacular two-man races for the batting championship. You won't find many takers—maybe none at all—if you wager that Williams or DiMaggio will be the AL batting king next year.

The "Why" of Ted Williams

BOB CONSIDINE

1946

In 1946, Ted Williams made a spectacular return to baseball following three years of service in World War II: he hit .342, with thirty-eight home runs and 123 runs batted in, and led the Red Sox to the pennant.

But regardless of his accomplishments on the field, to many Ted Williams was primarily a puzzle begging to be solved. The enigma of his often contradictory behavior presented a challenge that prompted sportswriters to go beyond game accounts and statistics in an attempt to find out what made Williams tick.

Though briefer than most, this article by one of the most illustrious journalists of his time is representative of the numerous psychological analyses that would be written about Williams.

Considine provides an interesting comment on the mood of postwar America, and on the magnitude of Williams' celebrity, with his observation that the Red Sox hero is "an unconscious victim of a nation's hunger for a superstar to match the frenzied mood of a postwar culture."

I believe I have discovered why Ted Williams sometimes considers himself persecuted. The reasons are manifold.

He is a mixed-up adolescent who recoils from the vivid daffiness of his idolators. As a ball player who served his country and hit .340 in his first postwar year he instinctively resents abuse from fans whose lives were unaffected by the war. His sense of hearing is so acute he hears every blunt remark. And his eyes are so sharp he can read between the lines of every Boston baseball writer's story.

He is a bed of assorted neuroses as are all artists, from painters to adept street cleaners. To this condition has been added the free advice of countless fans, friends, well-wishers and the frankly hostile. He has been over-written, over-publicized—an unconscious victim of a nation's hunger for a superstar to match the frenzied mood of a postwar culture.

Because he is box office, and with a winner, he has been assaulted from all sides by those who sought to use him for their own gain. At long last he has wisely chosen one man—Fred Corcoran—to handle his outside interests. Yet he still needs police cordons to break back the opportunists and the delirious.

Because the nature of his life has mitigated against his having too much maturity, his balance is lopsided, his sense of values distorted. He is a reluctant hero, faintly reminiscent of Lindbergh, and a disgruntled loser—as are all outstanding men.

But of all the things he abhors most, he abhors himself when he fails to achieve the things his body and reflexes are suited to achieve. His loathing for exhibitionist fans who hound him after he has been especially bad on the baseball field is an all-consuming surge which on occasion—such as one day on a train platform in Philadelphia—has caused him to blaspheme them and drive them away, frightened.

He lacks the inherent worldliness of a Ruth, who was able to face and kid with vastly lesser-paid teammates who had performed better on a given occasion. In his mixed-up mind, he believed some of his Red Sox teammates were silently condemning him when he failed this season, and resented their guts and ignored them.

When he made his two $100 bets with friends that he

would be traded it was in each instance a case of wishful thinking. The pastures at Detroit or New York, where there is less intimacy between customer and laborer, must have seemed green and inviting to him. Anything quiet seemed desirable to him. Just as he once honestly hoped to become a fireman in some sleepy red building where he could lean against a wall and blend into anonymity.

He longed for the fireman's life during the first blush of his success for a simple and direct reason. The quietest, most solid person he knew as a boy was a fireman in San Diego. The man once wrote me a letter which revealed a lot of Ted's childhood, in which the only solidity there was came from the tambourine collections of his mother.

The first real money he made in baseball was used in renting a house and furnishing it for his mother. But once, while she was off some place, another relative of Ted's sold all the furnishings of the house to a secondhand man. Ted began to feel anchors around his lean, brown neck.

He is far removed from feeling underpaid. As a matter of fact, most of the stories about his "demands for 1947" are made of the stuff that has no truth. He made $40,000 flat salary from the Red Sox for this season. In addition, Tom Yawkey twice called him in and gave him bonuses of $5,000. When Ted contemplated joining Bob Feller's barnstormers, at $15,000, Yawkey gave him $20,000 not to play with them.

Under the astute management of Corcoran, he has grossed about $20,000 more out of endorsements of various types. There is more to come, from radio and other sectors. But if he stopped working today he still would have made about $90,000 this year.

He may deny the above figures, on the ground that their publication will boomerang against him whenever he is less than terrific. They happen to be accurate.

When he is going right and doing things on the ball field which warrant his income and the respect for him, he is the most genial soul in baseball. He loses his shyness, the fog clears out of his character and he is at peace and in balance with life, the bursting life of a healthy young giant. When he is bad he is even badder than the becurled little girl, and he can see no reason for his existence as a hero.

He was awful in the first of what should be several World Series for him. Adolescently, he was swinging for the more or less unattainable right-field stands, hoping to justify his unwanted role with one lethal swat. Such eager beavers are putty in the hands of any man who pretends to be a big league pitcher.

I saw Ted Williams the first day he played in New York. In the locker room before the game I asked him to name the hitter he had imitated—knowing that, however great, all ball players try to imitate some childhood hero.

"Who do you hit like?" I asked him.

He thought a long time, then said, "I hit like Ted Williams."

But that was when life wasn't too complicated for him. Now, because he thinks people expect it, he is trying to hit like Ruth. And only Ruth could hit like that.

Open Letter to Ted Williams

GRANTLAND RICE

1947

In 1946 Williams won his first MVP award and the Red Sox won their first pennant since 1918. But the World Series against the Cardinals would prove to be one of the biggest disappointments of his career. In his only World Series he hit .200 (five for twenty-five) with no home runs and only one RBI.

The archetypal American sportswriter, Grantland Rice was both a maker of legends and a legend himself—setting the standards by which all other sportswriters would be judged.

In this "open letter" published in *Sport*, Rice offers consolation and encouragement to Williams following his disappointing performance. What is particularly striking about Rice's letter is the fatherly and affectionate tone adopted by the quintessential sportswriter in addressing a ball player renowned for his hostility toward sportswriters. Rice also makes it clear that his affection for Williams was not unique among baseball writers.

Dear Ted—

I have certain reasons, Ted, in writing you this letter. Here they are:

In the first place, I wanted to tell you that I had missed our visits through the last World Series, which I enjoyed. So did Frank Graham, Arthur Daley, and Johnny Drebinger, from the *Journal-American* and the *New York Times*.

In the second place I'd like to add that this is no letter trying to give you any advice, except possibly along lines you and I have talked over. It is my opinion that you have received too much advice, all of which you can throw out.

You have your way of life—and you have your way of baseball. In a free country you are entitled to your way of doing things, as long as this way doesn't affect the play of your team.

This last certainly couldn't have happened, since you were picked as the most valuable player in the American League on a team that ran away with the pennant and came within one base hit of winning the World Series.

You didn't happen to have that hit in your system. But neither did any one else on the Red Sox squad. Brother, you were not alone, not with Harry (The Cat) Brecheen feeding up stuff that was hard to hit.

Almost every one, Ted, seems to think you are high hat, a bit surly, hard to get along with. In my book you are just the opposite. But you don't quite believe in your own ability.

Remember the night in St. Louis when I knocked on your door and no one answered? I walked in and you were pacing the floor in the dark. You were lonesome. You said so.

I remember doing that to Babe Ruth, who was never lonesome. Who was sure of himself. Who wanted everybody around. Babe was what you might call a potentate, welcoming his subjects. You were alone and lonesome, looking for a friend. And yet one season you hit over .400—something Babe Ruth never did. In the home-run department, of course, there has only been one Babe Ruth. And here's one big difference between you and Babe, if you care to look it up, for I'm not quite sure about it. Babe was an extrovert, you are an introvert. Babe thought outwardly, you only thought inwardly. Babe's main thought was the masses, the crowds, the big show. Your main thought has been Ted Williams. This of course is not an exceptional human trait.

When I saw you through and after the last World Series, you were on what I might call the low side. You felt badly over your late-season slump. You felt even worse over your World Series showing, which, of course, was none too hot.

But I want you to think over a few details. You broke in with the Red Sox in 1939 where you batted .327. You hit for .344 in 1940 and you moved up to .406 in 1941. In 1942, before entering the service as a flyer, you finished at .356.

You finished your first years at .356, only 11 points back of Ty Cobb's all-time record, the best in baseball, with something to spare. But remember this—your first four years in big-league baseball (as I recall, and I may be wrong) were something like 10 points above Ty Cobb's first four years with the Detroit Tigers. You were away to a great start before the war years took you away from the game. You returned last Spring in a season where stars were flopping all over the landscape. The power-hitting Yankees fell away from 30 to 60 points at the plate. This was a tough season for servicemen who had been out of action for over two seasons.

In spite of this, you finished your season at .342, a great performance in my book, and you hit almost 40 home runs, your best home-run season. Facing handicaps that few know about, you were still good enough to be named the most valuable player in the American League. There isn't anything in this record about which you need feel ashamed.

Your all-time record, to date, is fourth to Cobb, Hornsby, and Jackson, three of the great hitters of all time. That isn't so bad. I know your slant, Ted, and I admire it. I found this out last Spring in Florida when you told me your goal was to be the greatest hitter of all time. No sane person can quarrel with that ambition, especially one who has your skill at the plate. There was only one thing in Florida that worried me a little.

You kept asking me how Cobb handled a bat—what Joe Jackson did—the way Babe Ruth stood at the plate—how Hornsby used his hips and hands. You were talking about great natural hitters. I think you overlooked the fact, Ted, that you also were and still are one of the great natural hitters. According to Bill Dickey, a smart judge, you're one of the best natural hitters he ever saw.

Great natural hitters, like great golfers, have styles and form of their own. I can see no reason why you should copy anyone. I recall the time when Gene Sarazen, a natural golfer, who won the U.S. Open and the P.G.A., beat Walter Hagen in a challenge match before he was 22. At that point Gene began to study his swing, to take it apart, and it took him four or five years to get back to the natural Sarazen swing, which carried him to one of the greatest rcords in American golf and which has stood up for over 20 years.

"The mistake I made," Sarazen told me, "was in not sticking to the swing I had—and trusting it. As Bobby Jones did." You get the idea, Ted. You came to big-league ball with one of the soundest swings in the game. You had and still have the fastest hand and wrist action.

So the best suggestion I can give you is to stick to the Ted Williams system and forget about Cobb, Hornsby, Ruth, and Jackson.

Charlie Wagner, your roommate for many years, told me: "About as nice a fellow as I ever met. Sure, he gets moody at times and a little low after a bad day, but what ball player doesn't? Ted is still my favorite roommate."

Remember those few lines of verse I wrote about you, when you were thinking of the booing?

THE WAY OF THE MOB

*All you who get the cheering and the
    plaudits from the mob,
Who shrink because they bawl you out
    upon some off-day job,
Who scowl because they call you names
    that no one likes to hear,
Who keep the welkin ringing from the
    hoarse hoot to the cheer,
Who build you up and knock you down,
    from here to kingdom come,
Remember as the game goes on—they
    never boo a bum.*

*I've heard them hiss Hans Wagner and
    I've heard them snarl at Cobb,
I've heard them holler "Take him out,"
    with Matty on the job.
I've heard them curse when Ruth struck
    out—or Speaker missed a play.
For forty years I've heard them ride
    the heroes of their day.
I've heard their roaring welcome switch
    to something worse than hum,
But Eddie, Ted, and Joe, get this—they
    never boo a bum.*

I wrote that for you, Ted, and for Joe DiMaggio and Eddie Arcaro as well.

Here's the main point, Ted. Baseball needs outstanding stars. Baseball can always use a Ty Cobb, a Babe Ruth, a Dizzy Dean—players who have color as well as top skill. You are still young, strong, and keen. You don't drink or smoke. Physically you have many years ahead. The only thing that can hurt you is yourself. You'll find that neither life itself nor any game has any place for self-pity, for lack of confidence, for sensitivity. I don't know exactly what color is. No one does. But you had enough color to dominate the World Series headlines when you were still a World Series "flop." But don't forget that Ty Cobb and Hans Wagner were also World Series "flops" some thirty years ago. Later on, they managed to do pretty well.

I have an idea that this new season of 1947 may be your best year. Whether it is or not will be up to a fellow by the name of Ted Williams. You've got all it takes, Ted, if you will only give the game all you have. Which is plenty.

In a way, baseball needs you more than you need baseball. For we have all too few colorful characters left who can catch the fancy of the crowds. This is the year to show the mobs that you belong with the great hitters of all time. Forget the World Series, just as Ruth, Cobb, and Wagner forgot their flops. I can't recall another ball player who ever had the chance you have this season to steal the show. And more than a few of us have full faith in your ability to prove this point once and for all.

Sincerely your friend,
GRANTLAND RICE

Two Guys Named Ted Williams

ED FITZGERALD

1948

A more detailed "psychoanalysis" than that of Bob Considine's appeared two years later in this feature for *Sport*. Fitzgerald sets out to do what many would attempt over the years: "Find the answer to the riddle of Ted Williams." The answer to that riddle, concludes Fitzgerald, can only be found in Williams' private life.

Williams' "split personality," alluded to in the earlier article by M. J. Brandt, here becomes the primary focus, with Fitzgerald concluding that it is "undoubtedly an outgrowth of his unhappy, insecure childhood."

Fitzgerald's analysis is a classic example of the type of journalism that Williams denounced as an unwarranted invasion of his privacy. Because Fitzgerald quotes an interview with Ted's mother in San Diego, this article spawned what Ed Linn would describe, thirteen years later (in "The Kid's Last Game"), as Williams' "abiding hatred" for *Sport*.

What kind of a guy is Ted Williams? Brother, all I can say is he can play on my team any day in the week. Didja ever see that guy hit? I'm tellin' ya, he ain't human. They say he's got camera eyes, and I'm willin' to believe it. I seen him in that All-Star game—you know, when he got them two homers and two singles. That was the day he belted one off Rip Sewell's blooper. Happy?

*He laughed all the way around the bases. He's another Babe
Ruth, that kid.*

*What kind of a guy is Ted Williams? Listen, Mac, when
bigger jerks are made, I don't want any part of them. That
guy's nuts. He oughta be put away. Sure, I know he can hit.
But only when he feels like it. And did you ever see the bum
in the field? He couldn't catch a ball with a bushel basket.
And what's more, I hear the other guys on the club hate his
guts. I guess he thinks he's too good for them or something.
All I know is if I was Yawkey I'd can the bum. He'd never
play ball for me.*

This is an attempt at an honest report on the most controversial baseball figure of our time, Ted Williams of the
Boston Red Sox. It's a report a lot of people may not like,
because most fans already have formed violent opinions of
their own about the Boston slugger. And this is neither a
pro-Williams nor an anti-Williams article.

I approached this assignment with an open mind. I had
never met Ted Williams. All I knew about him was what
I'd read in the newspapers. And I've known for a long time
it doesn't pay to believe everything you read in the papers.
I had, of course, seen him play, many times. Sometimes I
admired what I saw him do on the field; other times I was
unimpressed.

So I started from scratch. First I read all the books and
articles I could find that contained material on Ted. Then
I invaded newspaper morgues, poring over stacks of clip-
pings about his career. I studied record books, publicity
handouts, and baseball trade publications, soaking up information about things he'd done and things he'd said.

Then I stuffed my pockets with blank sheets of paper
and started talking to people. I went to Boston and talked
to the Red Sox official family. I talked to the guys who ran

the elevators and sold newspapers and tended bar in Boston's old Copley Plaza Hotel. I talked to cops, taxi drivers, and shoe-shine boys around town. I talked to Johnny Orlando, the Red Sox clubhouse boy. I talked to newspapermen and I talked to fans. I asked them all what they thought of Ted Williams—and I collected such a bewildering variety of answers that for a while I thought I was worse off than when I started.

Then I took a week off. I dropped the story completely. I'd been so close to it for so long, I was afraid maybe I couldn't see the forest for the trees. Then I picked up my notes and went over the whole business again. And suddenly I began to see things weren't as confused as I feared. When I looked at what I had objectively, without passion, I realized I could stop trying to make up my mind whether this complex character was a hero or a heel. I saw, suddenly, just what the real story of Ted Williams was.

It takes a lot of telling, because there's a lot to tell. The long, lean, 29-year-old athlete who wallops baseballs out of the ballpark in exchange for a paycheck of approximately $75,000 from the Boston Red Sox is one of the most fascinating characters in American sport. It's possible to love, or at least admire, him, and it's equally possible to hate, or at least dislike, him. The problem, therefore, is—why?

To make the two definite sides of the Ted Williams story easier to follow, I propose to take up his case the way you might take it up in a court of justice, with the prosecution—or anti-Williams—side first. Then we'll hear from the defense—or pro-Williams—side. After that, we'll look at the guy himself and see if we can figure out what it all adds up to.

Briefly, here's the case for the prosecution:

Ted, who is known as The Kid in Boston, has never grown up. He is subject to childish fits of temper and is inconsistent in such departments as good humor, cooperation, and perseverance. At least three times he's been yanked from ball games by Joe Cronin for offenses like failing to run out an infield hit, loafing after fly balls, and swinging half-heartedly at pitches when he was in one of his frequent tizzies. He has never shown himself able to take adversity like a man. He invariably yaps back at any fan who has the nerve to criticize his not-always-flawless play.

The ancient right of the customer to beef at the performer is as much a part of baseball as the three-strike rule. Terrible Ted, however, does not recognize this right. He has often demonstrated that he would like to have it changed so that any jeering fan would be hauled out of his seat, given two in the chops, and dragged off to the pokey.

Needless to say, many fans disagree violently with Ted's viewpoint. For instance, Curt Noyes of Marblehead, Massachusetts, wrote a letter to Dave Egan, sports editor of the Boston *Record,* which said in part:

"Williams, the all-time, All-American adolescent, will never wear a necktie, unless he wears it to bed. He'll never tip his cap to the guys who pay his overstuffed salary. He'll never bunt, steal, hustle, or take a sign . . . unless it suits his own royal convenience. In short, he'll continue to be just what he's always been . . . the prize heel ever to wear a Boston uniform . . ."

Egan himself, the stormy petrel of Boston's sportswriters (and that's saying a lot, because the journalists in that town are not renowned for their gentle nature), has for a long time campaigned to get Williams out of the Hub. Blunt, plain-talking Dave thinks the lanky kid from San Diego does the Red Sox more harm than good, even if he does swing a mean bat.

Unquestionably, thousands of Boston fans agree with Egan. Many of them like Ted, of course. But an awful lot of them would just as soon spit in his eye as shake his hand.

This troubles The Thumper not at all. "Damned New England buzzards," is one of the more polite phrases he has used to describe the paying customers.

It's not easy to find out exactly what relations prevail between Ted and his teammates. After careful investigation, I reached the conclusion that it's like everything else about the guy—a little of this and a little of that. Some of the players like him fine, some of them think he's a little unusual but all right, and some of them would like to kick him in the pants.

I talked to a couple of Red Sox ballplayers about Ted, but they were understandably reluctant to say much. That is, except the ones who liked him. The others changed the subject. One of them though, who for obvious reasons will have to remain anonymous, admitted there are plenty of guys on the club who could do without Williams very well.

You get nowhere, of course, pursuing this line of questioning with the Red Sox officials. It is impossible to guess whether they really mean it or not, but they all religiously follow the party line. Williams, they will have you know, is not only the greatest ball player of his generation, but also the greatest guy you'd ever want to meet. He has no faults. He's just misunderstood. The writers pick on him. He loves everybody, and everybody loves him.

There may be some truth in all that, but for my dough it's mixed up with a hell of a lot of hogwash. The most charitable explanation I can see for the party line is that it stems from overenthusiasm blended with a natural desire to look after one's investments.

When Ted first hit a Red Sox training camp, he picked up a reputation as a "fresh guy" that he's never been able to shake. You know the stories that are told about his antics in that Spring of 1938. He's supposed to have run into Bobby Doerr, a friend of his from the Pacific Coast League.

"Wait till you see this guy Foxx hit!" Doerr raved.

"Wait till Foxx sees me hit!" bragged Williams.

That kind of stuff follows a guy around. The first thing he knows, the boys are lying in wait for him, baiting him, encouraging him to say something even funnier. And all the time they're going around spreading the word that he's a clown, and it isn't doing his reputation any good. That's part of what happened to Ted Williams. But it's only part of it. Most of the Williams legend was hand-tailored by Teddy himself.

The fireman story, for instance. Back in 1940, Ted visited an uncle of his who was a fireman in Mount Vernon, New York. He must have liked what he saw because a few days later he petulantly complained to a reporter that he'd a lot rather be a fireman than a ball player. Of course, he didn't really mean it. It was just that his fireman-uncle had been lounging comfortably in the sun in front of the fire-house when Ted saw him, and Ted—who was having his troubles getting a hit in a series at Yankee Stadium— thought it looked like an ideal existence.

Like so many other things he has said or done impulsively, Ted lived to regret the fireman crack. Jimmy Dykes, the fun-loving manager of the Chicago White Sox (now he runs the Hollywood Stars), went to work on him with a vengeance. When the Red Sox visited Chicago, Dykes out-fitted his bench jockeys with fire helmets and raincoats, and equipped them with a loud siren which they operated glee-fully every time Williams came to bat.

A story that reflects the opinions of some of the Red Sox players about their big star concerns a day the Boston club was playing the Athletics at Shibe Park in Philadelphia. Ted was one of the first Boston players to walk into the dugout before the game. Dom DiMaggio, Bobby Doerr, and Johnny Pesky were with him. DiMag, Doerr, and Pesky jumped out on the playing field and were greeted by a friendly chorus of cheers. Seconds later, Williams stuck his head above the dugout steps. The house shook under the impact of a barrage of sincere boos.

Said a Red Sox player sitting on the bench: "That's an excellent example of the early worm catching the bird."

I asked the Boston front office for some help in locating Ted a couple of months ago. "Well," I was told, "he's either in Princeton, Minnesota, which is his wife's hometown; the Black Hills of South Dakota; or Florida. At least, probably he is."

Which gives you a reasonably clear idea of the degree of responsibility Ted feels toward his ball club. The Red Sox pay him lavishly for working six months out of the year, but he doesn't think it's necessary (or even advisable) to let them know where he is at any given time.

Few of his fans thought any more highly of Ted when it became known last Winter that the great man went fishing in Florida while his wife journeyed to Boston to await the birth of their first child.

The fans and writers who were dismayed by Ted's unpaternal behavior while his wife was awaiting their child got really harsh in their judgments when the Williams baby, a daughter named Barbara Joyce, was born prematurely on Wednesday, January 28—with Ted still in Florida! Even the more charitable observers shook their heads and said: "You'd think he could have interrupted his vacation long enough to be around when the kid was born!"

Not since the Sacco-Vanzetti case has Boston been rocked so severely by a single controversy. Well, not since *Forever Amber* was banned there, anyway.

Harold Kaese, writing in the Boston *Globe,* said: "Everybody knows where Moses was when the lights went out, and apparently everybody knows where Ted Williams was when his baby was born here yesterday. He was fishing."

Instantly leaping to Ted's defense, the Red Sox front office insisted the baby wasn't due until February 15, that Ted had planned to fly to Boston on February 5 to be on hand for the big event, and that it was a tough break for him when the child was born almost a month ahead of time.

The young woman most concerned about it all seemed the least concerned. Doris Williams, interviewed at the hospital, was as happy as any young mother.

"She has Ted's eyes and my mouth," she told reporters, "but she really doesn't look like anybody yet."

Mrs. Williams confirmed the club's statement that the baby hadn't been expected until February 15. Just the same, the incident didn't make Ted look any better in the eyes of his fans.

Informed of the public's reaction when he finally arrived in Boston to see his wife and newborn child, Ted growled: "To hell with the public. They can't run my life." He told reporters he planned to visit briefly with his wife and daughter, then return to Miami because "this place is too cold for me, and besides, the fishing is great down there."

Writing about the mighty macer's odd behavior, Paul Gallico said sternly: "You are not a nice fellow, Brother Williams. I do believe that baseball and the sports pages would be better off without you.

"Where you are wrong in saying that the public cannot run your life is that we can. For I am a part of that public and I would no longer invest ten cents to see you ply your trade because I have an aversion to finding myself in the same enclosure with a self-confessed mucker."

Then Paul let go with his high, hard one. "When, oh when will you thick-headed athletes catch on that the public is your darling, that you may not disillusion us, that you cannot live as other men but dwell in glass houses and that this is the price you pay for wealth and success?"

Williams has a positive genius for getting into situations. In his first years with the Red Sox, he got into trouble not only with the fans, but even with the law, for persistently shooting the pigeons which nest in all the nooks and crannies of Fenway Park.

Decidedly not on the good side is Ted's conspicuous coolness to rival stars on his own team. Boston writers noticed that Williams was anything but encouraging toward little Johnny Pesky when the sharp-hitting shortstop was pressing him for the club's batting leadership in 1942.

It may not mean much to the average fan, but most sportswriters agree that Ted's unwillingness to cooperate even a little bit with the press detracts from his value to the Red Sox. One Boston writer told me he went into the club's dressing room with a few of his colleagues one day when Ted was in a batting slump, hoping to interview the slugger. When the request was conveyed to Ted, his prompt and gracious reply was: "Throw the bastards out."

The editors of *Sport* magazine learned something about Ted's unreliability last year when they tossed a large luncheon for advertising executives in Beantown. A Boston representative of the magazine got in touch with Sergeant John Blake of the Massachusetts State Police, who is one of Ted's closest buddies. Sergeant Blake was asked if he thought Williams could be coaxed into making an appearance at the luncheon.

"I don't know," he said. "But I'll ask him."

Subsequently the sergeant called the magazine representative and told him it was okay, Ted would be there. Sergeant Blake explained that Williams had to go to a baseball dinner that night, but he would come to the luncheon as well. Everyone thought it was mighty cooperative of Ted.

It would have been, too, except that he didn't show up. There were about 800 important Boston businessmen at the luncheon, all of them expecting to see and maybe hear the great Ted Williams. Almost any responsible person would have notified the people in charge that he couldn't make it. But not Ted Williams. He just didn't bother to go. Nobody, of course, ever has accused Ted of being a responsible person.

If you're a Ted Williams fan, you may chuckle at such stories and say, "Well, the kid's a little eccentric, but he doesn't mean any harm." The trouble is, when he insults the customers, alienates the reporters who publicize the games, and allows his fractious disposition to interfere with the efficiency of his play, he's giving neither the Red Sox nor the fans full value for their dough.

I found Ted's part-time business manager, Freddie Corcoran, of the PGA, extremely friendly. But he wouldn't give out any information covering the interesting parts of Ted's life.

"He doesn't like to get into anything at all controversial," Corcoran said. "He'll be glad to talk about the Boudreau Shift, and how it's hard for a right-field hitter to try pushing them into left. And he'll talk about Joe McCarthy, and how he's always had a lot of respect for Joe, for whom he once played on an All-Star team. But nothing personal, you know."

And, of course, it was only the personal stuff I wanted. All the rest of it—the averages and the home-run totals and the runs-batted-in—you can find in the record books. But you'll never find the answer to the riddle of Ted Williams in anybody's record book, and finding that answer was the only thing that interested me.

Corcoran couldn't help me get in touch with Ted's wife, either. "Ted wouldn't like that," he said. "He wouldn't like that at all . . ."

Shifting now to the defense, we find that the witnesses here all feel just as strongly about Ted as those who enjoy taking potshots at The Kid. But that's the only common ground shared by the pro-Williams and anti-Williams camps.

Sam Mele, who plays in the Boston outfield with Ted, looked around the neat brick interior of Toots Shor's and gave his roast beef hash a few minutes to settle while he thought about what to tell me.

"It's hard to say just what I feel about Ted," Sam said. "He's done so many nice things for me. He's gone out of his way to help me, to give me tips, to make me feel at home on the club. Things he didn't have to do. He's a great guy. No kiddin', I love him."

Sam was scornful of the oft-repeated story that Ted refused to associate with his teammates off the field. "Well," he said, "all I know is he had me up to his place for dinner a lot last year. And I went to the fights with him and his wife, not only in Boston, but in Sarasota, too, during Spring training. I had a lot of fun with them. They're swell people."

Sam reported that when he was a rookie, first up with the Red Sox, he was in the batting cage taking a few cuts at the ball when he was bawled out by Al Simmons. Mele had been fouling off a lot of pitches, so he was staying in there until he hit his quota of fair balls. But Simmons, waiting to hit next, got impatient.

"Hey!" he yelled. "You gonna stay in there all day?"

Williams, waiting behind Simmons, strode up to the cage and called in to Sam: "Stay right in there, kid. Hit all you're supposed to hit!"

That doesn't sound like the action of a selfish jerk with a king complex, does it?

You should hear Johnny Orlando, who takes care of the Boston club's equipment, on the subject of Ted Williams. Johnny is sold on Ted—with a capital "S."

Orlando has been around Fenway Park since 1925, so he's seen a lot of them come and go. "I was batboy for the Sox," he told me, "when Eddie Collins was playing second base for Chicago, and I was here when Joe Cronin was the Washington shortstop."

Johnny thinks Ted Williams is not only the greatest guy who ever played ball, but one of the most misunderstood persons who ever walked the face of the earth. He has nothing but contempt for the way newspaper reporters criticize the slugger from San Diego.

"It ain't that he don't want to be friendly," Johnny explained. "It's just that he hates front-runners. He don't like people who run up and make a big fuss over him when he's done something good. Now, take me. I never shook his hand once after he hit a home run. Never once. He don't need it then. It's after he goes oh-for-five that I talk to him. That's when he needs it, not when he's doin' good. But a lot of people don't understand that."

Johnny, who is no raw youngster and who unquestionably knows the score, insists that underneath his sometimes brash exterior Ted is essentially a shy guy. "He don't hang out with the big shots, like some guys do. He hangs out with the kids in the clubhouse, with cops, firemen, and taxi drivers. You know, the plain people. That's the kind of people he likes. On the road, he eats most of his meals in his room because he don't like to have everybody making a fuss over him in the dining room."

It's a cinch Johnny knows Ted well. He pals around with the celebrated slugger about 90 percent of the time. The two are fast friends. And when you listen to this hard-working guy talk about Williams, you can see genuine devotion in his eyes. To him, Ted can do no wrong.

"When he first came here," said Johnny, "he used to take a bunch of us clubhouse boys out fishing. He'd hire a boat and the crew, all the tackle, and lay in sandwiches and stuff for the whole gang. Must have cost him three or four hundred dollars. And you didn't see him calling up the newspapers to come and take pictures, either."

Johnny runs out of adjectives when he tries to tell you how generous Ted is with money. Searching for the right way to say what he meant, Orlando told me: "All I can say is, he gave money before he got in the money." Which says a great deal.

As most baseball fans know by now, Williams handed Johnny a modest tip of $2,500 after the Red Sox lost the 1946 World Series to the St. Louis Cardinals. And each Boston player's cut in that Series was exactly $2,077.06! (I mention that, by the way, not to discredit Orlando's testimony, but rather to prove the accuracy of what he says.)

Tom Dowd, the good-natured traveling secretary of the Red Sox, has nothing but praise for the Splendid Splinter—both as a ball player and as a man.

"In the three years I've taken this club on the road," says Dowd, "he's never objected to his room location, never been critical of his rail space, though it's true he always gets a lower, and never offered any complaints at all about the way he's treated. If a guy is a prima donna, which is the rap the newspapers try to hang on Williams, this is where it usually shows up. Lot of guys behave themselves in public, but act up something fierce when they're out of the limelight. I found that Williams is always easy to get along with."

It seemed to me that Tom had his finger on something

important when he said the writers who are critical of Ted simply refuse to allow him the frailties of ordinary human beings. "Other people can pop off, or throw things when they get angry," Tom pointed out, "and it's okay. But let Williams show the slightest sign of temper, and they pounce on him." Dowd may have something there.

"I've never known him to utter any bitterness toward a fellow player or toward any other player in the league," said Tom. "There's not an ounce of braggadocio about him. He even walks with his head down, looking at the sidewalk."

Dowd undertook to straighten me out on one point which had interested me particularly. Whenever I talked to a hotly pro-Williams man, I wondered how he'd explain Ted's absence from the victory party the Red Sox staged in Cleveland the night they clinched the American League championship in September 1946. That seemed to me to be a clear-cut indication that Ted leans toward the antisocial side.

The Red Sox, you'll remember, were breezing home to their first pennant in 28 years. For a while it looked as though they'd nail down the flag as early as September 6 or 7, but the club ran into an unaccountable bad streak. Washington beat the Sox once, and the Athletics put the boot to them twice.

Undisturbed, the Bostonians headed for Detroit, where they were certain they'd clinch the pennant. Tom Yawkey made elaborate plans for a big victory party there. Dowd was ordered to put a stack of champagne on ice and hold it in readiness, which he did. But the Red Sox promptly lost two straight to the Tigers. It was getting embarrassing.

It got more embarrassing when the boys moved to Cleveland and had their ears pinned back by Rapid Robert Feller. That made it six in a row on the losing side—and the champagne was still on ice. Tom Yawkey was traveling with the club, itching to throw the big binge, and he was getting more impatient every day.

The suspense ended finally on Friday, September 13, when the Red Sox spilled the Indians, 1–0, on a Ted Williams home run. The homer was hit to left field against the Lou Boudreau Shift, sailing safely over Pat Seerey's head into the undefended territory where Ted wasn't supposed to hit. That afternoon, the Yanks licked second-place Detroit, and the Sox were in.

Actually, the Boston boys had to huddle by their radios for a couple of hours before they knew they had the flag. The Yankee–Tiger game started later than the game in Cleveland. But when the final out was made at Detroit, the lid was off for the Red Sox. It was a joyous occasion for them, and the champagne started to flow at a party hastily arranged in the Hotel Statler by Secretary Dowd. The only trouble with the party was that Williams didn't show.

Dowd explains this by saying the interval between the finish of the Boston–Cleveland game, and the finish of the New York–Detroit game, left time for the Red Sox to scatter. It was, he points out, a tough job to round them all up for the party. "I couldn't find Pesky until seven o'clock," he told me, "and I wasn't able to get Williams at all. He was visiting some old fishing friends, and I didn't locate him until he returned to the hotel that night to go to bed."

That's Dowd's story, and he ought to know. But there are other stories, too many of them not to make a dispassionate observer wonder a little. For instance, it was reported at the time that Ted was visiting a hospital. And it has been said by reliable newspapermen that Ted was still in the Hotel Statler—and very much aware of what was going on—when the word came that the Red Sox were in. Certainly it would not require much deduction for him to assume there would be a party that night.

No matter how "the defense" explains the story of the victory party, it's hard to make it come out to Willliams' credit. After all, the Red Sox had carted that champagne around for almost a week. It was no secret to Williams that a big bust was scheduled for the hour the pennant was won. The casual observer cannot help but feel he didn't try very hard to get there. In fact, it's hard to disagree with the people who insist he tried very hard *not* to be there.

Ed Doherty, who used to be publicity director of the Red Sox and now runs their farm club at Scranton, Pennsylvania, in the Eastern League, told me some interesting stuff about Ted. Ed, who had something to do with getting Williams into the Navy (from which he transferred to the Marine Corps after winning his wings), says: "I like the perseverance of the kid." Which is interesting, because a lot of people don't think Teddy is much of a hand at persevering.

Doherty points out that Ted had the benefit of only two years in high school as far as education was concerned. Yet he was able to win a commission in Naval Aviation. "He did it by hitting the books like mad," says Doherty. "He went to school at night after ball games back in 1942, and he didn't play ball in the service because he had to work like hell to make the grade."

It was to Doherty that Ted made his famous statement: "I don't see that hitting .400 is so hot. It's only four out of ten. You work for Yawkey, too. You do four out of ten jobs right, and you're out in the street on your tail. I do four out of ten jobs right, and I'm a great hitter."

Doherty told me, "I know all about the stories they tell blasting Williams, but on the level I think he's a great kid. The newspapers brought this thing on themselves."

By "this thing" Doherty meant the hard-to-handle reputation that has been draped around the Boston Beauty. Ed compared the newspaper treatment of Williams to the way the scribes used to go to work on Lefty Grove. "It's the same situation," he insisted. "It took Grove a dozen years longer to mellow than it would have if the baseball writers had left him alone."

There may be a lot to be said for Doherty's point of view. Certainly it is shared by many another competent observer. But it's difficult to prove that a writer is guilty of any moral crime—or is even off base—when he hasn't done anything but tell what happened.

Sure, the writers whooped it up in the public prints when Ted first showed signs of what may charitably be described as an unusual personality. What else could they be expected to do? News is where you find it, and nobody would read the sports pages if the boys never wrote about any but well-behaved athletes. Does Tony Zale get as much space as Rocky Graziano?

It is, however, unfortunate that Ted got in bad with the typewriter brigade at the very start of his career. A collision like that leaves lasting effects. Because all sportswriters have been accustomed to think of Williams as a pouting schoolboy, they instinctively think the worst whenever he becomes involved in any new incident.

For example, I noticed that one famous writer waxed poetic in print over the sad lot of Joe DiMaggio, who has to hang around the clubhouse for two or three hours after every game lest the autograph hounds tear the poor guy limb from limb.

And then I read the indignant, sizzling prose of another accredited critic who stormed in print that Ted Williams was an arrogant, spoiled so-and-so who would sit in the clubhouse for hours after a game rather than do his bounden duty by the cute little tykes hanging around outside with their pads and pencils. You'd think what's good for the goose would be good for the gander, but it ain't necessarily so.

How can smart baseball people hold stubbornly to such opposite viewpoints on Ted Williams? How is it possible for one man to tell you vehemently that he's a no-good bum who should be dunked in the nearest lake, and the next man to argue just as passionately that he's the greatest hitter *and* the greatest guy baseball has ever known, adding bitterly that the poor kid is just misunderstood?

That's the big Williams question, and it took a lot of soul-searching before I finally arrived at a satisfactory answer. My answer is that both men are right.

They're both right because Ted is in all truth two entirely different people. Sometimes he's happy and sometimes he's blue. Like Dr. Jekyll and Mr. Hyde, one day he's charming, the next day he's mean. And like the little girl who had a little curl right in the middle of her forehead, when he is good he is very, very good, and when he is bad, he is horrid.

Believe me, a practicing psychiatrist would have a field day probing into the subconscious of Ted Williams. The Kid, who, as Milton Gross once wrote, has done everything in baseball but grow up, is the victim of an oppressing sense of insecurity, a terrific inferiority complex, and a basic distrust of his fellow men.

All of which is undoubtedly an outgrowth of his unhappy, insecure childhood. Ted Williams is, as any working sportswriter will tell you, one of the hardest guys in the business to interview no matter what you want to talk to him about. But if you try to get him to tell you anything about his background that's when he'll clam up on you for keeps. Which, when you think it over, is interesting in itself.

Ted's mother, Mrs. May Williams, is an ardent Salvation Army worker in San Diego. Up and down the Southern California coast she's known as "Salvation May," "The Sweetheart of San Diego," and "The Angel of Tia Juana."

As single-minded about her religious work as her famous son is about his hitting, she is proud of her reputation for being able to force her way into any kind of an establishment in behalf of the Salvation Army, and she has laid claim to the world record for selling the Salvation Army newspaper, *War Cry*.

I didn't get a chance to go to San Diego to see her, but my friend and colleague Hannibal Coons took care of that detail and came up with some interesting information.

"Mrs. Williams is extremely friendly and pleasant to everyone," he reports, "but by now she is a little hipped on the Salvation Army, and if you so much as say hello she will gladly leap aboard the conversation and talk both your legs off about the Salvation Army and its glories."

May Williams not only satisfied her spiritual desires through her Salvation Army work, but also used it to earn a living for herself and her two boys. That was a little detail that apparently didn't always appeal to Ted's father.

Sam Williams, a confirmed wanderer to whom a house was a prison, played virtually no part in the little family's life. He and his wife have been separated for nine years and are now officially divorced. Sam is in the photography business in San Francisco and is very proud of his boy Ted. He sticks his chest out every time he hears of some new exploit by The Kid.

A corps cadet as a little girl, Mrs. Williams has been in the Salvation Army for 44 years. She graduated from the Salvation Army Training College in Chicago in 1910, and spent three years on duty in Honolulu, where she met her future husband. Later, she was assigned successively to San Francisco, San Jose, Santa Barbara, and San Diego. (For the benefit of any provincials who may think the Western border of the United States is at St. Louis, all those are cities in the sovereign state of California.)

•

Mrs. Williams was an officer in the Salvation Army for years. She is now an envoy—a noncom, something like a sergeant. She told Coons, "When I didn't marry an officer in the Army, I lost my rank."

Playing the cornet in the Salvation Army band, and occasionally picking up extra money by entertaining prisoners in nearby jails, May Williams took care of her growing boys. But the haphazard conditions of their life must have made an indelible impression upon young Teddy's character. It doesn't take a psychiatrist to see the effects of those impressions in the person that Ted has become.

"Ted is a wonderful son," Mrs. Williams said. "He's never given me a moment's worry, and he's been a wonderful provider. He loves baseball just like I love my Salvation Army work."

When he was a small boy, his mother used to give Ted 30 cents a day to buy his lunch. One day the school nurse called her and asked what arrangements Mrs. Williams was making for Ted's lunch. The nurse explained her concern by adding that the boy never seemed to go near the school cafeteria, and was obviously losing weight.

Mrs. Williams investigated and found that Ted was giving away his daily 30 cents to other kids who had no lunch money. He was going without lunch himself. This action didn't especially surprise his mom, who says: "Ted is very generous, and always has been."

Mrs. Williams didn't have as much luck with her other son, Danny. With their mother so busy, both Ted and Danny were pretty much on their own. Ted went whole-hog for baseball, while Danny proceeded to drift into difficulties.

There's no question but that Ted has been exceedingly generous to his mother, even though he seldom goes to see her. He has sent her sizable sums of money ever since he started making it. A few years ago he had the old family home on Utah Street in San Diego completely remodeled for her. She knows what she's talking about when she tells you he has always been a good boy.

"Don't say anything about Teddy except the highest and the best," she told Coons. "He's a wonderful son." And as Hannibal says, "You can't beat that!"

When Ted was a little boy, he was "dedicated" to the Salvation Army by Commissioner Estill of San Diego. It didn't take. As soon as Ted discovered that the Army had no baseball team, he was through with it.

Ted's mother made no objection when he began playing ball at an early age. She didn't even object when he plastered the house with pictures of Babe Ruth, who is probably still Ted's number one idol. The first time she put up a kick was when Ted told her the Texas Liquor House in San Diego wanted to pay him two dollars a game to play on its team. May Williams wouldn't stand for that at all. "I'll sweep the streets first," she said, indignantly.

But by and large she was very tolerant of his all-out attachment to the game. In fact, as he grew a little older, Mrs. Williams took an active interest in his baseball career. Her demand for a $1,000 bonus for signing caused Bill Essick of the Yankee scouting staff to drop Ted like a hot potato. And when, at 17, he was signed by the San Diego club, she made the owner of the club—Uncle Bill Lane— promise not only that he wouldn't sell Ted until he was 21, but also that he'd give her a piece of the purchase price when he did.

Uncle Bill apparently forgot both promises. He peddled Theodore to the Red Sox in the middle of his second semester with the Padres, and he neglected to cut in Mrs. Williams. A big rhubarb resulted, and Mrs. Williams went all the way to Eddie Collins, the vice president of the Red Sox, with her complaint. The word around the baseball circuit is that she came away from that interview richer by $2,500.

So many things become clearer to you when you weigh all this information about Ted's background. You can understand, for instance, why he is so eager to make big money. There never was any money around the Williams house and there must have been times when the lack of it was a constant worry. Every time he endorses a fat paycheck, Ted becomes that much bigger in his own eyes. He justifies himself that much more.

Knowing the kind of mold that shaped him, it's difficult to dismiss Ted's tantrums as the actions of an unmitigated jerk. He isn't a jerk. He's a badly mixed-up young man who is just beginning to get his bearings and is trying hard to draw up on even terms with his inferiority complex. You've got to keep in mind that a guy who feels inferior will often attempt to make up for this by doing things that make people complain: "Who does that guy think he is?" In other words, he tries to cover his burning sense of inferiority with a veneer of superiority. It's a hard thing to get away with, and Ted is no master at it.

Now that we know something about the origins of this young man with a bat, and a bit about what different people think of him, let's shift our spotlight to Williams himself.

Ted's a fiend for exercising. He does pushups almost every day, though he laughs off the stories that he does 50 every morning. "I wouldn't be able to swing a bat if I did," he says. He gets plenty of sleep, being no part of a nighthawk, and he eats enough to feed two ordinary men.

He's always buying new exercise gadgets that strike his fancy, especially ones that he thinks might strengthen his wrists and his forearms. That's where he generates the power that sends the ball screaming over the fence—and he's always in the market for more power.

The stories you've read about the way he's always practicing his swing are largely true. He'll stand for an hour in front of a hotel-room mirror swinging a bat, and any by-standers are strictly on their own. Once he misjudged his distance and crashed his bat into the bed, wrecking it with one stroke. Broadway Charlie Wagner, who was rooming with him, dropped to the floor in the middle of the debris. Ted stood with the bat in his hand, looking at the unhappy Wagner in the ruined bed. And all he said was: "Gee, what power!"

Ted likes to read, but he'll never make the Book-of-the-Month Club happy. His taste runs to hunting and fishing magazines and sports publications. He may look at a comic book or two on the side, but it's the sports stuff he goes for mostly. Newspapers, too. He reads the papers religiously, although it probably would be better for his disposition if he didn't. He agrees with the writers about as often as Molotov agrees with Marshall.

Except for baseball, the Red Sox slugger has only one sports passion, and that's hunting and fishing. Give him a new gun or a new reel, and he's the happiest guy in the world. He's an absolute nut about the two outdoor sports. And good, too. Competent observers have said he is one of the finest fly-casters, if not the finest, in the United States.

When it comes to being entertained, he'll settle for the movies. He's crazy about Wild West pictures, but will compromise on a good, bloody murder picture. As long as it's got plenty of gunfighting, Ted will say it's okay.

Ranking right along with his passion for the movies, but not as frequently indulged in, is Ted's love for prize fights. His wife, Doris, shares this enthusiasm with him, as she does his delight in hunting and fishing. The Williamses rarely miss a good—or even mediocre—fight.

Ted will strike a fighting pose at the drop of a hat, and make like Joe Louis, whom he admires intensely. He picked Rocky Graziano to beat Tony Zale in their second fight in

'47 and was tickled pink when the New Yorker came through in that memorable Chicago bout. Ted, incidentally, bought $30 tickets to that fight for a flock of Red Soxers who couldn't afford such a luxury.

When it comes to money, as to so many other things, Ted is a strange guy. He'll break your arm before he'll let you pick up a check, but he'll endorse anything or participate in any kind of a stunt to make a fast buck. When I first went to work on this story, I was warned by the Boston front office that Ted might demand a fee for being interviewed. He doesn't miss any bets. Fred Corcoran, his business agent, gets paid to hustle extracurricular fees for him.

But if Ted is an eager beaver when it comes to making money, he has few peers in the technique of spending it. He tips lavishly and he stubbornly refuses to let anybody in his company pay for anything. If you insist, you're in for trouble, because Ted's method of settling such an argument is to wrestle you for it.

As far as his baseball pay is concerned, the best guess seems to be that Ted wants to get his hooks on the biggest paycheck in baseball history not only because he's hungry for the cash, but because he's hungry for the prestige such an arrangement would carry for him. He wants, more than anything else, to be known as the top hitter of all time. And, quite logically, he figures that if he can pull down the biggest salary of all time, he'll have made his point.

Except for the tantrums he directs at the fans and at himself, nobody can say Ted is a bad actor on the playing field. He never bothers the umpires and he never gets belligerent toward the guys on the other team. Nobody at Boston can ever recall seeing Ted in a rhubarb with an umpire—and there are very few players who can make that statement.

Ted never wears a hat or a necktie, which leads many

observers to wonder how he'll get along with Marse Joe McCarthy, who always insisted that all his New York Yankee ballplayers "dress like big leaguers."

The one thing he didn't like about his service in the Marine Corps was the regulation that forced him to wear a field scarf. "Field scarf, hell!" he still complains. "As far as I was concerned, it was just another goddam tie!"

Williams has no permanent home. He lives most anywhere the fishing is good. He hasn't bought or built a house yet, and if he has any ideas in that direction, he hasn't told anybody about them. During the season, he rents an apartment or a small house in Boston, picking it off the listings kept on file in the Red Sox office.

He has a car, but there's nothing Hollywood about it. It's a dark blue sedan, of a medium-priced make, and it looks like any brush salesman's piece of transportation. There is little outward fuss and feathers about Williams.

Ted has no business interest outside baseball. Last year some people in Boston tried to interest him in an automobile agency, but he turned the proposition down. "I'd rather go off some place and fish when the season's over," he told them.

Nobody ever has heard Ted speak of any baseball ambitions extending beyond his playing days. It's unlikely that he'd have the patience to take on a coaching or managing job.

Ted's reluctance to make public appearances is well known, but a lot of people don't know that he's a wonderful after-dinner speaker if you can get him to do it. He has a ready wit and a gift for repartee that enables him to hold his own with the best professional speech-makers. But he hates it, hates it like poison, so it's a rare occasion when he sits down at a banquet table.

He's a rapid-fire talker when you have him off by himself. Especially if he's not just making polite conversation, but is really interested in the subject being discussed. Get him talking about hunting or fishing, or batting, and he bubbles over with excitement. He tries to tell you six things at once, and his personality is at its effervescent best.

A swing music fan, Ted has no use for the quiet tunes that are generally piped into Fenway Park the afternoon of a ball game. "Geez, that stinks!" he'll complain loudly.

Ted's idea of a wonderful way to spend a rainy day in Boston is to hustle down to the Police Department range and shoot at targets for hours. The cops love him. They've always got a gun and a flock of bullets for him—and that's not a crack.

When you look at him, or study a picture of him, there doesn't seem to be anything especially unusual about Ted Williams' ears. They don't stick out from his head at right angles like Ewell Blackwell's do. They aren't mashed to pulp like a punch-drunk prizefighter's. On the contrary, they're a good-looking pair of ears. They fit close to his handsome head and they go well with his regular features.

But the fact remains that they are highly unusual ears. They're the most sensitive organs of hearing baseball has known in recent history. To put it in the language of the dugout, they're "rabbit ears." Each one is equipped with a natural radar set that makes it possible for Ted to pick a single raspberry out of a booming roar of approving cheers.

Young Mr. Williams is an artist in this department. Standing in deep left field, he can hear a mildly sarcastic comment originating in the last row of the grandstand on a cloudy day. And what he does when his sensitive ears tune in on the wavelength of the booing fan is a caution. No man alive can guess what form his savage counterattack will take. It's a good bet, though, that the counterattack will come.

The consuming passion of this young man's life is hitting, and that means he has apprenticed himself to a tough trade, one that imposes harsh restrictions on him. It has made him a perfectionist, like Bix Beiderbecke was with trumpeting, or Bobby Jones with golf.

Ted not only dislikes himself when his hitting falls off—he's positively intolerant of himself. It's this ingrained compulsion to be the best man at his trade in the world that has made him such an irascible character. When the homers aren't rattling off his mace, he can't stand anyone—including himself. When a fan barks a querulous jibe at such a time, Williams is goaded into turning on his tormentor with a spitting, scathing stream of searing profanity that would burn the ears off a mule skinner.

When he's hitting, it's a different story. Then he's the picture of the complacent artisan, the satisfied workman who has just finished a good day's work and is ready, even eager, to accept compliments from all hands.

There is nothing malicious, I am sure, about the occasional princely rages he directs at jeering fans. They are, rather, wholly defensive in character, another product of that whopping inferiority complex.

Ted made his first ripple in the baseball world back in 1935 when, as a 16-year-old pitcher-outfielder at Herbert Hoover High School in San Diego, he murdered opposition pitching for a sensational .586 batting average.

According to people who ought to know, it was right at this time that the New York Yankees muffed a chance to wrap him up in cellophane for future delivery. One of Ted's buddies, a fireman named Elmer Hill, is reported to have touted the kid slugger to Bill Essick, who makes his living hunting ivory for the Yanks. Essick was interested in young Ted, but he lost interest fast when he learned, as mentioned previously, that Ted's mother wanted a cash bonus of an even thousand bucks for signing. Essick didn't think the gangling youngster was worth that kind of dough.

This is strictly hindsight, and not meant as a slam at Essick's scouting talent, which is considerable, but it's a fact that a quarter of a million dollars wouldn't buy half of Ted Williams today.

Ted had a terrific slump in his 1936 high school season. He only hit a feeble .403! But even that anaemic mark was good enough to catch the eye of Bill Lane, who at that time owned the San Diego Padres of the Pacific Coast League. The Padres signed Williams to his first professional baseball contract.

Fran Shellenback, who later became a coach for the Red Sox, was managing the Padres at the time. Williams reported to him as a pitcher, but Shellenback wasted no time switching the kid to the outfield. For one thing, Frank wanted to exploit Ted's batting power, and for another he was worried about the kid's health.

"I wanted him to have a long life,"he says now, "and I knew he wouldn't have as a pitcher. The balls were going back to him a lot faster than he was serving them up."

The only time Williams has pitched since was one desperate afternoon in 1941 when the Red Sox mound staff had been exhausted by the Detroit Tigers, and Ted took over. In one inning, he fanned Pinky Higgins, made Hank Greenberg pop up, and struck out Rudy York. For weeks he talked about nothing else.

There was no indication in Ted's first season as a minor-leaguer (he finished out the '36 campaign in the uniform of the San Diego club), that he was going to grow up into the most feared slugger since Ruth. Ted hit .271, including exactly no home runs. But there was something about the way he leaned into the ball, something about his nonchalance on the firing line, that made you look twice at him.

Certainly Eddie Collins, then the general manager of the Red Sox, looked twice. And again, and still again. Collins finally grabbed Williams after he finished the 1937 season with the Padres. That year, his first full season as a pro, Ted belted 23 homers and hit a respectable .291. He hit his way right into the Boston organization.

It would make pleasant reading to say that the Red Sox rushed Ted straight to Fenway Park, and that his bat rocketed home runs into the bleachers there with the consistency of an 81-millimeter mortar. But that didn't happen. Instead, the Sox took a look at Teddy in the spring of 1938 and promptly dispatched him to Minneapolis in the American Association.

Ted came of age as a hitter in Minneapolis. All the pitchers in the circuit—and the American Association is not known as an easy league—were cousins to Thumping Theodore. He walloped the ball at a merciless .366 clip and included 43 home runs in his production of hits. Not bad for a growing boy.

While he was playing for the Millers, he met Doris Soule, who lived in nearby Princeton, Minnesota. He married her in 1944.

Though his hitting was good in Minneapolis, his behavior was extremely bad for Manager Donie Bush's peace of mind. Ted had a habit of wandering around in the outfield taking imaginary swings with an imaginary bat that almost drove Bush nuts. He would be swinging away, and practicing his footwork, even while a fly ball was soaring toward him, which is a brand of outfielding difficult for the most broad-minded manager to endorse.

Bush sputtered with indignation one day when Ted belted a double, then took a short lead off second. The third-base coach hollered instructions to him, and Ted turned on the offending citizen angrily.

"Hey!" he yelled. "Shut up, willya? I got myself out here, and I'll get myself in again!"

But Teddy learned a lot in Minneapolis, enough to help him stick with the Red Sox when he reported for duty in the Spring of 1939.

His first season with the Red Sox didn't seem to be getting off to an especially good start when he was yanked from an exhibition game in Atlanta for throwing the ball into the stands after missing a foul catch. Joe Cronin didn't waste a second pulling him out of the lineup after that outburst, and the square-jawed Irishman from San Francisco pulled no punches explaining to the recruit that if he was going to play in the big leagues he'd have to learn to act like a big leaguer.

Whether or not Ted ever has learned is open to question. But he hasn't been yanked from any ball games recently.

Although Ted had a good season with Boston in 1939, his first year up, he wasn't able to take the spotlight away from Foxx. The fading Jimmy, nearing the end of his career, walloped 35 home runs as he fashioned a batting average of .360. The kid from Minneapolis hit .327, chalked up 31 homers, and batted in the astounding total of 145 runs.

That was a reasonably happy year for Ted. Everybody liked him, despite his cocky attitude and his forthright manner of speech, and certainly everybody respected his ability. But the next season marked the beginning of his unpopularity. It was in 1940 that the fans began to ride him and he began to snarl at them like a caged lion. The relationship established that year hasn't changed materially since, though it has its high and its low points. Ted and the customers rarely enjoy any degree of intimacy beyond the status of an armed truce.

It was in 1940 that he first decided he wouldn't tip his cap to the crowd, and he has stuck to that decision.

If it weren't for his unfortunate actions, Ted would have been the hero of Boston in 1940. He hit a rousing .344 and smote 23 home runs, 14 triples, and 43 doubles. He drove in 113 runs. On all sides he was gaining recognition as one of the game's outstanding hitters, but in few quarters was he winning friends or influencing people.

The year 1941, of course, was a great one for The Thumper. That .406 batting average stands out in the record books like a beacon light, and you've got to admire the way Ted put it together. With a week to go, his average was .406, and since the Red Sox had no hope of changing their position in the race (they were second to the Yankees), Cronin offered to let him call it quits in order to protect his average. Ted refused instantly.

"If I'm a .400 hitter," he told his manager, "I'm a .400 hitter for a whole season, not for part of one."

For a while after that it looked as though he wasn't going to make it. His average slipped to .399, which is what it was on the last day of the season as the Red Sox went into a doubleheader with the Athletics at Philadelphia. There was no longer any interest in the American League pennant race that day, but there was plenty of interest in Ted Williams' bid for immortality. Eerybody waited to see if he could do it.

He did it—and then some. Ted collected four hits in five trips to the plate in the first game and got two out of three in the nightcap. That was a total of six hits in eight tries for the day, and it left his 1941 average at a spectacular .406. One of the hits, incidentally, was a booming homer, his 37th of the year.

Ted had another fine season in 1942, his last before entering the service. He hit .356, driving in 137 runs and showering the stands with 36 homers. (It's interesting to note that

Williams invariably keeps his home-run production around the middle thirties.)

He was involved in a bit of a fuss that year when he applied for deferment from the draft on the grounds that he had to support his mother. His already widespread unpopularity caused a lot of people to mutter about him, but the muttering died down when Ted enlisted in the Navy as an Aviation Cadet. Later, of course, he moved over to the Marines, for whom he flew an F4U. Ted holds the Marine Corps all-time gunnery record for firing at a towed sleeve, which is not surprising when you remember what an amazingly keen pair of eyes he possesses.

The Navy doctors who gave him his entrance examination said his eyes would occur only six times in 100,000 persons. American League pitchers will nod sagely at this information and tell you they knew it all the time.

While we're on the subject of Williams at the bat, they say around the league that the only way to pitch to Ted, other than walking him, is to keep the ball well inside, on the handle of his bat. It's hard for him to get enough leverage to lift the ball into the stands if you watch your control and keep it well in there. But look out if you miss by so much as an inch. The ball will zoom past your ear like the Santa Fe's Super Chief rocketing through New Mexico hell-bent for L.A.

Ted's fielding is a different story. His philosophy holds that fielding is a relatively unimportant art, so he refuses to knock himself out in pursuit of defensive distinction. He leaves that to the DiMaggio boys.

"They'll never get me out of the game running into a wall after a fly ball," he says. "I'll make a damn good try, but you can bet your sweet life I won't get killed. They don't pay off on fielding."

Despite this attitude, he's not as bad out there as he's

sometimes painted—even if his favorite fielding pose *is* a disinterested slouch with his arms folded across his chest after the manner of a cigar-store Indian.

When Ted came back from the war and rejoined the Red Sox at Sarasota in the Spring of '46, he seemed to be happy and friendly. The sportswriters turned out barrels of material on "The New Ted Williams," and speculated about whether his marriage or his service experience should get the credit for his reformation.

Then things began to go wrong again. It's generally true that a Williams rampage has its beginnings in a frustrating event. Well, the big frustration of 1946 for Teddy was the Lou Boudreau Shift. It just about drove him out of his head. The shift came into being at Fenway Park on a hot day in July, 1946. Ted had enjoyed a spectacular first game in a scheduled doubleheader with Cleveland, powdering three home runs. Desperate for some means of stopping the Boston clouter, Lou Boudreau, the Indians' manager, tried over-shifting his defensive lineup to the right. He hoped to rob Williams of a lot of infield hits that way—and he did.

He also gave Ted a new bone to worry over. Williams could have discouraged the shift idea that first day by the simple expedient of bunting down the unprotected third-base line, or slicing a hit into the wide-open spaces of left field. But he didn't. Instead, he got proud, and he slashed away furiously at the heavily populated right side of the diamond, trying to prove he could hit the ball into the stands. He's been trying to prove it ever since—and, of course, he has succeeded quite well. But the shift has hurt him just the same. Most experts agree that it robbed him of anywhere from 15 to 20 base hits in 1947. And it bothers the daylights out of him, even though he hates to admit it.

Of course, when Williams is having a good day, there is no defense against him. It's illegal to put an outfielder in the right-field grandstand.

Ted did all right in '46 despite the handicap of the new shift. He hauled the Red Sox to the pennant on the wings of his .342 batting average, his 123 runs-batted-in, and his 38 homers. He didn't win the batting championship, which went to Washington's suddenly inspired first-baseman, Mickey Vernon. But he did everything that was expected of him, and more, until he hit the World Series. Then he went into the most woeful tailspin of his career. He couldn't hit the St. Louis Cardinal pitchers for beans, and he came out of the series the undisputed goat of the beaten favorites.

Some observers thought his sobering World Series experience would work a change in Ted's approach to the game, but no such change was visible last year. He was the same old Ted. His batting average was about the same, his RBI total was about the same, his home-run production was about the same—and his disposition was exactly the same.

It's too bad it had to be that way, for Ted has the makings of a great American sports legend. He has created something of a legend already, but it's not a pleasant one. He had the opportunity to do much better. He has known some great days on the diamond, this stringbean who comes from California and plays in Boston. He has accomplished some feats that no amount of eccentricity will be able to erase from the literature of baseball.

There was, for instance, the day Ted broke the hearts of all National Leaguers in the 1941 All-Star game at Detroit. Leading by 5–3 with two out in the last of the ninth, the Nationals seemed to have the ball game all wrapped up. But they had forgotten about Ted Williams. With one magnificent poke, Terrible Ted changed everything.

You probably recall what happened. In that fateful ninth, Frankie Hayes was first up for the American League. He popped to Billy Herman at second. Kenny Keltner, the Cleveland third-baseman, batted for pitcher Edgar Smith and drove an infield hit to Eddie Miller at short. Joe Gordon singled to right and a walk to Cecil Travis filled the bases.

The stands were seething with excitement as Joe DiMaggio, the Yankee Clipper himself, strode to the plate with that purposeful, businesslike air. But DiMag didn't have a hit in his system. The best he could do was hit into a force play that pushed Keltner over the plate. As Travis went into second base he bothered Billy Herman just enough to make that marvelous second-sacker throw a little wide on the attempted double play. That was the National League's big mistake, for it brought up Ted Williams again.

Bill McKechnie, the wily NL manager, could have walked Williams. But Claude Passeau had struck him out in the eighth—and besides, Dom DiMaggio was up next, and that could hardly be regarded as a picnic. So McKechnie crossed his fingers and ordered Passeau to pitch to the Boston star.

Ted stood up there in that wiggly, waggly, way of his, fidgeting and stretching and squirming. You could hear the people in the stands talking. "Loose as a goose up there, ain't he?"

With the count two balls and one strike, the mighty man swung. He kissed the ball with the fat part of his bat and that was all. Into the right-field stands whistled the tiny pellet, and the ball game was over. Grinning and dancing happily, The Kid circled the bases behind Gordon and DiMaggio, and dented the plate to make the score 7–5 for his league.

It was a tough game for the National League to lose, but they learned the hard way what the boys in the other league have known for a long time—that the only way to get Ted Williams out is to hit him on the head with a blunt instrument.

Then there was the 1946 All-Star game, in which Ted took the gentlemen from the National League, stirred them up with a few pokes of his bat, and hung them out on the line to dry. It was plain murder, what he did that July 9 in his own ball park.

Principally because of the way Ted Williams swung his dynamite-laden bat, the National League went down that day to a humiliating 12–0 defeat in the annual mid-Summer classic. It was, by anybody's standards, a rout. And Williams was the chief router. (There isn't any such word, but in this case there ought to be.)

While Bob Feller, Hal Newhouser, and Jack Kramer were handcuffing the NL hitters with three stray singles, the AL power erupted like Mount Vesuvius. Williams went up to bat five times, and each time he got on base. He walked in the first inning, hit a home run in the fourth with nobody on, singled home a run in the fifth, singled off the great Ewell Blackwell in the seventh, and hit his famous homer off Rip Sewell's blooper in the eighth.

It's doubtful if any baseball crowd ever got more of a kick out of a hit than the Fenway Park throng got out of Ted's clout off Sewell in that game. Remember, it was no longer a contest at that stage. It was simply an exhibition. Without anything specific to root for, the fans loaned their affection to Williams and implored him to hit another homer.

When he teed off on Sewell's teaser, supplying all his own power to propel the ball into the seats, the crowd roared until it sank back exhausted. It was a great moment for Ted.

In any study of this amazing character, you've got to spend a little time on the Most Valuable Player situation. It's important to note that despite his fabulous batting feats, the Red Sox hero has won the MVP award in the American League only once. He was voted the honor in 1946 for his work in sparking the Sox to their first pennant in 28 years. The writers overlooked Ted's miserable World Series performance (he batted .200 against the Cardinals).

But in 1941, the year Williams blasted American League pitching for a .406 average, the first .400 mark in the majors since Bill Terry hit .401 for the Giants in 1930, he didn't get it. Joe DiMaggio did. That was the season Joltin' Joe hung up his consecutive game batting streak of 56 in a row as he slugged the Yanks to the flag. The decision was received with an ominous quiet in Boston.

Last year, it was almost like a replay of the '41 affair. Ted monopolized the slugging titles in his league, but Joe DiMaggio led the Yankees to another pennant. DiMaggio hit .315, and Williams hit .343. DiMag collected 20 home runs. Williams hit 32. DiMag drove in 97 runs. Williams batted in 114. But when the writers filled out their ballot slips, DiMaggio was named the Most Valuable Player by a one-vote margin over Ted.

What does this mean? In Boston they'll tell you it means nothing except that "those goddam prejudiced New York sportswriters are at it again." The 1947 MVP announcement got a different reception from the 1941 result. That time there was stunned silence. This time there was an anguished outcry. "We was robbed!" the Red Sox shouted, as they staggered from the blow.

The truth of the matter is, of course, that the small group of New York City sportwriters participating in the poll cannot possibly wield enough influence to swing the election to their candidate. Williams was defeated because a great many conscientious sportswriters do not consider him the Most Valuable Player in any league. The chances are good they wouldn't consider him such if he hit twice as many home runs. They think he's a poor team man who cares only for his own batting marks and nothing for the success of the unit.

But this is for sure. No matter how complicated are the wheels that go around inside Ted Williams' head, no matter how many rhubarbs he stirs up either on or off the field, he is still the greatest batsman of his time. With that Louisville Slugger in his mitts, Ted is absolutely the best.

There are few players in the game today who can equal the impression of controlled violence that you see in Ted Williams' every gesture as he steps up to the plate.

He's as loose as ashes up there, wiggling his bat incessantly, swinging his arms, fidgeting this way and that. The wiry grace of his body carries an explosive air. You sit in your seat and you begin to tingle. It's something like the feeling you get when the bathrobes come off the two antagonists just before a heavyweight championship fight. It's a feeling anyone who ever saw Babe Ruth bat will remember clearly. Something is going to happen . . . you can feel it . . . you wait for it . . . and when Ted leans into the ball, the swish and the smash remind you of the lash of a giant bullwhip.

It's an indescribable relief when you know he's hit the ball. . . . You wanted him to hit it badly, and you half-rise out of your seat when you see the ball fly off the fat of his bat, soar into the blue sky like a homesick star, and dip purposefully into the stands where dozens of people knock each other over in a mad scramble to recover it.

The deep roar that accompanies a Ted Williams home run comes from the pit of the fans' stomachs, and you don't have to be an amateur psychologist to guess that his blast has made them a little bigger in their own eyes. It's as though the crash of his mighty bat made them feel they had managed to belt savagely all the obstacles and troubles in the world, driving them out of sight and out of mind.

Many people have compared Ted Williams to Babe Ruth, on two counts. They claim he hits like the mighty Bambino, and he has the same colorful temperament.

That's a swing and a miss, the way I see it. Williams may grow up to be a hitter of Ruthian proportions, but he's got a heap of growing to do first. The Boston thumper is a whale of a man with that bat in his hands, but, good as he is, he has yet to prove he belongs in the same class with Ruth.

As a person, Ruth was a man of huge appetites, a man who ate and drank like Gargantua, out-playboyed Tommy Manville, and rode through life on a cloud of casual good humor that left no room for thoughts of a serious nature. Williams, on the other hand, trains religiously, never lets himself pick up excess weight, carefully respects his eyes and his wind, and gets plenty of sleep. He's no girl-chaser, no lover of nightclubs, no devourer of hot dogs by the dozen. His claim to the rating of "character" is based on one trait, and one trait alone—his petulance.

Petulant is a word that means sulky, bad-tempered, irritable, huffy, fretful, moody, peevish, cross. All those words fit Ted Williams. Because he owns these unenviable qualities, Williams has enlivened his baseball career (but not enhanced it) by a bewildering array of incidents that have made him look like nothing so much as a small boy who gets sore when things don't go exactly his way. He's the archetype of the kid who has to be treated with kid gloves because he's liable to get mad at the gang, pick up his marbles, and run home.

That's not the kind of ball player Babe Ruth was. It is, unfortunately, the kind of player Ted Williams is—or, at any rate, has been until now. When and if Ted grows up, the chances are good his ability will improve side by side with his character.

But that's pure speculation. You never know what the guy is likely to do next. Even the Williams-hardened people in the Red Sox front office were slightly surprised to see him take up a position in the boxes behind first base one day a few years ago and calmly point a shiny new pistol at the scoreboard in left field. Shooting deliberately, Ted proceeded to shatter some $400 worth of electric light bulbs!

Then there was the day the Red Sox were playing a doubleheader with Cleveland before 35,000 paying clients in Fenway Park. It was the same day that Lou Boudreau first sprang his shift on Williams.

Between innings during the first game—in which, as mentioned before, he hit three homers—Ted stepped to the scoreboard instead of heading for the Boston bench. Slipping out a trapdoor leading to the street, he ran across to a small restaurant and asked the waiter for a dish of ice cream. Everybody in the place had been listening to the radio and discussing Ted's home runs. They sat openmouthed at the spectacle of the uniformed ball player sitting next to them while the radio blared an account of the game in which he was supposed to be playing.

Ted paid no attention to their astonishment. Parking his spikes on the foot rail, he gobbled up his ice cream, handed the waiter a coin, and dashed back across the street. He ducked through the trapdoor and into the ballpark just in time to resume his position in left field.

I ask you, what the hell are you going to do with a guy like that? Especially when he's a couple of guys.

Why We Pick on Ted Williams

HAROLD KAESE

1949

In this analysis of Williams' relations with the press, Kaese divides Boston sports-writers into two camps: those who deify Williams and those who treat him as an "ordinary mortal." (Kaese does not quantify his division, but he does place himself in the latter group.) While he acknowledges that heroes such as Williams have real value to society, Kaese also insists on the right, and obligation, of journalists to be honest in their portrayal of celebrities.

Kaese, a Boston sportswriter and columnist for thirty-seven years, covered baseball throughout Williams' career. While his portrayal of Williams was generally evenhanded, he did incur Williams' wrath on more than one occasion by committing the unpardonable sin of writing about his personal life. In the preceding article, Ed Fitzgerald quoted Kaese's sarcastic comments on Williams' late arrival for the birth of his first child. Kaese also chastised Williams in 1940 for "not visiting his father and mother all last winter." In *My Turn at Bat,* Williams writes that until that remark was printed he had been "willing to believe a writer was my friend until he proved otherwise."

A good many people seem to think that admission to big-league press boxes should be restricted not only to members of the Baseball Writers' Association but also to bona fide members of the Ted Williams Chowder and Marching Society.

Even as one who thinks he has done his share in glorifying the Red Sox swatter, I am opposed to this attitude. Such discrimination would rob the press box of much of its remaining character and dignity, leaving it populated with backslappers and flatterers.

Of course, I grieve for Williams and his followers. It is unfortunate that only 95 percent of the publicity given him is favorable, and that something cannot be done about the remaining 5 percent. But even he probably would agree that to abolish the minority, to keep its members out of the press box and their animadversions out of the papers, would be to create another distasteful baseball monopoly. Fans who ask, "Why don't the writers leave Ted Williams alone?" do not really want writers to leave him alone. They want them to leave Williams alone only when he does, or says, something of which they cannot feel proud.

In a like category is the woman who wrote, "I'm a Ted Williams rooter. I wish you would write something about him in your column every day." She should have written, "I wish you would write something *nice* about him in your column every day."

A writer *could* compose something nice about Williams every day, but it would get very monotonous and, as far as reporting went, dishonest. It is an inner compulsion to be honest that makes some writers present the seamy side of life, and some others the shortcomings of potent personalities like Williams. Such writers are often charged with "picking on" Williams, as if they were innately cruel.

THE TED WILLIAMS READER

●

Obviously, it is wrong to distort any man's character. But because it is more repulsive to distort it in the direction of the bad does not mean that it is of little significance to distort it in the direction of the good. Too often great athletes are glorified and falsified for no good reason and to no good purpose, but there are always opportunists ready to meet the demand for heroes.

Ten years ago, Ted Williams broke in with the Red Sox. I have known him and—I'll confess—liked him for a decade. I feel pretty certain that his fame is explained only by his ability to hit a baseball. Otherwise, he is neither better nor worse than most men. He has a quick mind, but there are quicker. Even his capacity for fishing is not unique.

Oh, the writers will be leaving Williams alone soon enough. Just let him stop hitting the baseball. Let him retire to the fields and streams, the woods and marshes, and he will be left as alone as Lefty Grove, Paul Waner, Grover Cleveland Alexander, and Jimmy Foxx.

There will be plenty of time for leaving Williams alone. But now he is one of baseball's showpieces, a man who earns at least eighty-five thousand dollars a year with a thirty-five-inch billet of wood that weighs only thirty-five ounces. He can't be left alone any more than a Truman, Eisenhower, Einstein, or Sinatra can be left alone. He means much to society, and society has the right to know him—as he is, not as the sycophants would like us to have him.

In Boston, a man does not qualify as a baseball writer until he has psychoanalyzed Williams. Some of the more analytical scribes dissect him once a week, and a couple are suspected of taking him apart twice a day, partly for the edification of their readers, but largely for their own amusement.

There seem to be, roughly, two schools of Boston writers: those who treat Williams as an ordinary mortal and describe his pluses and minuses, and those who treat him as an immortal and describe only his pluses. I know of no Boston writer who devotes himself entirely to Williams' minuses, but among those who have not neglected them are such sterling columnists as Dave Egan of the *Daily Record,* Austen Lake of the *American,* and myself of the *Globe.*

We do not agree on Williams, naturally, except to agree that he should not be immune to criticism. Egan acquired a formidable reputation for being anti-Williams, which he fondly nourished. Yet he has written many favorable accounts of the player, especially when Williams was being abused for his draft deferment in the 1942 season. And late last season, Egan came right out and said that Williams was improving as a team player—which that writer had never thought one of his strong points.

As a writer, Lake is as rugged as they come. His honesty is never questioned. He has powerful convictions, one of which is that athletes, owners, and other sports figures must take the bitter with the sweet. Lake is not anti-Williams, but occasionally his columns can be so interpreted.

In August of last season, after Williams had apparently twice cold-shouldered Vern Stephens—once after Stephens had hit a game-winning home run and again after Williams had hit a home run—Lake wrote: "The blunt truth is Williams, hitting maestro that he is—and one of the best— cannot brook competition in a field that he considers his personal monopoly. Any teammate who steals his thunder, be it home runs, RBI's, or batting average, is thistle under his skin."

But Lake has also praised Williams, calling him the Albert Einstein of the batting profession, admitting that he has grown "mellow, smarter, and more temperate through the years," granting him the right to call newspapermen a "bunch of bubbleheads" if he so chooses, and concluding, "I wouldn't have Ted any other way than he is. As copy he's priceless, among a lot of drab, colorless, journeymen Red Sox."

And what of Kaese? I have stuck up for Williams in a variety of arguments, rated him ahead of Stan Musial as a hitter, advertised the animosity that has kept him from winning more than one Most Valuable Player award, and in general helped tell the world of his genius as a player. Alas, I too have incurred his displeasure, which can be done simply by (1) contradicting his baseball theories, (2) psychoanalyzing him, (3) referring to his conduct on or off the field in anything except flattering terms.

Going to work one evening in January, 1948, I was engulfed by a wave of wrath that seemed to hit me from six directions at once—because Ted Williams was fishing in the Everglades when his daughter was born in Boston. When asked if he would rush to Boston, he had replied, "I don't know. What good can I do?"

Williams' presence did not seem essential to me—a crusty bachelor—but I was startled by the indignation of the people I had met and I was amused by Williams' characteristic indifference to public opinion.

"Is everybody in Boston as mad as these people here in the office?" I asked myself. I decided to find out.

At random, I called a dozen or so people—a telephone operator, a glue salesman, a baby-sitter, etc. The baby-sitter said she not only knew nothing about Ted Williams' baby, but knew nothing about Ted Williams—a most unusual baby-sitter. Sentiment revealed by the poll was about two–one against the player. The males were more indignant than the females. I wrote their reaction, did no moralizing of my own, and concluded that these same overwrought citizens would soon be cheering Williams when he was again hitting home runs. This was the case.

But many people, including Egan, Lake, and Williams, thought I was trying to make a bum out of Williams. I still think it was a good idea for a story. If the poll favored the player, everything no doubt would have been ducky. At least, Williams would not have given me the deep-freeze chill he did most of last season.

To offend Williams usually is to be ostracized by him. Sometimes he lashes out, as he did at a writer who wrote that Joe McCarthy had won the first skirmish from Williams by limiting the star to three swings when he batted in Spring training. "I've had no skirmish with McCarthy," roared Williams. But he favors the ice-box treatment, and after the baby episode he got even with the Boston press by giving exclusive interviews to out-of-town and news-service writers.

Williams is one of the few top-notch big leaguers to stand up and fight the press. Joe DiMaggio, Stan Musial, and Lou Boudreau are so popular they do not have to. Bob Feller, who is frequently blasted in print, seldom hits back, but Williams from the very start has waged war on his critics. Some players admire him for it.

"I'll say one thing for you, Ted," Dom DiMaggio once told him. "You took everything the press could throw at you, and then you shoved their words right back down their throats."

And Johnny Beazley, the Braves pitcher, once said, "I admire Ted Williams. If he doesn't like a sportswriter, he tells him to go to hell and doesn't care what he writes. Not many fellows are good enough to do that. If he was an ordinary player, though, they'd run him out of the league."

After the Red Sox had beaten the Indians in Boston last August, a group of home writers walked into the Sox clubhouse and Williams abruptly called them "a lot of front-runners." This provoked another Red Sox regular, whose name is not vital to the story, to say, "Ted, why don't you smarten up?"

There was a brief exchange, and Williams went to the showers. Complimented on his attitude, the regular shrugged his shoulders and said, "Somebody's got to tell him off some time."

Williams, when the thumbscrews of pressure are being twisted, is not the same charming young man who in the off-season has no worries except what fly he'll try next on the baby tarpon. At the Boston Baseball Writers' Dinner in 1947, Ted made his usual modest and captivating appearance. A writer began his story, "Tuxedoless but tie-wearing Ted Williams—the real Ted Williams—won the friendly applause of 950 baseball fans . . . Ted, the smiling kid. . . ."

A few months later, in the heat of the 1948 pennant race, this admiring writer asked the kid a simple question and almost had his head snapped off by the reply. He had a different version then of "the real Ted Williams."

Allowances, I agree, should be made for athletes competing under pressure. And let the athletes make some allowance for writers who are also working under pressure.

The "real Ted Williams" is the man some of us have been trying to reveal to the public, and it has not been easy because of the many facets to the player's personality. Thus, Grantland Rice wrote during the 1946 World Series, won by the Cardinals from the Red Sox: "The prevailing belief that Williams is swell-headed is entirely incorrect. The main trouble is that Ted suffers from an inferiority complex. He also admits he does things he shouldn't do, and doesn't do things he knows he should. 'Boston fans,' he said, 'were swell to me all through our series at home, where I was a flop. I wanted to lift my cap to their applause. For some reason I couldn't do it. And I knew I was wrong.'"

Williams during the war explained his attitude toward

newspapermen when he told Huck Finnegan of the Boston *American* that, "every time I go up to the plate in batting practice, some guy I never saw before comes up and says, 'I'm from such and such a paper, or news service. My managing editor sent me out to get a story on you and your girl friend.' So I burn up and say, 'I'm not looking for any story about your managing editor and *his* girl friend, so scram.' Then they all get on me, and I'm never the Most Valuable Player because I don't want writers butting into my personal affairs. Why can't they stick to baseball?"

When Williams does not tip his cap to the applauding multitude, or ignores a photographer, or mixes little with his teammates off the field, he is declaring his independence. Williams is honestly independent, and it's his hard luck that he has one of the world's worst jobs—as Paul Gallico told him—for being independent.

"I don't want a manager's job or a coaching job," he said last Spring. "You're generally indebted to somebody for a job like that, and I've always been independent. That's the way I'll always be."

Most writers sympathize with him, possibly for the same reason advanced by Bill Cunningham of the *Herald* when he wrote: "I think it's because I see so many of my own eccentricities, inferiority complexes, and damn-the-torpedoes defense mechanisms in him."

Despite my sympathy, as a writer I cannot join the school which calls him Teddy-boy-you-great-big-dear, wildly endorses his virtues and blandly ignores his faults, and basks blissfully in a warm glow created by the fuel of their own words. They have my envy, not my allegiance. To see only the good, to think only the best—what a blessed quality!

Of Williams' virtues, I am well aware. His unpublicized trips to hospitals; his kindnesses to Red Sox clubhouse boys; the time he spends giving autographs; the critics whose rebukes he has forgiven, including myself; his faithful application to the art of hitting; the stories he has given writ-ers; and the pictures he has given photographers are all clear in my mind.

"I'd like to get a series of batting practice pictures. Will you pose for me?" asks Abe Fox, the Associated Press pho-tographer in Boston.

"Not today. Don't feel like it," replies Williams. He adds, "Tell you what. Come out at 10 tomorrow morning and I'll give you all you want."

At 10 o'clock, Fox appears, figuring that Williams has probably forgotten. But there is Williams, waiting, ready, eager. Fox gets a mess of pictures.

Or, the Red Sox beaten in a play-off game for the pen-nant by the Indians, a writer pays a rare visit to the club-house to say adieu to a couple of players he knows.

Williams: "What's the matter? Aren't you going to speak to me?"

Writer: "I don't know if I dare to."

Williams: "Why? We've never had any arguments, have we?"

Writer: "No. I don't know you well enough. But I've heard about your moods."

Williams (laughing): "Oh, you have? Those damn things!"

This is Williams at his best, the Williams who can be glorified, but it is not all of the profile. If some writers persist in portraying Williams as they see him, do not conclude that they despise him. Did Rembrandt, painting the Man With a Gilt Helmet, hate his model? Did Shakespeare hate the rebellious Hotspur? I submit that a Williams depicted in true, bold, brave colors makes a greater picture than a pastel goody-boy.

Why I Would Trade Ted Williams

JOE WILLIAMS

1951

The powerful lineup that won the pennant in 1946 led many to believe that the Red Sox were on the verge of a dynasty. Instead, the 1946 pennant proved to be a tantalizing prelude to a series of agonizingly close but frustrating finishes. In 1948 the Sox lost a one-game play-off to the Indians, and in 1949 they lost the pennant by one game after losing the last two games of the season in New York.

In this article Joe Williams provides a simple answer to explain the Red Sox failure: Ted Williams was not a team leader and could not deliver in the clutch.

To prove his point, the writer cites Williams' poor performances in the 1946 Series, the 1948 play-off game, and the 1949 pennant stretch. Other writers have attempted to balance the record by pointing out that Williams went six for eight in the final three games of 1948 to force the play-off game, and that in 1949, in the eleven-game Red Sox winning streak that led up to the showdown with New York, Williams won four of the games with home runs.

For three years in a row, the Boston Red Sox have been the team to beat in the American League. And that's just what happened. They got beat.

This is a phenomenon in frustration that has baffled the baseball world, driven Joe McCarthy, the game's best manager, into exile, busted chalk-eaters from coast to coast, and sent owner Tom Yawkey out looking for new gold deposits.

What's wrong with the Red Sox? Why don't they win? It can't be their hitting. They swing the most trenchant bats in baseball. Last year, their .303 led both leagues. Even when they get superlative pitching, as in '49 when Kinder and Parnell racked up 48 victories between them, they miss out. Their defense is alert and adroit, and in Ted Williams they have one of the greatest hitters baseball has ever known. Still they don't win. Why?

I think the answer is Williams. Or mostly Williams. It has been popular in making the Red Sox favorites year after year to say they have "everything." This isn't true. If they had "everything," there would be no excuse for this thesis. There would be no Red Sox mystery. The fact is the Red Sox do not have "everything." They do not have team spirit. As Detroit's Dick Bartell said to me last Summer, "You can make 'em quit."

Remember, there is more to winning than what you see on the ball field. More than the basics—hitting, fielding, running, and throwing. A team must have pride, character, and ambition. In a word, it must have a soul. Such a team doesn't need a bench packed with stars to win. It will beat a team of superior players who lack the will to win. It will show to its best advantage under pressure. Somehow, with the chips down, it will play better than it knows how.

What gives a team character? How is this quality distilled. Where does it come from? It comes from the players themselves. Once in a while, it comes from the manager. This happens usually when he is a playing manager. Bucky Harris, in his younger days, had this gift. So did Frank Frisch. And Lou Boudreau was a vivid example in '48 when he almost literally carried the Cleveland Indians to victory, first in the pennant race, then in the World Series.

That was the year the American League had a play-off for the first time. The Red Sox were in the other corner. They lost. They lost for a variety of reasons. One of the most important was the fact that they had no one in the field who could match Boudreau's inspirational fire. If they had had a Boudreau, there never would have been a play-off. The Red Sox would have won by six or eight games. Their defeat in the play-off was incidental.

This was, however, the first enlightenment the baseball world had that the team which had "everything," and which had been picked to dominate the pennant race, was in reality suffering from a mighty serious malady. You didn't have to look too close or too long to realize what was wrong—the Red Sox had no sparkplug. This is a defect, a character deficiency, really, which cannot be perceived in the standings. It is not visibly present in the won-and-lost columns. But it beats more teams than key injuries, gopher balls, and myopic umpires. The Red Sox took no known steps to combat the disease. They lost again in '49 and yet again in '50, close ones both—the kind where character tells.

You'll find a take-charge guy on all winning teams. He may not be a great star. Eddie Stanky is the soul of the New York Giants. The only quality which makes him stand out is hustle and team spirit. I don't care how great a player is, if he's not a team player, he isn't going to help you much, and the chances are he won't help you at all when you need help the most. I think this describes Ted Williams. He's the most flagrant individualist I've ever seen in baseball—and I was traveling with big-league clubs as far back as Larry Lajoie's active days. All Williams is interested in is his hitting. This is another way of saying that all Williams is interested in is Williams.

Yet Williams will give you the most vehement argument that there is no more devoted team player in baseball, and he will be deadly serious, too. According to his lights, he *is* a team player. His lights just aren't blinding. Oh, he plays to win all right, and generally gives his best—or what he considers his best—but there is something lacking. The dimensions of the performance are heroic, but the effect isn't moving or genuine. It is like watching a superb Hollywood duelist in action. Wonderful. But you wouldn't want to bet on him to get you out of a jam.

"Trouble with Williams," commented an old ball player as we sat watching the Red Sox and the Indians play a game last Summer, "trouble with him is he ain't got a drop of Joe DiMaggio blood in his entire system."

Williams presents a complex study. For one thing, he has never grown up as a ball player. Essentially, the fault is his. Still, he might have had a more helpful, understanding start. If he has cost the Red Sox pennants, as I believe, then the Red Sox, or more specifically Joe Cronin, must plead guilty as an accessory to the fact. From the beginning, Cronin elected to pamper an outrageously talented young man. It was a mistake.

It is quite conceivable that if Williams had started under Joe McCarthy, he would have had a happier life, perhaps even a more brilliant career. McCarthy would have cut him down to size quickly. There would have been no time for him to indulge his monumental peeves and morbid moods. Either he would have fitted into McCarthy's way, or he would have been on his way. By the time he did come under McCarthy's direction, it was too late—and by then, Marse Joe probably didn't care very much anyway.

Hindsight tells us that Cronin's baby-sitter policy wasn't bright. What is that line Yogi Berra quotes? "As the twig is bent, etc." Only a player who was coddled as a beginner could be guilty of some of the things Williams does, and the only reason I mention them here is that they are pertinent to my theme: is Williams a handicap to the Red Sox?

Can you imagine him, as a member of the Yankees or the Tigers, thumbing his nose to the home customers and escaping with a contrived and counterfeit apology which the front office—not Williams—issued? The Yankees would have hit him with a fine which would have shaken him to his heels, and I frankly believe old man Briggs of Detroit would have kicked him off the team.

Only a player who holds his manager and the broader interests of the team in disdain, or else is just plain stupid—and I would have to doubt Williams is that—would have popped off to Florida newsmen that he would play or not play in the Spring exhibition games, depending on how he felt about the whole dreary nonsense. If my old friend Steve O'Neill had any previous doubts as to who was managing Williams, it was dispelled in a way which could have added nothing to his peace of mind.

So, as we progress in this study of the most controversial ball player of our time, we find Williams isn't a team player, isn't a take-charge guy, and isn't above putting the manager in his place. These are not admirable qualities. But that isn't the whole of it. Williams is responsible for the worst press relations any Boston club ever has had.

You are told that much of the criticism directed at the young man—who is graciousness itself off the field, by the way—is brewed of personal antagonisms. This could be. Still, when you go looking for trouble, brother, you can't miss finding it, and Williams, especially in recent years, has seemed to take a bitter, neurotic delight in saying and doing the wrong thing at the right time. He does not seem happy unless he has a feud on with the baseball writers, for whom he professes and manifests rhapsodic contempt.

All of which is his privilege, of course. But no ball club ever has prospered on a bad press—and the Red Sox press grows increasingly less complimentary. Indeed, the situation as applied to Williams has reached a point where the attitude of the writers is that if they can't say anything bad about him, they won't say anything. Sooner or later, Boston must feel the effect of this situation at the box office, just as the Giants did some years back when relations between Bill Terry and the New York press became intolerable. Eventually, Terry was dismissed. It simply isn't good business or good baseball to heckle the press, and a club owner who encourages this sort of thing on the part of one of his stars ought to have his head examined.

And I'd like to confess in this connection that there are more than several men in my profession for whom I have not the slightest esteem.

I do not wish to give the impression that Williams is universally unpopular. On the contrary, despite his sophomoric outbursts, his dubious value as a team player, and his occasional displays of coarse manners, which he seems to employ to describe his scorn for the people who pay his large salary, he somehow commands a fiercely partisan following. How big, I don't know. But they know how to write, and their epistolary angry blasts scorch the seat of your pants as they rush to the defense of their strange hero.

I know. I've had my full quota of these letters. Williams, parenthetically, means nothing to me personally, and I'm positive I mean infinitely less to him, though we speak as we pass. Like any objective reporter, I try to see a guy as he is, be he a .400 hitter or a bullpen catcher. And I surely don't pretend to know it all, though once in awhile, I'll admit, I do try to cover too much ground. However, it has been my notion for some time that Williams bulks large in the monstrous defeatist complex from which the Red Sox suffer. It was this conviction which inspired me unhesitatingly to pick the Yankees to beat them in my column in the New York *World Telegram and Sun* last April.

Nevertheless, when a writer makes the charge that the greatest hitter in baseball is a burden to his ball club and that the only way the ball club is ever going to win a pennant is to get rid of him, he should have something more substantial to stand on than his own personal appraisal. It develops I have. I have the opinion of a number of men with responsible connections in the American League, some club owners, some front-office men, some managers—enough, all told, to arrive at a cross-section, composite judgment. To these gentlemen, I presented two questions:

(1) If you had the Red Sox, would you get rid of Williams?

(2) If you could get Williams in a trade, would you take him?

It was agreed that I would not use names, for it is not considered good Emily Post for one club to engage in public debate about the chattel of another. And protocol, not to mention the Commissioner's office, frowns about anything which may smack of tampering. Even imaginary trades, identifying the party of the second part, might come under this heading. I do believe, however, that it is safe to make one exception. Besides, Joe Cronin's words may be comforting to the Ted Williams-can-do-no-wrong club. His comment: "Why don't you see a psychiatrist?"

To the question would you trade Williams if you had the Red Sox, the answers ranged from probably to positively. Incidentally, it became known as the symposium extended that the idea of trading Williams wasn't altogether new. The details did not emerge in full, but it appears that a deal was broached at the end of the '47 season with the Yankees offering DiMaggio and Berra, the latter an in-coming big-leaguer at the time.

If this deal was proposed and Cronin rejected it, I must believe there were times in the days that followed when he wished he had gone through with it. It could be, of course, that Cronin was overruled by Tom Yawkey, who not only rates Williams with Ty Cobb, his boyhood idol, but has a personal affection for him. Such a deal, incidentally, would have put the two great slugging rivals in home parks more suited and inviting to their hitting capacities, the short left-field fence in Fenway Park for DiMaggio and the short right-field wall in Yankee Stadium for Williams. Undoubtedly, this thought was a pivotal point in the discussions of what must be listed as the biggest abortive deal for king-size hitters in the history of the game.

Most of the "trade Williams" responses sounded a familiar note. Lack of hustle. Too much of an individualist. Unproductive in the pinches. Here's a quote from a manager in the West: "The only way Williams can ever help you is with the bat. On a contender, this isn't always enough. Check the records and you'll find Williams seldom comes through in the big situations. I suspect he's a front-runner. The Red Sox were nowhere in the race when he had his .400 year, and the only time they've won with him they got off to such a big lead they never were crowded. I actually think he hurts you rather than helps you when the pressure is on. Besides, he's soured on something in Boston, the newspapers largely, I guess, though it may be the town or the team or even himself. Anyway, if I were Cronin, you could do business with me and you wouldn't have to give up too much."

Here's a quote from a general manager, also in the West: "The feel and attitude of a ball club is best exemplified, I think, by the way the dugout reacts to a home run. Particularly when it is hit by their big man, the fellow they look up to and depend on to carry them over the hump. When Williams hits a home run, the Red Sox players sit on their hands. But let one of the lesser Red Sox—Dropo, Doerr, or Stephens—hit one, and the dugout comes alive with emotion. This can mean only one thing. Nobody cares whether Williams hits or not."

Nevertheless, this same gentleman—and he's been in baseball 30 years and more—admitted that he wouldn't hesitate to deal for Williams. "I'd gamble that a change in scenery would have a tonic effect on him. I wouldn't worry that he would impair the morale of my club. My players all hustle. They'd shame Williams into some semblance of team interest. It's my notion that hustle can be as contagious as complacency. And I think it's only fair to mark that Williams hasn't been exposed to an abundance of the old up-and-at-'em stuff in Boston."

If the Red Sox were to bow to the weight of critical opinion and offer Williams in trade, what would be his most probable destination? I asked contributors to my Gallop Poll to suggest some deals that would be attractive enough to warrant serious consideration by the Red Sox front office. Because of economic factors, three clubs—Browns, Athletics, and Senators—were excluded. Two collateral conditions, the importance of which might not occur immediately to the layman, were underscored. First, the Red Sox, as an appeasement gesture to the fans, would have to get a name player in return. Second, any club dealing for Williams would have to be prepared to assume his enormous salary. Of the dozen or so suggested deals, it was agreed that these would stand the best chance of getting Williams:

From the Yankees—Joe DiMaggio, Ed Lopat, and Charley Silvera. DiMaggio's the name; Lopat helps a weak staff; Silvera's better than any catcher Boston has got.

From the Tigers—Hal Newhouser, John Groth, Myron Ginsberg. Newhouser's the name; Groth could take over for Williams in the outfield; Ginsberg is a good catching prospect.

From the Indians—Bob Feller, Bob Kennedy, and Jim Hegan. Feller's the name; Hegan is big league behind the bat; Kennedy's a journeyman outfielder.

If you took Williams, what would you be getting? You'd be getting at once the greatest hitter in baseball, a headache, and a player who is suspect in more ways than one. You would be getting a player whose record for clutch performance is, to be charitable, not impressive. "Check the records," my manager friend in the West advised. Once you have done that, you must doubt that it is mere coincidence that Williams goes into a sad slump just when the Red Sox need his bat—all he's got to help with—the most.

Consider:

There was his flop in the 1946 World Series when he hit only .200 and arrogantly jested at the shift the Cardinals used against him. There was his one, lone shabby hit in the historic play-off game in '48.

There was his bloomer-girl mark of .215 down the stretch in the steaming '49 race, capped by his utter helplessness in the two wind-up games with the Yankees with the pennant virtually hanging on every swing of his bat.

Finally, there are the accusing figures of '50, which saw the Red Sox play so much better with him out of the lineup (.721 for 61 games) than with him in the lineup (.537 for 93 games).

Yet, in the face of these damning implications and the knowledge that in other ways he is no bargain, there isn't a qualified club in the league that wouldn't trade for him. Both as a writer and a fan, I'd like to see him traded. Just the realization that the Red Sox would even attempt to get along without him might give him a jolt and set him to taking inventory of himself. In the end, Ted Williams might even reach the conclusion that he isn't completely perfect himself.

Ted Undeserving of Fans' Tribute

DAVE EGAN

1952

Dave Egan, the Boston columnist known as "the Colonel," was the most persistent and acerbic of all Williams' press antagonists. Everyone, including Williams, acknowledged Egan's talent as a writer, but they also acknowledged his consistently brutal treatment of Williams. In commenting on the viciousness of the Boston press in the '40s and '50s, David Halberstam writes in *Summer of '49*: "In a culture of journalistic scoundrels, the greatest scoundrel of them all was Dave Egan. . . . What he did, especially to Williams, was not pleasant for anyone who cares about the American press."

Ironically, on two occasions when Williams was attacked by the press—his 1942 draft deferment (enabling him to provide financial security for his mother) and his late arrival for the birth of his first child—Egan came to his defense, arguing that those were private affairs that did not concern the public.

The Boston *Daily Record* column that follows appeared the day of Williams' final game (April 30, 1952) before he left to report to the Marines for active duty in Korea. Prior to what many believed might be his last game ever, Williams was honored at Fenway Park by the mayor and the governor and presented with a memory book signed by more than 400,000 fans. A resolution introduced in the Massachusetts Senate cited Williams as "an inspiration not only to the youth of the country but to the youth of Massachusetts." Egan obviously disagreed with that assessment.

Incidentally, Williams, who had not started since opening day because of a pulled muscle, hit a home run off Virgil Trucks in his last time at bat to beat the Tigers, 5 to 3.

There must be thousands of boys exactly like him, up and down the country.

He was pointed out to me at a high school banquet recently. Where or when makes no difference. Neither does his name. He is just a boy who idolizes Ted Williams. Swings left-handed like Williams. Wears his pants long, like Williams. Plays the outfield, like Williams. And will not wear a necktie even when the occasion insists upon a necktie, simply because the great man will not wear a necktie.

The skies will not tumble down upon us, whether a boy wears a necktie or not, but I have the right and the duty to ask where Ted Williams is leading this boy. Does he also refuse to tip his cap, does he feel that even the most indecent gesture will be overlooked, so long as he can hit a baseball with a piece of wood? Is he to be a rebel against conformity, simply because the man after whom he models himself has successfully rebelled, and may he expect to be honored by municipal big wheels at a later date, if he follows the pattern set by Williams?

It seems disgraceful to me, that a person such as Williams now is to be given the keys to the city. We talk about juvenile delinquency, and fight against it, and then officially honor a man whom we should officially horsewhip, for the vicious influence that he has had on the childhood of America. Mayor John Hynes and troughman Mike Kelleher and the other members of the committee are making it more difficult for every one of us who is trying to bring up a child in the right way.

We want our children to respect the rights and the feelings of others. We want them to have ordinary good manners. We want them to conform to the good code that society has established, for we feel that this is of the highest importance in the molding of a good citizen. Then men who call themselves community leaders insult the decent and intelligent fathers and mothers in the community, lavishing honors on a man who consistently and over a period of many years, has set the poorest possible example to our children, and if this is leadership, I'll have strychnine.

Nobody ever objected when Babe Ruth was honored, for in more ways than one, he never threw to the wrong base. Like me, and like many another sinner, he was far from being a model in his private life, but I repeat that, in public, he never threw to the wrong base, and never made the wrong move. He was not a mental giant, but he knew enough to know his responsibilities to kids who adored him. He sold raw drama, and high heroics, and performance in the pinch, and technical brilliance, but most of all, he sold plain decency. He came out of a reform school, and was the great American underdog, but he never permitted himself to forget for one moment that the eyes of millions of children were upon him, and he lived up to his obligations, in a manner that made him one of America's best-loved and most valuable citizens.

It would be much easier, and much more pleasant, to say the expected thing, and to praise Williams, but I don't peddle insincerity. I try to give you a nickel's worth of truth when I sit down to a typewriter, and though this has won me no popularity contests, at least I have the satisfaction of knowing that I'm being true to myself and to my own principles.

Therefore I say that I shall pay no honor to Ted Williams, for the reason that I cannot honor a man whom I do not respect. I respected the Babe, respected him enough to cover his funeral, and to ride with him to Valhalla, and to add my tributes to those of millions more. I felt that I owed it to the man for his many contributions to the richness of our lives. Chief of these was that he preached a fine, good sermon to kids of all creeds and all colors, and so left behind him a better America than the one in which he had entered.

Williams has stubbornly and stupidly refused to recognize this responsibility to childhood. The kid has set a sorry example for a generation of kids. He has been a Pied Piper, leading them along a bitter, lonely road. He has done much harm, and now it is one minute before midnight. If this is to be his final hour, then he should capitalize on it by apologizing to all boyhood everywhere, and by telling them that the social niceties are of the utmost importance, if only because they raise man above the level of the beast.

Return of the Master

ARTHUR DALEY

1955

A columnist for the *New York Times* for thirty-one years, in 1973 Arthur Daley became the first sportswriter to win a Pulitzer Prize. He was one of the many writers that Williams respected throughout his career, and he, in turn, respected Williams. His columns provide some of the most objective and insightful portraits of the controversial slugger.

This column is about one of Williams' many returns to baseball. Following his combat tour in Korea, he returned to the Red Sox lineup in August, 1953, hitting .407 with thirteen home runs in ninety-one times at bat. The following April, after breaking his collarbone on the first day of spring training, he announced that 1954 would be his final season. He changed his mind early in the 1955 season and on May 13 (the day this column appeared) signed a one-year contract for $98,000.

The pitchers won't like it," said Casey Stengel, "but everyone else in the league will. It's the best possible thing that could have happened for our league."

Ol' Case was referring to the news that Ted Williams would rejoin the Boston Red Sox.

"There's a feller," continued Stengel, "which has tree-mendous ability with the bat. He's not a singles hitter but a distance slugger which leads the league in power. He kin hit singles, doubles, triples and home runs and kin beatcha on days when he gets only one little single 'cause he also gets three walks. A great hitter. I'm glad he's comin' back, even though there may be times later on when the sight of him wavin' that bat will give me the creeps."

Al Lopez of the Cleveland Indians said practically the same thing and there was considerable rejoicing in every front office in the American League at word that the big fellow was on his way. Frank Lane of the White Sox estimated that Williams would be worth half a million dollars extra at the box office.

Some fans will come to cheer and some to jeer. It's almost impossible to feel neutral about the stormy, controversial Williams, an outspoken man of many moods. Most baseball writers dislike him, but a few hold him in affection and esteem. The baseball players—and this may be highly significant—regard him with great admiration.

In the first place, he's not only the best hitter in the sport but is the most stylish natural hitter since Shoeless Joe Jackson. The statistics prove his eminence. His lifetime average of .348 is surpassed only by Ty Cobb with .367, Rogers Hornsby with .358 and the Shoeless One with .356.

No man in baseball has studied the batting art with the avidity of the ever-curious Williams. He'll talk hitting with anyone from the drop of a bat and he'll share his vast knowledge with any ball player who asks his advice. Often he does it without being asked.

His tips last year made a formidable hitter out of young Al Kaline of the Detroit Tigers. At the All-Star Game last July, Al Rosen of the Indians was in a horrendous slump. Williams straightened him out in a minute's conversation and Rosen hit two homers that day.

Although Ted made a formal announcement last season

that 1954 would be his final year, no one who knew him well believed it.

"Williams is a fellow who lives for his next time at bat," once remarked Eddie Collins, then general manager of the Red Sox. Ted was only a mere stripling when this description of his character was offered. It still holds for the man of 36.

When Williams hesitated about returning to the sport during spring training, there were some folks who thought he was coyly playing hard-to-get. That was arrant nonsense. This was strictly a personal problem, predicated on what financial settlement would be forthcoming to his wife in their divorce proceedings. If she were too demanding, he would refuse to earn any salary. It was as simple as that. Aware of his blind stubbornness, she was not too unreasonable.

It's the Williams stubbornness that has his critics, friendly and otherwise, at odds. When Lou Boudreau devised an overshifted defense against him, Ted rockheadedly refused to slice it to ribbons by slicing the ball to the opposite field. Instead, he tried to overpower it.

"If they ever used that defense against me," Ty Cobb dreamily told this reporter, "they'd never have got me out."

"I can't rate Williams as a great hitter," said the blunt Rogers Hornsby, "until he learns to hit to the opposite field. I once hit homers in succession over the left, center and right field fences. That's what I call hitting." The Rajah never could be termed overly modest.

Williams has the keenest eyesight in the big leagues and he steadfastly refuses to swing at a ball that is even an inch wide of the plate.

"Once in a while," reluctantly admitted Joe DiMaggio under the pressure of a pointed question, "a batter has to go for a bad pitch if a home run will win a ball game and a walk won't."

"He's wrong," heatedly declared Williams in rebuttal. "If a hitter starts swinging at pitches an inch wide, these smart pitchers begin to give him pitches two inches wide. It keeps getting worse; you become a bad-ball hitter and down goes your average. Ask Stan Musial. It happened to him."

"He's right," said Stan the Man, "although I still will go for a slightly wide pitch if it might win a ball game."

But Williams won't. He's a perfectionist and the acknowledged master of his trade. No one in baseball knows more about hitting than Theodore Samuel Williams.

Handsome Bad Boy of the Boston Red Sox

AL HIRSHBERG

1956

Readers may be surprised that a story on Ted Williams appeared in *Cosmopolitan*, whose audience as well as its editorial policy has obviously changed considerably. Its publication is a reminder that Ted Williams was not only a sports hero but a "matinee idol."

While it repeats some of the details and conclusions found in Fitzgerald's essay ("Two Guys Named Ted Williams"), Hirshberg's story is distinct in that it is explicitly targeted to a female audience. Considering the author's approach—"Williams is every woman's dream of the male animal she secretly yearns for"—this article reveals as much about the era in which it was published as it does about its subject.

Ted Williams of the Boston Red Sox is baseball's greatest slugger and the game's most baffling character. At thirty-seven, an age when most ball players have hung up their spikes, Williams is still the most feared hitter in the business. Beyond that, he is, as he has been since he broke into the Red Sox lineup as a brash rookie in 1939, one of the most thoroughly misunderstood figures on the American sporting scene.

He is a shy, stubborn, proud, unhappy man, a man with

THE TED WILLIAMS READER

everything and nothing, a man who has always wanted to live and let live but who can't understand himself or his fellow man. He says what he thinks and does what he pleases, and he sees no reason why he shouldn't be permitted to continue to do so without interference. Those who understand him and thus willingly put up with his idiosyncrasies love him. Those who don't, hate his guts.

Product of a divided home, victim of an unhappy childhood, subject of some of the most bitter criticism ever leveled at a professional athlete, Ted Williams today is a part-time recluse, a self-appointed pariah, who, as soon as the baseball season is over, seeks peace of mind on an isolated Florida key.

He collects over $100,000 a year in salary from the Red Sox and makes, perhaps, as much again from outside interests; yet as far as his personal needs are concerned, he could live on the pittance of a street sweeper. Here is a man who could have had the world at his feet, who could have become as beloved a baseball personality as the immortal Babe Ruth. Instead, he is a bitter lone wolf, subject to moods as changeable as the tides and not nearly as predictable.

The man is more than a great ball player, more than a controversial character, more than a celebrity. His brain is sharp, yet he can do brainless things. His magnetism is enormous, yet he can express himself in the vernacular of a dockwalloper. He has the instincts of a gentleman, yet can show the manners of a lout.

This last seems to make no difference whatever to his female fans. He is perhaps the greatest single drawing card for women in the major leagues. His clean-cut good looks, his boyish grin, his thick, curly, brown hair, and his rugged build combine to serve as an automatic attraction. But beyond that, Williams is every woman's dream of the male animal she secretly yearns for—a handsome, disdainful, nonconforming, uninhibited, unmanageable, unpredictable, and utterly charming individual. Three-quarters of the huge pile of letters addressed to him at Boston's Fenway Park are mash notes from unknown female admirers.

• HEARTBEATS IN THE BLEACHERS

"The man drips with magnetism," a respectable young Boston matron remarked one day last spring. "Maybe he's impossible to live with, but I'd gladly spend a weekend with him. I challenge you to show me a woman with an ounce of femininity who wouldn't."

If the lady ever were granted the chance she yearns for she very probably would come away adoring or loathing him. With Williams, there seems to be no middle ground of opinion—and no agreement among those who know him. He is as complex as a mechanical brain, the answer to an analyst's dream. If he ever stretched out on a psychiatrist's couch—which he would not do—the findings would fill several volumes.

Today some of his friends say he has mellowed a little, but he is no less complex. He dislikes attention and resents the printed word, even when it is written in praise.

One day last year, when Billy Klaus, who preceded him at bat, broke up a ball game with a ninth-inning home run, Williams rushed from the on-deck circle to congratulate the little shortstop as he crossed the plate. The next morning, a Boston reporter wrote, "Williams is a team man now."

Williams sought out the writer later and grunted, "What's the idea of saying I'm a team man *now?* I've always been a team man."

He once reveled in praise, basked in the light of the special adulation reserved for American sports heroes. Today he asks only to be left alone.

It is too much to ask. As long as he plays baseball, as long as he lives, perhaps as long as baseball itself lives, people will want to read about Ted Williams. He objects to almost every word written. If it's praise, the writer is trying to get something out of him. If it's criticism, the writer is a no good so-and-so.

When plans for this article were mentioned to him during spring training in Sarasota, Florida, last March, Williams snapped, "What can you write that hasn't been written before? Aren't people sick of reading about Ted Williams?"

His pet peeve is the "front-runner" who fawns all over him after a big day and ignores him after a bad one. Johnny Orlando, the Red Sox clubhouse attendant, is one of his favorites principally because Orlando works in reverse. When Williams goes hitless, Orlando is the first to greet him in the locker room. When Williams plasters the ball all over the lot, Orlando ignores him.

Williams has dozens of favorite characters today—and not one truly close friend. Other celebrities travel around escorted by a retinue of admirers and hangers-on. Williams travels alone. Other celebrities like to be seen in public places. Except for the ballparks, Williams shuns all public places. Other celebrities gravitate toward people of means. Williams gravitates toward policemen, firemen, garage mechanics, waiters, ushers, servicemen. Other celebrities make it their business to keep on good terms with the press. Williams doesn't care what the press thinks, and actually goes out of his way to antagonize the Boston newsmen.

Yet to say, as has been said over and over, that Williams hates all newsmen is a canard. It is even wrong to say that he hates the Boston press. He is very close to Arthur Sampson of the *Herald,* and has no axes to grind with one or two others. But he does hate Austen Lake of the *American* and Dave Egan of the *Record* with an abiding passion. In 1939, when Williams was a rookie and first began having trouble with the fans, Lake wrote, "Ted Williams is a grown man with the mind of a juvenile." He has harped on that theme ever since, often with justification, more often without.

Egan, never noted for his velvet touch, incurred Williams' wrath early in his career by writing, among other things, "Williams is the all-time, All-American adolescent, the prize heel ever to wear a Boston uniform." The *Record* columnist repeatedly twits Williams for his miserable showing in the 1946 World Series, and always refers to him in print as a "choke artist."

• RASPBERRY AND LEMON

But his dislike for the newsmen isn't nearly as intense as his dislike for the fans. "They're a bunch of sheep," he says. "When one starts giving me the business, the whole bunch joins in. Every time I look at them, I feel like vomiting."

Which is why he never looks at them. His psychopathic hatred for the people who pay his freight dates back to incidents that occurred during the 1939 season—his first year in the major leagues.

• IN LIKE A LAMB

In those days, Williams was a right fielder. In Boston's Fenway Park, the right fielder can become very chummy with the fans, since a section of the grandstand is close beside him, and a bleacher section is just behind him. Williams and the fans *were* chummy during the first few weeks of his career. He always ran out to his position with a big grin on his face, and the fans, in turn, took him to their hearts. This happy state of affairs was intensified every time Williams hit a home run. He would cross the plate waving his cap, and he'd wave it again in response to cheers when he moved out to right field.

But one day he let a ground ball go through his legs, and, as he chased it, a few scattered boos issued from the bleachers. After throwing the ball to the infield, Williams turned, cupped his hands, and shouted a stream of profane invective in the direction of the bleachers. This brought forth a chorus of bazoos, and the battle was on.

He was openly swearing as he came in toward the dugout at the end of the inning. He moved to the bench, yelling, "The hell with all of them. I'll never tip my cap to them as long as I live."

Up to that point, Williams was regarded as a happy-go-lucky, somewhat eccentric, but thoroughly refreshing kid. He was forever swinging a bat, whether he had one in his hands or not. Often, to the delight of the fans and the consternation of his manager, Joe Cronin, he stood in right field during a ball game and swung an imaginary bat at an imaginary ball. He aimed the thumb of his glove at pigeons atop the fence and "shot" them off. He grinned after reaching a base safely. And when he belted a ball out of the park, he laughed as he crossed home plate.

He even practiced swinging a bat in front of a mirror in his hotel room. One night he came too close and smashed the mirror. Turning to his roommate, Charlie Wagner, he grinned and exclaimed, "What power!"

● *"I'LL NEVER TIP MY CAP"*

When he returned to Boston for the 1940 season, he was shifted from right field to left, but there was no shift in his absurd feud with the fans. He not only wouldn't tip his cap or look toward the stands except to answer boos with chilling curses, but he went out of his way to antagonize the public.

"Why do you call the fans such names?" he was asked one day.

"Never mind the names I call them," he countered. "Go out there and listen to the names the dirty, miserable unprintables call me!"

He kept a jealous watch on his personal affairs, deeply resenting the slightest intrusion on his privacy. He refused to recognize that lack of privacy is the price of fame. When it was pointed out to him, he snapped, "Who the hell asked for fame anyhow?" It took much digging to uncover and piece together the pathetic story of his unhappy childhood.

• CHARITY BEGAN ELSEWHERE

Ted's father, Sam Williams, was a drifter who often left his home in San Diego, California, for long periods of time. He finally left permanently around 1937. Ted and a brother were brought up almost exclusively by their mother. Mrs. May Williams was and is a most remarkable lady, completely dedicated to the good works of the Salvation Army. She spent her life helping to raise derelicts from the gutter and trying to set them on the right track. No human wreck was too hopeless for her. Beloved by society's forgotten dregs, she was known all over southern California as a kind, generous woman who could not turn down an appeal for help. There was only one thing wrong. She was so wrapped up in her work that she had little time for her children.

This neglect of the child must have had a shattering effect on the character of the man. Williams grew up insecure, and he remains insecure to this day. He has no roots, no place to light. He never considered San Diego his home after he joined the Red Sox, and, so far as is known, hasn't even visited there for many years. In spite of the fact that he rarely sees her, he has a deep affection for his mother. Mrs. Williams, on her part, adores him.

"Ted is a wonderful son," she said. "He's never given me a worry, and he's a wonderful provider. He loves baseball the way I love the Salvation Army."

Separated from his wife because of difficulties which he refuses to discuss, Ted now lives a bachelor life in a house of his own in Islamorada, in the Florida Keys. He has a housekeeper who lives there permanently. He works and plays in private, and, on the few occasions when he ventures abroad, something almost always happens that makes him wish he hadn't.

One day last spring, a middle-aged man stormed into the lobby of the John Ringling Hotel in Sarasota, where the Red Sox make their headquarters, and, buttonholing a ball player, snapped, "That Williams is no good for baseball."

"Why?"

"Well," the man declared, "my wife and I just saw him on Lido Beach listening to the radio with a woman."

"The poor guy can't even sit on the beach with a girl without antagonizing somebody," the ball player commented later. "The man walked away before I could point out Ted is legally separated from his wife and has a perfect right to take out a girl—as if it was anyone's business."

Insecurity as a child was only one of the factors in the development of the enigma of Ted Williams. As a boy, his ears rang with the gibes of other children because his mother was a Salvation Army worker, and her charities became a source of shame to him. As a man, he shows no interest in religion and hides his own charities beneath a hard shell of surly secrecy. As a boy, he developed an abnormal sensitivity to insult. As a man, he became famous as the possessor of the worst "rabbit ears" in baseball. As a boy, recognition came hard. As a man, long after he had achieved it, he never stopped trying to prove that he could do things better than anyone else.

His refusal to talk about his background, his parents, or his personal affairs, has resulted only in unhappiness for him. His father died, presumably in poverty, several years ago in San Francisco while Williams was at the peak of his career. The son flatly refused to deny accusations that he had neglected his parent, although he had repeatedly financed his father in unsuccessful business ventures, and continued to send him money to the day of his death.

In May of 1944, while still in the Marines, Williams married the former Doris Soule, stunning brunette daughter of a hunting guide in Princeton, Minnesota, where Williams spent his winters from 1938 on. He began going there at the time he played for the Minneapolis ball club. Somewhat like her husband, Doris was quick-tempered, shy, and suspicious of strangers. In Boston where, as Mrs. Ted Williams, she was a marked woman, she kept pretty much to herself.

• PEN IS MIGHTIER THAN TRUTH

In January of 1948, the couple's daughter, Barbara Joyce, was born in a Boston hospital while her father was on a fishing trip in the Florida Everglades. The newspapers castigated the Red Sox star as an inexcusably neglectful husband and father, and he became a subject of controversy in new circles. Housewives who didn't know a home run from a strikeout exploded with indignation. What manner of man was this who went fishing while his wife was having a baby?

As usual, Williams offered no explanation because, as usual, he resented the invasion of his privacy. He felt that such items as the confinement of his wife and the birth of his daughter were his and their business, and nobody else's. Only when the attending physician explained that the infant had arrived several weeks prematurely and that Williams had planned to be in the city in plenty of time for the event did the storm subside.

He kept his wife and daughter in a cocoon of isolation, carefully shielded from the contaminating glare of the public eye. Doris had never shown much interest in baseball; now she stayed away from games altogether. She was in complete agreement with her husband on the subject of publicity. She abhorred it.

She also apparently grew to abhor baseball. One evening, during dinner with two other couples a year or so after Barbara Joyce was born, Williams was asked, "If you had a son, would you like him to be a ball player?"

"If he were a good one," Ted replied.

"Well, would you like your daughter to marry a ball player?"

Before he could answer, his wife snapped, "I'd see her dead first!"

Williams' stubborn disdain for explanation got him into trouble on the day the Red Sox clinched the American League pennant in Cleveland in 1946. The players had a victory party at the Hotel Statler that night, and Williams was conspicuous by his absence. His failure to attend the party commanded almost as much space in the Boston newspapers as the winning of the pennant, and left him with a reputation of being anything but a team man.

He had spent the evening at the bedside of an incurably sick child in a Cleveland hospital. He hadn't bothered to mention it because he didn't think it was anyone's business.

• WILLIAMS' TIN CURTAIN

He loves to plague the press. In 1950, at his instigation, the Red Sox players voted to ban the press from the locker room before games and for an hour following. Williams gleefully helped to enforce the rule. Day after day, as the deadline minute approached and the writers waited outside, he stood at the entrance, clad only in a towel, and, pointing to the clock, repeated, "Not yet, you chowderheads, not yet!"

There are some signs that Williams has changed a bit in his own press relations. Last summer, when his daughter visited him in Boston, he asked that newspaper photographers leave her alone. But the little girl, who lives with her mother in Miami, was big news at the time. One afternoon paper took a set of posed pictures of her, and ran a panel of them on page one. Williams was not happy about it, but he didn't blow his top, as he would have in previous years.

In general, the Boston newsmen go out of their way to protect Williams, in spite of his open contempt for them. When Williams and his wife separated in the spring of 1955, very little publicity was given the split-up. Even when he handed the press a direct insult last winter, it continued to protect him. Voted an award for being the Red Sox's most valuable player, he didn't even show up to receive it at the newsmen's winter dinner, yet he appeared in Boston the very next morning to sign his 1956 Red Sox contract. His arrival in the city was played up, but the slap was ignored.

● *A THROWBACK TO PECK'S BAD BOY*

So, too, was an astonishing example of childishness hardly worthy of baseball's first citizen or, for that matter, of any grown man. The writers, not knowing whether to expect him or not, asked Johnny Orlando to see what he could find out. Orlando contacted Williams at his home in Florida, and asked, "Are you going to the writers' dinner?"

"Why," Williams declared, "I wouldn't give those clowns the right time. Of course I'm not going!"

"O.K.," said Orlando. "Send them a wire and tell them so."

"The hell I will," Williams said. "Suppose I change my mind?"

This masterpiece of infantile idiocy is a prize example of Ted Williams at his worst today, but it is a far cry from the Peck's Bad Boy that he used to be. At twenty-one, he swore aloud. At thirty-seven, he swears under his breath. At twenty-one, he was a perpetual motion machine. At thirty-seven, he moves more slowly. At twenty-one, baseball was a pleasure for him. At thirty-seven, it's a business. At twenty-one, he was obscene with strangers. At thirty-seven, he ignores them.

His last public visit to the gutter in Boston occurred in the 1950 season. He had had a bad day, both in the field and at the plate, and the wolves were working overtime on him. When an opposing base runner took an extra base while Williams was leisurely going after a ball, the stands rocked with a chorus of deep-seated bazoos. As Williams reached the dugout after the inning was over, he stopped, then spat and made a vulgar gesture in the direction of the fans.

Tom Yawkey, owner of the Red Sox, sitting in his box on the roof of Fenway Park, was as disgusted as everyone else present. At his insistence, Williams issued a public apology the next day. It was the nearest thing to disciplinary action the Red Sox had taken on him in years.

Only once before had Williams ever apologized to anyone in baseball. That was in 1942, after Joe Cronin, then the Red Sox manager and now the club's general manager, fined him $250 for loafing during a game in Washington. Cronin had disciplined him a few times before that, but has never done so since. Neither has any other Red Sox manager.

Williams' relations with his managers, with the exception of Lou Boudreau, who ran the club from 1952 through 1954, have been uncommonly good. Williams never forgave Boudreau for devising a highly successful and widely copied defensive shift against him when Boudreau managed the Cleveland Indians. Boudreau packed the right side of the diamond with fielders, leaving the left virtually unprotected. Not for years did Williams wreck the shift by hitting to left field. Instead, he tried to ram the ball through the heavy defense. He succeeded often enough, but he lost dozens of base hits on balls fielded by men who ordinarily would have been positioned elsewhere.

Williams was flying for the Marines in Korea during much of the time that Boudreau was the Red Sox manager, but the two studiously avoided each other after Williams returned. If Boudreau had not been fired at the end of the 1954 season, Williams probably would have stuck to his announced intention of retiring. But he likes Mike Higgins, the current manager. He and Higgins were teammates in the 1946 World Series.

• THE MANAGEMENT OF MANAGERS

Williams also deeply admired Joe McCarthy, who succeeded Cronin in 1948, partly because McCarthy had won eight pennants with the New York Yankees, but mostly because McCarthy showed enormous tact in resolving at the outset what could have become a ticklish situation. Williams has always refused to wear a necktie. McCarthy had always demanded that his players never appear in public without one. On the morning of the first day of spring training in Sarasota, McCarthy came down to breakfast in a sports shirt open at the throat.

If Williams' career had not been repeatedly interrupted, he might have set records that could stand for years. He is baseball's only active .400 hitter. He batted .406 in 1941. He led the American League in batting four times and on two other occasions lost the title because he did not have the required 400 times at bat. He has a lifetime average of .348, a lifetime slugging percentage of .642, a lifetime home run total of 394. He has led the league in homers and in runs batted in four times. He has twice been named the American League's Most Valuable Player and once missed by a single vote. Last July, he played in his twelfth All-Star game.

Injuries and war service have cost Williams the equivalent of about five complete baseball seasons. He was a Marine flight instructor in World War II, during which he lost three seasons. He broke an elbow in the 1950 All-Star game and was out most of the year. He was recalled into the Marines in May of 1952, saw action as a jet pilot in Korea, and didn't return to baseball until July of 1953. He broke his shoulder on the first day of spring training in 1954, and was on the shelf for two months. Last year, because of problems resulting from his marital embroilment, he didn't report to the Red Sox until late May, and he was out for ten days in June with a back injury.

• *A LONG, INTERRUPTED CAREER*

Yet, in 98 games, he hit 28 home runs, which was only nine less than the league leader, Mickey Mantle, who played in 147 games. At the end of 1955, Williams' lifetime home run total was surpassed only by Babe Ruth, Jimmy Foxx, Mel Ott, and Lou Gehrig, all of whom enjoyed long, uninterrupted careers.

Williams' one remaining baseball ambition is to star in a World Series. He was a sensational flop in 1946, when the St. Louis Cardinals beat the Red Sox in four of seven games. St. Louis pitchers, backed by a variation of the Boudreau shift, held him to five singles, one a bunt. Williams had ended the season in a bad batting slump, and it stayed with him throughout the series. His only comment was, "I was lousy."

He remembers that series with burning humiliation and wants another chance to prove that he can dominate a World Series the way he has dominated almost everything else in modern baseball.

He has a warped, bitter outlook on life, yet is an astonishingly well-rounded individual. He is one of the world's leading authorities on deep-sea fishing, and owns a fishing tackle business in partnership with Sam Snead, the golfer. He is a student of aviation; and has flown all types of airplanes. He is something of a financial wizard, with a sound knowledge of the intricacies of the stock market. He is a surprisingly good public speaker, and has a keen sense of humor.

A few years ago, right after a Japanese runner had won the Boston Marathon, a road race of over twenty-six miles, Williams was asked whether he objected to the great number of intentional bases on balls given him by opposing pitchers.

"Why should I object?" he said. "That guy just ran 26 miles, 385 yards, for a medal. Look at the dough they give me for walking 90 feet!"

When Ed Doherty, then the Red Sox publicity man, congratulated Williams for hitting .406 in 1941, Ted replied, "When a guy hits .400, it means he's had four hits for every ten times he's been up. How long would you last in your job if, out of every ten assignments you were given, you only did four of them right?"

• EASY MARK FOR A SOB STORY

Williams has a heart as big as his pocketbook, but he refuses to admit it. He barks invective, but has no bite. A sob story, personally substantiated, will move him to tears.

Once, in Washington, he was asked to allow his name to be used in connection with a movement to raise funds for the family of a deceased policeman. Williams, taken to meet the widow, who was faced with the prospect of trying to support four children on a meager pension, gave her every cent he carried. "I'm sorry," he said, "This is all I've got. I'll send a check later."

He once paid the hospital bill of a former Boston baseball pressman who had been one of his bitterest critics. After his recovery, the pressman went back to his practice of beating Williams' brains out in print at every opportunity. To this day, the man doesn't know the identity of his benefactor, and, if Williams has his way, he'll never find out.

Williams has little patience with juvenile autograph-hunters, yet will travel miles to comfort a sick child. He once flew from Washington to Raleigh, North Carolina, after a night game, arrived at four in the morning, spent five hours with a dying youngster, then flew back to Washington in time for an afternoon game.

His favorite charity is the Jimmy Fund, sponsored by Boston's Variety Club for the benefit of the Children's Cancer Research Foundation. Only the patients and nurses know how much time Williams spends in the Jimmy Fund Building, adjoining Boston's Children's Hospital. His efforts alone have been responsible for the raising of more than a quarter of a million dollars.

Since Williams refuses to answer telephone calls, he is practically incommunicado to strangers. If he wants to talk to a party trying to reach him, he will call back. His buffer is the nearest telephone operator. Once sloppy and forgetful about his commitments, he now keeps a careful check on his schedule. When a visiting columnist asked him for an appointment after practice in Sarasota one day last spring, Williams said, "Meet me at 1:30; I'll give you half an hour." The two met in front of Williams' locker in the Red Sox clubhouse. Precisely at two o'clock, Williams stood up and headed for the showers.

He and his business manager, Fred Corcoran, who has some foibles of his own, have a strange but very close relationship. Corcoran, like Williams, is inordinately sensitive, with the result that each is always a little annoyed at the other for some real or imagined slight. But they respect each other's judgment and rarely disagree over matters of business. Asked one day whether he advises Williams about what to buy on the stock market, Corcoran replied, "He advises me."

Corcoran's standard reply to routine requests for appearances by Williams is, "I doubt if he'll do it, but I'll ask him." Williams has two methods of turning down requests that don't appeal to him. One is a flat refusal. The other is, "I'll take it up with Fred."

But if Williams is interested in a project, he will agree on the spot, whether Corcoran likes the idea or not. One day last winter, when the two were sitting side by side at a banquet in Washington, Williams was asked to attend the opening of an annual sailfishing tournament in Stuart, Florida, a month later.

"I'll be there," Williams said.

"Write me a letter and check on it," Corcoran told the man making the request.

"The hell with that," Williams said. "I said I'd be there, didn't I?"

And he was.

Williams hasn't had a close friend in baseball since Bobby Doerr retired after the 1949 season. Doerr, a teammate of Williams both in San Diego and Boston, was a remnant of the old guard, the last of the Red Sox to have preceded Williams into the major leagues. A quiet, steady man, he was the only person who could make Williams exercise even the slightest restraint.

● *THE CROWD IS A LONG WAY OFF*

Now Williams walks alone. He has had no roommate for two years. He has no teammate who considers himself his equal. The other members of the Red Sox treat him with an awe born of hero worship. They respect his ability, marvel at his durability, seek his advice, appreciate his help, even exchange wisecracks with him when he's in a happy mood, but they have no true, give-and-take affection for him. They are Johnny-come-latelies. He is an elder statesman. They are the little guys. He is the big guy. They are only human. Williams is a living legend.

Ted Is Hope

ROBERT CREAMER

1956

The final years of Williams' career were spent with mediocre teams that were but a faint echo of the powerful lineup of the late forties. In this "hopeful outlook" piece typical of spring training reports, Robert Creamer sums up what the presence of a mature Ted Williams means to a now youthful team.

Spring is here, and with it the Boston Red Sox and hope. Hope for the Red Sox is spelled T-E-D. It stands 6 feet 4 inches high, weighs at the moment a bulky 224 pounds and swings a baseball bat as perfectly as a herring gull flies.

Hope stood in short left field in Payne Park in Sarasota, Florida last week, flopping around after fly balls and grounders, smiling, talking with this player and joking with that one, laughing, sweating under the sun. People watching practice from the grandstand looked mostly at the batting cage and the man currently at bat, but eyes kept straying out to left field, and newcomers to the stands were nudged and told, "There's Ted. That's Ted Williams out there in left."

When it was near time for his turn at bat, Williams loped in to the batting cage. He dropped his glove, picked up the little red shin guard he uses to protect his left leg from fouls glancing down off his bat and leaned over to strap it on.

Joe Reichler, an Associated Press sportswriter, was on the other side of the cage.

"Hi, Bush," he said to Williams. Williams looked up from the shin guard, his face alert, and saw Reichler.

"Hi, Joe," he said. He finished buckling the strap and walked over.

He stood leaning against the cage, making small talk, occasionally interrupting himself to comment on the action. Leo Kiely, the lean Boston left-hander, was on the mound. Williams indicated Kiely with a nod of his head.

"That guy there. He's as thin as a damn rail."

He shook his head as if in worry, like a parent disturbed by a child who won't eat. A batter hit a sharp line drive.

"Base hit," Williams announced approvingly. "Dandy."

• *A HARD SWING*

Then it was his turn and he hopped into the cage. Bill Henry took over the pitching chores. Williams bunted the first pitch and took the second. He swung hard at the third pitch but missed it completely, grunting from the effort.

"Attaway, Bill!" he called out to the pitcher. Then to himself: "Same old Williams."

He popped one up, fouled one off, rapped two or three "base hits," then swung and missed again.

"How can you miss those?" he asked himself. He talked constantly while he was at bat, to the pitcher, to the catcher, to the other players around the cage. He set himself as Henry threw again. "I won't miss this one."

He hit the ball hard but on the ground.

"One more," he called out to Henry.

He topped it and it bounced off to the left. Williams jumped back into the batter's box for still one more pitch. He set himself, swung hard and hit the ball with a sharp *whack!* The ball towered high, high into right field and the outfielders turned to watch it drop beyond the fence.

Sammy White, the catcher, said slowly in open awe: "For God's sake."

"Nope," said Williams, walking briskly out of the batter's box and around to the back of the cage. "Didn't hit it good."

Somehow, it did not appear that he had entirely convinced White, who was still looking at the distant outfield fence.

The high regard that Sammy White and the other members of the Boston Red Sox feel for Ted Williams is not based solely on esthetic appreciation of Williams' great skill with a bat, though no ball player could watch Williams' hitting and not admire it. No, for the Red Sox the presence of Williams in spring training means something else: very possibly the fulfillment of a frequently frustrated dream. Yogi Berra of the New York Yankees was, with considerable logic, named Most Valuable Player in the American League last year, but let no one tell you that any player in the league means more to his team's chances of success than Theodore Samuel Williams.

● *A "YOUTH MOVEMENT"*

For four seasons now (this will be the fifth), the Red Sox have been pushing a "youth movement" designed to bring honor and quite possibly an American League championship to Fenway Park. It began in 1952. That year, with Williams away in Korea flying a jet for the Marines, the great Red Sox team that had fought the Yankees tooth and nail for years finally came apart. Lou Boudreau, now with Kansas City but then manager of the Red Sox, wasted no time trying to nail things back together. He ripped out the deadwood on the roster and replaced it with with a cargo of youthful innocents: Sammy White, 23; Jimmy Piersall, 22; Dick Gernert, 22; Ike Delock, 22; Ted Lepcio, 21; Faye Throneberry, 20; Bill Henry, 24. White had played in four major league games prior to 1952, Piersall in six. None of the others had played an inning in the majors.

They were too green. One day they would look great, the next day miserable. It was fun for a while and pretty exciting, but then they began to lose; and they lost much more often than they won. Capable veterans like Mel Parnell and Billy Goodman contributed good seasons, but the final result was disaster: sixth place, the worst, except for the war years, that a Red Sox team had finished since 1936.

But if the results were disastrous, the feeling about the future was bright with confidence. The argument in Fenway Park went like this: "The experience these kids are getting is invaluable. By the time Ted gets back, they'll be ready, and with Ted we'll have a great team." More youngsters were added: Billy Consolo, Milt Bolling, Frank Sullivan, Tom Brewer, Tom Umphlett. Trades brought in Jackie Jensen and Grady Hatton.

But Ted never got back, not really. In 1953 he returned from Korea in time only for the last quarter of the season. (He batted .407 and hit 13 home runs in that brief stretch.) In 1954 he broke his collarbone on the first day of spring training, and before he was well enough to get back in the lineup (he hit .345, with 29 homers), the Red Sox were hopelessly behind. In 1955, reluctant to sign a baseball contract until the financial details of his divorce were settled, he missed the first 46 days of the regular season and once again returned to a team that was out of the pennant race (he hit .356 and 28 home runs). For three years the youthful Red Sox had acquired age and experience, but they finished fourth, fourth and fourth.

The fourth-place finish last season, however, had meaning. If earlier years had a gleam in the eye, this one was pregnant with the future. At the same time that Williams returned to the lineup, a catalyst named Billy Klaus—a journeyman infielder with eight years in the minor leagues behind him—took over at shortstop and jarred the infield and the team into cohesion. The Red Sox came alive and raged through the rest of the season like the club the Boston fans had so long hoped they would become. From deep in the second division they rose high enough to close in on the teams fighting for the pennant.

• A TRULY SOLID TEAM

Now, in spring training, the Red Sox for the first time in five years have a truly solid team. Late-blooming, youth movement boys like Lepcio and Gernert and Throneberry are still there, threatening to burst into stardom, but this season they are supported by a bedrock of proven skill in the infield and the outfield. Catcher Sammy White is, after Berra, probably the best catcher in the league. The pitching staff, led by 18-game-winner Frank Sullivan, was superb last year and has been bolstered since by the addition of Bob Porterfield and Johnny Schmitz from Washington.

More significantly, Mel Parnell appears to be back in shape. Parnell, who averaged 18 victories a year from 1948 through 1953, broke his arm in 1954 (he won only three games all season) and injured his knee last year (he won only two). Last week, for the first time in a long, long while, he was throwing the ball with his natural overhand delivery. Parnell is almost too much. If he is indeed himself again, the Red Sox cup will run over.

Because, as any Boston fan will point out, beyond the solid infield and the brilliant outfield and the topflight catching and the deep pitching, Ted is there, too. And this year, for the first time since 1951, he'll be there right from the beginning.

Ted Williams Spits

RED SMITH

1956

Ted Williams' legendary spitting episodes in 1956 provided his detractors with some of their most potent ammunition. When Williams, now thirty-seven years old, got off to a slow start, some writers suggested it might be time for him to retire. On July 18, as he crossed home plate after hitting his 400th home run, he spit toward the press box. Three days later, on Joe Cronin Night, he repeated his gesture of contempt and vengeance.

Then, on August 7, angry because the fans had first booed and then cheered him in the same inning, he spit toward the crowd. Spitting at writers was one thing, but spitting at the fans crossed too far over the boundary of permissible behavior. The Red Sox fined him five thousand dollars (which they never collected) and the writers took their revenge.

The barrage was immediate and heavy. Dave Egan called Williams an "overgrown, adult juvenile delinquent" and concluded "it will be a good day when he retires and stays retired." Harold Kaese, normally less judgmental than Egan, advised Williams to "quit baseball before baseball quits him." Milton Gross of the *New York Post* prophesied: "The end is near for Ted Williams."

Red Smith, the Pulitzer Prize–winning columnist, took a more temperate view of Williams' antics.

By now some modern Dickens, probably in Boston, must surely have brought out a best-seller entitled *Great Expectorations*. It was a $4,998 mistake when Ted Williams chose puritanical and antiseptic New England for his celebrated exhibition of spitting for height and distance. In easygoing New York's unsanitary subway the price is only $2.

It was bush, of course. There is no other way to characterize Williams' moist expression of contempt for fans and press, even though one may strive earnestly to understand and be patient with this painfully introverted, oddly immature thirty-eight-year-old veteran of two wars.

In his gay moods, Williams has the most winning disposition and manner imaginable. He can be charming, accommodating and generous. If Johnny Orlando, the Red Sox maître de clubhouse and Ted's great friend, wished to violate a confidence he could cite a hundred instances of charities that the fellow has done, always in deep secrecy.

This impulsive generosity is a key. Ted is ruled by impulse and emotions. When he is pleased, he laughs; in a tantrum, he spits. In Joe Cronin's book, this falls $5,000 short of conduct becoming a gentleman, officer and left fielder.

The price the Boston general manager set upon a minute quantity of genuine Williams saliva, making it the most expensive spittle in Massachusetts, suggests that the stuff is rarer than rubies. However, this is one case where the law of supply and demand does not apply.

Actually the $5,000 figure is a measure of Cronin's disapproval of his employee's behavior and an indication of Ted's economic condition. Rather than let the punishment fit the crime, Cronin tailored it to the outfielder's $100,000 salary. As it is, considering Williams' tax bracket, chances are the federal government will pay about $3,500 of the fine, though it may cause some commotion around the Internal Revenue Bureau when a return comes in with a $5,000 deduction for spit.

Baseball has indeed put on company manners since the days when pitchers like Burleigh Grimes, Clarence Mitchell and Spittin' Bill Doak employed saliva as a tool of the trade and applied it to the ball with the ceremonious formality of a minuet.

Incidentally, the penalty was applied after Williams drew a base on balls which forced home the winning run for Boston against the Yankees. He must have realized that a few more victories at those prices would leave him broke, yet the next night he won another game with a home run. With Ted, money is no object.

Nobody has ever been able to lay down a rule determining how much abuse a paid performer must take from the public without reciprocation. It was either Duffy or Sweeney, of the great old vaudeville team, who addressed an audience that had sat in cold silence through the act:

"Ladies and gentlemen, I want to thank you for giving us such a warm and encouraging reception. And now, if you will kindly remain seated, my partner will pass among you with a baseball bat and beat the bejabbers out of you."

Baseball fans consider that the price they pay for admission entitles them to spit invective at a player, harass him at his work and even bounce a beer bottle off his skull. It is not recalled that Williams' hair was ever parted by flying glassware, but verbal barbs from Fenway Park's left-field seats have been perforating his sensitive psyche for years.

There are those of a sympathetic turn who feel it was high time Williams be permitted to spit back. Miss Gussie Moran, trained in the gentle game of tennis, remarked on the radio that she approved, "as long as he didn't spray anybody." As in tennis, Gussie believes, marksmanship and trajectory count.

All the same it is a mark of class in a performer to accept cheers and jeers in stride. One of the soldier citizens of the Boston press—it could have been Johnny Drohan—pointed this out to Williams years ago. Ted was a kid then, a buff for Western movies.

Hoots and jeers were a part of the fame, the man said, and everybody in the public eye had to learn to accept them.

"Take actors, for instance, Ted. You see one in a good show and you applaud and go around talking about how great he is. Then you see him in a bad vehicle and you say, 'He stinks. Whatever gave me the idea he could act?' "

"Oh, no, Johnny," Ted protested, "not that Hoot Gibson. He's *always* great!"

Sidetracked Again

ARTHUR DALEY

1957

In 1957, after hitting .388 at the age of thirty-nine, Williams finished second to Mickey Mantle in the balloting for the Most Valuable Player award. It marked the fourth time that he had finished second to a Yankee—twice to Joe DiMaggio, in 1941 and 1947, and to Joe Gordon in 1942.

In this *New York Times* column Arthur Daley argues that Williams deserved to win the 1957 award.

It was just ten years ago that a Boston baseball writer committed the unpardonable sin of allowing a violent personal prejudice to warp his judgment and perpetrate an injustice.

"I don't like Ted Williams," he said, "and I refuse to vote for him."

Unfortunately, the small-minded man from the Athens of America was one of the three Boston members of the twenty-four-man committee from the Baseball Writers Association who were balloting for the Most Valuable Player in the American League for 1947. What were Williams' credentials in that campaign? He'd merely won the Triple

Crown, the batting championship, the runs-batted-in championship and the home run championship.

Joe DiMaggio beat Tempestuous Ted for M.V.P. honors by the fragile margin of a point, 202 to 201. If the biased Bostonian had even tossed Williams the sop of a tenth place, the Splendid Splinter would have tied DiMadge. If he'd given Ted a ninth place, the picture hitter from Back Bay would have won. Wouldn't you think that a Triple Crown winner deserved at least some mention for the distinction?

• ***THOSE CENTER FIELDERS***

It must seem to Theodore Samuel Williams that Yankee center fielders are a constant source of frustration to him. Back in 1941 the smooth swinger from the Hub batted a mere .406. Did that make him most valuable? Don't be silly. DiMaggio got that one. But at least there were extenuating circumstances because the Jolter had his record fifty-six-game hitting streak that season and hit a handsome .357. But in 1947 the Yankee Clipper was a .315 hitter, although a timely one.

Now DiMaggio's successor has taken his turn in muscling past Williams as the M.V.P. Master Mickey Mantle has achieved the honor for the second straight year and it has to come out slightly tainted. His margin was not a measly point. It was 24 points. But there was one aspect of the balloting which cannot help but point accusingly at Ted's unpopularity with the ink-stained wretches of the Fourth Estate.

One voter threw him a bone with a ninth place. Another voter threw him another bone with a tenth place. That's disgraceful. Williams had a truly remarkable year. At the age of 39 the best natural hitter of this generation ripped off an astonishing .388 average and thereby won his fifth batting championship. Not even Ty Cobb, the hitting superman, was so proficient at a similar age.

• LAST CHANCE

The election of the M.V.P. never should degenerate into a popularity contest, but the brusque, outspoken Williams has never concealed the contempt which he holds for so many of the press box tenants. This is one way for returning the compliment. By some odd quirk this reporter and Williams have been friends from the start, thereby making the relationship an island in the journalistic sea.

He's a strange, complex character who is filled with many inherent contradictions. No one in baseball can be more charming than he. Few can be nastier. It's the stubborn streak in Tempestuous Ted that has kept alive his vendetta with the press and he shows only his more disagreeable side. If this handsome man with the winning smile would give with the charm only for one season, he could be as popular with the press as Stan Musial. And Musial doesn't even try. He just is himself.

It looks on the surface as though Williams has missed his last chance at the trophy. Fortunately he's twice won M.V.P. honors and on one occasion he really didn't deserve it especially. This was in 1949 when Ted had what he described as "a lousy season." He hit only .342.

The most valuable operative that campaign was either Phil Rizzuto or Joe Page, both of them Yankees. But that was the difficulty. The voters couldn't decide and wide diversity of opinion let Williams romp off. Nor did he refuse.

"They owed me that one," he said with a grin.

• A GOOD YEAR

The conviction here is that the Boston Belter was the most deserving of all the candidates. Yet there still isn't any tendency to disparage Mantle. The Boy Wonder had an extremely good year himself with a .365 average. In fact, the two were tightly bunched in a brisk battle for the batting championship into the homestretch. But Williams, rebounding from idleness caused by a chest infection, was a tremendous hitter when the chips were down. That's when he pulled away.

If a nonvoter can be allowed another second guess, he'd be more inclined to pick Gil McDougald over his more illustrious teammate. The handy man of the Yankee infield had another of his highly competent seasons, no matter where he played. If he ever had recovered fully from an injury which bogged him down in the latter stages of the campaign, he might have taken it all easily.

Personal prejudices should have no bearing on an election of this sort. But voters are human and they therefore let their emotions influence their reason. It's a shame that it has to happen that way.

The Ted Williams Miracle

ED LINN

1958

In chronicling the "miracle" year of 1957, Ed Linn tells why it may have been Williams' best season ever. He also reflects on Ted's relations with the press and the fans.

The 1957 season will always be recalled by us winemasters as a great year for the grapes that had been ripening on the vine. The batting champions were Ted Williams (39) and Stan Musial (36). The leading pitcher was Warren Spahn (36). The only no-hitter was thrown by Bob Keegan (36). And the league-leading bridegroom was Mike Todd (50), who married Elizabeth Taylor (36¾- 22-34½).

The most imposing figure, next to Miss Taylor's, was owned by Ted Williams, whose .388 batting average ranks as the highest in the majors since Ted himself hit .406 in 1941. It could well have been the best season he has ever had, for under today's conditions a .380 average undoubtedly equals a prewar average of .400. When Ted broke in, there were fast-ball pitchers and curve-ball pitchers; the fast-ball pitcher mixed his speciality with a curve ball, and the curve-ball pitcher mixed it with a fast ball. The batter had only to settle into a groove where he was ready for either. Any pitcher so creative as to throw a drop earned himself the title of "sinker-ball specialist" and was looked upon as romantic and maybe even eccentric. Sinker-ball specialists usually drank.

Since the war, all pitchers have developed three or four different deliveries and three or four different speeds. Add to that the break in the batter's routine imposed by the checkerboard schedule of day-and-night ball—plus the great improvement in fielding—and the drastically diminished batting averages of the day are easily accounted for. And Williams had a special problem: No 39-year-old man— unless his name is Enos Slaughter—is going to get many leg hits. There are very few cheap hits in Williams' .388 average.

The records bear out this postwar deflation. In the five years before Williams hit his .406, the league-leading averages were .388, .371, .349, .381 and .352, for an *average* average of .368. From 1952 to 1956, the figures were .327, .337, .341, .340 and .353, for an average of .342. In 1941, Ted was 38 points above the preceding five years; this year he was 46 points above it. (In the National League, the leaders from 1936 to 1940 averaged .359; between 1952– 56, it was .338.)

Perhaps the most remarkable of all the facets of Ted's 1957 "miracle" is that far from laboring as the season progressed, he came on strong over the last half. He came up to the All-Star game in a 1-for-16 slump and was so beat that he even thought about begging off. "Not seriously," he says, "but I will admit it went through my mind." After going hitless in the game, he flew to Detroit, checked into a hotel and stayed in bed for almost two days. "When I went out to the park, I felt good. Just great. I'd never felt better."

He broke out of the slump with two doubles, and over the last half of the season he hit a rousing .453. Rousing? Incredible!

The high point of Williams' season came after a bad chest cold knocked him out of the lineup. It was 17 days later before he got back in as a pinch hitter against Kansas City. Having blown a 6-2 lead, the Red Sox were trailing by a run. Ted tied it quickly by driving a tremendous 400-foot blow down the throat of the wind. The following day, he pinch-hit in Washington and walked. When Boston came up to Yankee Stadium—where, as everybody knows, Ted can't hit—he still wasn't ready to start. (Actually, Ted has hit .340 at Yankee Stadium during his career, as he himself will point out bitterly. This year he was .333 at the Stadium and .531 at Fenway Park.) Whitey Ford had a shutout when Ted came in as a pinch hitter in the ninth but he didn't have it long. Ted's king-sized drive landed in the upper deck.

Since nothing uncongests a chest faster than a couple of home runs, Ted was in the starting lineup the following afternoon. In the first inning, he came up with a man on second and one out: With first base open, he walked on four straight pitches—one of the many intentionally unintentional walks he received over the course of the season. The next time there were no bases open at all, and with the count two and nothing, he finally got a pitch he liked and hit a high, towering fly that dropped into the right-field stands for the 15th grand-slam of his career. It was the only ball thrown inside the strike zone to him all afternoon; the next two times, he was walked on four straight balls. In the final game of the series he walked, lined a homer into the seats, singled and walked. The home run was the fourth in four official times at bat, a performance which tied one of those miscellaneous records that keep radio announcers digging frantically into the record books. The Yankees never got him out in nine attempts. Before his streak ended, Ted had run that figure up to 16. From the time he returned to the lineup to the end of the season, he got 12 hits in 18 times at bat, for a .667 average. And, in 31 times up, he got on base 25 times.

Because the name of Ted Williams has been synonymous with hitting for as long as most of us can remember, there has been an inclination to feel that Ted sprang from the earth around home plate fully equipped to bang balls out of the park. That isn't precisely true. Williams is more than a machine; he became the best hitter of his time because he reduced batting, as no man has before or since, to a science. With all his natural ability to swing a bat, Ted's overall average at San Diego, where he broke in, was only .285. It is well known that Ted now has a micrometer eye for the strike zone; it is not so well known that when he came to the majors, the book on him said he would chase bad pitches. He stopped himself from chasing them as much by an act of will as by the gift of eyesight.

Ted has what baseball men call "great bat control"—by which they mean that he can wait until the ball is almost upon the plate and still swing easily and smoothly. But he has great willpower at bat, too. In Detroit this season, he took three strikes against Jim Bunning without taking his bat off his shoulder. The next time up, he got a base on balls, still without taking his bat off his shoulder. The third time up, he took five straight pitches, then hit a 3-2 pitch out of the park to give the Red Sox a 1-0 victory. What had happened was that Harvey Kuenn's positioning on the Williams shift had, through sheer accident, placed him in such a way that Bunning's sidearm delivery was coming right out of Kuenn's uniform. It had only been when the 3-2 count brought about a modification of the shift that Ted had got his first good look at the ball. What other batter could possibly have been that stubborn or that patient?

There are plenty of baseball men, of course, who do not

think that Williams helps himself—or his team—by being so patient. The big man, they say, is supposed to be up there to drive in runs, not to look for a base on balls. There is another theory, however, that says that the more bases on balls a batter gets, the higher he will eventually hit. This is a theory we find hard to buy since if it were followed to its ultimate end and the batter walked *all* the time, he would bat .000. Johnny Orlando, the Red Sox clubhouse man, has yet a third theory. "Think what this guy would bat," he says, "if they'd pitch to him!" That is precisely what the pitchers *are* thinking, and that is precisely why they don't pitch to him.

We have always felt that genius is nothing more than a lifelong retention of the child's first wide-eyed curiosity and wonder at the world in which he finds himself. The Kid—as Ted appropriately calls himself—still has that intense curiosity about his own world, the world inside the batter's box. At 39, he still thinks more about hitting than anybody else in the game. "You get to know 85 or 90 per cent of it after a while," he says, "but every once in a while something new comes up that you begin to wonder about. I always felt that you had to lift up on a low ball, for instance, but now I'm beginning to wonder whether maybe you shouldn't take the same slice on it. I'm not sure of it, now, I'm not sure of it at all; I'm just saying that I'm beginning to wonder. And I'm beginning to wonder whether a pitcher's motion might not be just as important a part of his equipment as his stuff. More and more, I'm beginning to think it is."

The Kid's pride in his hitting is such that he refused to bunt when Lou Boudreau first threw the Williams shift against him, even though Boudreau's original deployment put the third baseman at shortstop and awarded Ted the whole left side of the diamond. When he did begin to hit to left after he had hurt his elbow in the 1950 All-Star game, it was assumed that he had come to realize that he would have to keep the defenses honest. Ted denied it then and he denies it just as vigorously today. He does hit to left more than he used to, he admits, but that's only because he doesn't start off the year as strong or as sharp as he once did. It's not that he's *trying* to hit to left, Ted says, it's just that he's swinging a little late. "But," he says, "you'll notice that as the season goes along, I pull the ball more and more. Over the last half of the year, you'll hardly ever see me hit to left."

Except for the tag end of the season, Williams says, he has always done his best hitting after the All-Star game. "Over the last two weeks, there are too many variables. It gets colder then, usually, and you see a lot of new pitchers. Boy, that cold weather is tough on us old guys. Actually, though, cold weather bothered me even when I was a kid. Always."

Ted's resurgence as the undisputed king of the batters has been especially satisfying to him in that he has been written off as that kind of a batter so many times during the last few years. He finished the 1950 and 1951 seasons with averages of .318 and .319, and when a 33-year-old player hits a two-year slump, he doesn't figure ever to regain the powers of his youth. "What nobody wanted to remember," Williams says, with the bitterness that so often accompanies his references to the outside world, "was that I was playing with a busted elbow." He insists that the elbow began to loosen up during the last half of 1951 and had loosened up completely when the Marines grabbed him for his second hitch in the spring of 1952. Ted is not a man to give any credit to a situation he resented so deeply, and yet the records would seem to indicate that the return to uniform did give the elbow a chance to mend. At any rate, Ted came back hitting, and he has been hitting ever since.

Early in 1956, Williams was supposed to be slipping once

again. Age, according to the stories that began to appear, had rusted his reflexes so much that the pitchers were beginning to get the fast ball by him. Ted grins at the memory. "It was in Detroit and I wasn't sharp and they were throwing a lot of fast balls at me. They really thought they'd found out something. When that happens, word spreads through this league like wildfire. In a couple of days everybody knew that Williams couldn't hit the fast ball any more." The grin grew wider. "The only thing you can do when that happens is to show them they're wrong!" Since Ted, of course, has always murdered the fast ball, he had a lot of fun showing them the error of their ways before he began to see the same old junk again.

Unfortunately, Ted has no special formula for staying in shape beyond getting a reasonable amount of rest and maintaining a wholesome diet. A skinny kid when he first came up, Ted used to push around the body-building equipment; at this stage of the game, he has long since given that up. As far as physical condition is concerned, he is absolutely convinced that the legs of a ball player are the first thing to go. To keep his legs in shape, he does a lot of walking; in most cities he makes it a habit to walk from the hotel to the park. Clubhouse boy Johnny Orlando, who once tried to walk the route with him in Kansas City— where it is a long, long haul—had to give up and grab a cab. Ted's secret, if he has one, is that he is never really out of shape. Bob Feller, in his battles to get the owners to permit unlimited winter ball, used to tell them that what ruined a player was not overwork, but the pure agony of whipping the body back into shape after a winter of loafing around. Ted, who spends his winters fishing and hunting, is a prize exhibit for Feller's theories.

Before the season even started, the rumblings out of the South told conoisseurs of Ted Williams that it was going to be a great year. Ted got himself into a conversation with a

New Orleans sports editor. The conversation, much to Ted's surprise, turned out to be an interview—and before he had stopped talking and spitting, he had blasted the Marines, a couple of "phony politicians" named Truman and Taft, and the Bureau of Internal Revenue. Ted is at his best when he is under attack, so much so that it sometimes seems that when things are going along too placidly he will deliberately do something to stir up the animals. Since he had been introduced to the New Orleans writer by Hy Hurwitz of the Boston *Globe,* Ted blamed not his own big mouth but the Boston writers in general and Hurwitz in particular. His relationship with the writers, which had always been marked by a certain restraint, deteriorated completely.

Whenever a Boston writer approached him during the early part of the season, Ted would say, somewhat haughtily, "You know I'm not talking to you guys." As the year progressed, he began to answer simple questions—when he was in a kindly mood—but with the exception of a couple of close friends among them, Williams and the writers left each other pretty much alone. When Hurwitz, a pleasant little guy, approached him on the field for the first time, Ted cursed him out. "If you were bigger and younger," he raged, "I'd beat the hell out of you."

When Williams suffered a slight relapse during the course of his late-season illness, Hurwitz got hold of a medical report which led him to write that Ted was through for the season. "I'll be back now," Williams swore, "even if they have to carry me out there on a stretcher. I'll get back if only to show that so-and-so up."

If it pleases Ted to display his contempt for the Boston sportswriters, then the job has been made ridiculously easy for him by the Boston newspapers. No writer is allowed into the Red Sox dressing room for *two hours* before a game, which for all practical purposes bars them completely. Nor are they allowed in for 20 minutes after a game, which gives

Williams a chance to shower, dress and have himself smuggled out in a carpet. When you read a postgame interview with Williams, it is only because Ted has deliberately stayed in order to get something off his chest. Despite these minor obstacles the writers are expected to cover Williams completely, since every Williams gurgle is a roaring hurricane in Boston. When the Boston guys lose a story to an out-of-town writer, there is hell to pay. So when Ted sneers at the "gutless sportswriters," he is really looking past them to their "gutless bosses." If the sports editors of the city do not have enough respect for their writers to demand clubhouse access—in return for the million dollars' worth of publicity they give the club—then why should Williams have any respect for them, either? There is something a little ridiculous about newspapers righteously demanding that John Foster Dulles permit newspapermen into Red China but doing nothing about getting them past the flannel curtain of the Red Sox dressing room

At this stage in his career, it is obvious that Williams will do nothing about closing the breach. "The world's worst!" he shouts when he's asked about the Boston press. "No question about it, they're absolutely the world's worst. Not everybody, now. One or two of them are all right. But on the whole, the world's worst!"

Out of town, on the other hand, he can be the world's most charming man. His favorite gambit is to give a lengthy, sparkling interview to some old-timer from a little weekly newspaper. The old-timer then goes back to the Boston writers, smiles happily, and says, "Gee, what a great guy. What's the matter with you guys, you can't get along with a great guy like that?"

Even when he's in a dark mood, Williams will unbend for an out-of-town writer. He'll grouse and he'll growl, but if they'll stay with him and hear him out, he will eventually settle back and say: "Okay, okay, I suppose you've got a lot of silly questions to ask me." While the writer is trying to get the interview started, Ted will glare out at the writers huddled around the batting cage and bray: "They ought to keep writers away from the batting cage. We ought to do something about that." If the interviewer gets the impression that Williams is really trying to say that they ought to keep the writers out of the dugout, out of the park and maybe even out of the country, then that is exactly the impression Williams wants him to get.

If you ask a question that shows you know something about him and about baseball, you will get a thoughtful, forthright answer; if you ask a very general question, you will get a short answer. And yet, through it all, there is the sense that Williams is really putting on an act, that he is only doing what he knows is expected of him. A mannerly Ted Williams would be as much of a disappointment to a writer in search of a colorful story as a sober Joe E. Lewis. Williams would deny it, indignantly, but he is a great showman.

If there has been any mellowing in his feelings toward the fans, now that he is approaching the end of the ride, he won't admit that, either. When the announcer drones: "In left field, number nine, Ted Williams," and the roar of the crowd gathers force and descends upon the field, Ted is, he insists, unmoved. When he receives the tremendous ovations that now greet any of his home runs, it means, he insists, nothing at all. "Whether they cheer or boo," he says, "it's all the same to me." But then he adds, perhaps significantly, "Well, any player would rather be cheered than booed, but as far as meaning anything one way or the other, the answer is no."

You get precisely the same two-toned reaction when you ask him whether he is beginning to look back over his shoulder at his magnificent record, as would seem only natural now that it's all in the books for future generations to look upon. "Naw," he says, "I don't think like that." But then, once again, he pauses and adds: "Well, everybody is proud of what they accomplish. But I don't feel any different about my record than I ever have." With 456 home runs to his credit, he now ranks fifth behind Ruth, Foxx, Ott and Gehrig. Gehrig's mark of 494, only 38 ahead of him, would seem to be well within his reach, and Ted is frank to admit that he would very much like to overtake it. "But," he says, "I don't think I can do it. If I could get two good years . . . If I could have just had those two years I spent in the Marines that second time."

He was, at the end of the season, equally modest about his chance of getting the Most Valuable Player award for the third time. Without Williams, the Red Sox could easily have finished sixth, and it is difficult to think of any other player who meant three places in the standings to his club, but Ted only said, "Mantle certainly deserves consideration for the award, and so do Sievers, Pierce and Donovan."

The evidence is that he has begun to be much more concerned about public opinion than he used to be. Where he once was unbelievably profane in public, there was only one real incident this year. Ted seems genuinely sorry these days when that old, dark spirit sits upon him, and he generally will do something in a hurry to redeem himself. His special interest, as everyone knows by now, is the Jimmy Fund, the fundraising organization for Boston's Children's Cancer Hospital. Even when he was laid up with that chest infection, he was traveling around New England, addressing men's organizations and making appearances, and hearing himself being introduced as "a great humanitarian," a description which masters of ceremony seem to find irresistible even though it leaves Williams writhing in embarrassment.

Ted has always been a highly respected man among other ball players, almost an elder statesman, but he lost

a great deal of prestige after the spitting incident in 1956—
the incident for which he was fined a phantom $5,000. The
players have always been amused at Ted's passion for pop-
ping off, but they shook their heads in disbelief and mut-
tered "bush" when they heard about the spitting. For the
first time since the "fire chief" days Ted heard the sound of
opposing bench jockeys. This year he was on his good behavior. He took some riding about his spitting and about
being habitually given a fourth strike, but by the end of
the year it had pretty much disappeared.

He went out of his way to mend his fences with his own
teammates, too. Ted and Jimmy Piersall did have a mild
feud going in 1956, a feud which came about because Ted
is a great clubhouse needler, and Piersall was always ready
to needle him right back, louder and sharper. When they
first came together in Sarasota this spring, Ted put out his
hand and said, "For crying out loud, let's see if we can't get
along this year. This may be my last one."

He has also been observed shaking the hand of a teammate crossing the plate after a home run, even if he has
shaken it almost surreptitiously. And yet, he has no baseball friends off the field. He seems to prefer professional
people—businessmen, medical men, even "phony politicians."

Williams keeps insisting that he would have hung up
his spikes long ago if he didn't need the money. Whether
he would have or not—and it hardly seems likely that he
would have—his divorce settlement has made it necessary
for him to hold on to that baseball salary, which is usually
reported at $100,000. No one is more closemouthed about
finances than the Red Sox front office, but there have been
a couple of clues about the contract. Williams lives by himself on the road, and presumably pays his own expenses, so
he must have an expense allowance in his contract. It was
once thought to be $10,000, but with costs on the rise it is

probably closer to $15,000 now. Since he shows a great concern about attendance figures—as opposed to his lack of affection for the individual fan—we can assume that there is an attendance clause in his contract, too. Figure $40,000 as a base figure and another $40,000 or so in his attendance bonus and you probably wouldn't be very far off.

Certainly, no one ever deserved an attendance bonus more. There are only two true gate attractions left in the American League: Ted Williams and the New York Yankees. As a matter of fact, the other seven owners ought to pass the hat and give Ted a bonus for the fans he draws into their parks when the Sox come to town. The Sox home attendance was 1,181,087 this year; on the road it was 1,176,945. Most of them were there to look at No. 9.

Williams has been well paid by the Red Sox and he has always been easy to sign. There was one contract negotiation that still rankles him. When Ted returned from Korea he asked for a two-year contract. Cronin wouldn't give it to him. Ted signed, but he was unhappy. Throughout the year, whenever anybody congratulated him on a good day, he'd say, "Don't tell me, tell Cronin."

His annual coyness about stating definitely whether he intends to return the following year has probably been his way of getting some small measure of revenge. If they wouldn't give him the two-year contract, he seemed to be saying, let them sweat until April.

Ted has two businesses he can step into when he retires. He is president of Ted Williams, Inc., a company which manufactures and sells fishing equipment (Sam Snead is vice-president). He is also a partner in Southern Tackle Distributors, the largest tackle distributing firm in Florida. But with that .388 year in back of him, he is making no attempt to play it coy again. "Now would be a good time to step into my businesses," he admits, "because they're at a stage where my name would be a help. But why try to kid anybody, I'll be back. Oh, a lot of things can happen over the winter. I could always get cancer or something. But all things being equal, I'll be back."

Let's hope he feels that way at the end of the winter, too. Even the Boston writers, if backed to the wall, would probably admit that things would be pretty dull without him.

How Ted Williams Became Popular

MIKE GILLOOLY

1958

The title of this *Sport* article overstates the case, since Williams, in spite of his temperament, had enjoyed the support of most Red Sox fans throughout his career. But it is fair to say that as his career wound down the intensity of his fans' loyalty increased.

Mike Gillooly asserts that Williams silenced his critics in 1957 "with his strong bat and silent lip." By hitting .388 and avoiding controversy, even when denied the MVP award, he earned the fans' forgiveness of his past transgressions, and their affection for him made it "editorial suicide to needle Wiliams in print."

Whisper it or shout it, it still comes out as a phenomenon of our age when one considers what has happened to Ted Williams. A headline writer, enthusiastic to get down all the drama of it, might write: "Murderers' Row at Fenway Park has been murdered!"

In case you are a stranger to Red Sox owner Tom Yawkey's Little Acre in the Back Bay section, it would have to be explained to you that Murderers' Row in Boston is not like Murderers' Row anywhere in the majors. Normally, when a baseball fan speaks of Murderers' Row, he means a bunch of heavily muscled bat swingers who come up to the plate one after another and go bang-bang-bang to the opposition. Not so in Boston. There, Murderers' Row is a geographic location, a thin and treacherous section of the stands that encroaches upon the left-field area in Fenway Park where Ted Williams conducts himself defensively. It is the front row, far down the third-base line, where hecklers gathered on summer days to fling high-and-inside invective at leftfielder Williams. It was the closest they could get to him.

They arrived early and stayed late. They were, in their venom, accomplished and abusive, and Williams, who on good days admits to possessing rabbit ears capable of picking up even the crumpling of a bag of peanuts, needed no radar to pick out the gravel-voiced shouts.

For a long while, the language from this Murderers' Row was so obscene that the Red Sox management had to place a special detail of Boston police in plain clothes in the midst of the section to make arrests for the abusive talk that curled the ears of Williams and, more importantly, of other spectators. The Red Sox called out the militia not so much to coddle Williams—who may or may not have taken care of himself—but to try to throw a protective shield around those other customers who had paid to see the Sox play ball, not to be cascaded by the verbal garbage released by Williams' critics.

The taunts of these Murderers' Row characters were worse than the paper-clip snappers of Chicago, the beer-can throwers of Detroit, the orange-peel pitchers of Philadelphia, or any other crew of baseball vigilantes. These boys hurled personal insults with abandon, taunted Williams with challenges (which were sometimes accepted), and never let up.

Now Murderers' Row in Boston is dead, killed by the

hand of Ted Williams himself, who evoked this amazing transformation of public opinion by the remarkable exhibition he put on last year. This 39-year-old athlete, in his seventeenth season with the Red Sox, managed what had escaped him throughout his turbulent career. Suddenly, he got people to surge to his defense, loudly, boldly, and persistently, as they never had before.

Those people who were Williams rooters to begin with— and, understand, there were many of these always—had a powerful weapon to work with in 1957, Ted's .388 batting average, the highest in the American League since his own .406 in 1941. They had new records, established by Williams at an age when most athletes are struggling just to keep playing.

In the past, these Williams rooters found it difficult to pursue their hobby. Their hobbyhorse kept rocking the boat. Now, finding themselves with brigades of allies brought forth by Williams' 1957 success, they are willing to stand up and shout for justice for Ted—this in contrast to their silence of past years. In their enthusiasm, they are willing even to forget the unpleasantries of the past, and in their new dedication, they have become a potent and militant force of public baseball opinion.

As a consequence, it is doubtful that Boston's Murderers' Row will ever flare up again. There will be a few people, of course, who will go off on a tirade against Williams somewhere along this season. But the cops can be called off. The applause that Ted's bat (and his relative mildness) got for him will last, unless Ted manufactures a provocation, unless he takes a blast at someone, or unless he stops hitting altogether.

It is ironic that Williams' bat did so much for him so late in his career. It was as if Williams, with his strong bat and silent lip, was giving his supporters encouragement to get out there and root for him. People who stayed close to the Red Sox during the 1957 season were amazed by the change in the size and quality of Williams' support in the stands, and yet they were able to see signs of the shift through most of the year. There was a loud and notably unsubtle hint of the temper of the fans one night last August when Williams, hitting .392 at the time, went up against the Detroit Tigers at Fenway Park. There wre 30,000 people at the night game, drawn there (1) by Williams' magnetism, and (2) by an interest in a fair battle between the two teams for first-division spots. And about 29,000 of the fans went into a near riot against the Boston sportswriters when they felt that Williams had been deprived of a base hit by the writers, a hit that would have moved him closer to the coveted .400 mark.

When Williams came up to hit, the Tigers had shifted automatically into their overloaded-right defensive setup. This shift placed shortstop Harvey Kuenn on the first-base side of second base and second baseman Frank Bolling out in short right field. Williams hit a line drive toward right-center, and Kuenn, not timing his leap well, had the ball smash off his glove and carom into the outfield. The official scorer flashed "Error" on the scoreboard (he later changed it to a hit) and Fenway Park exploded instantaneously. Never before had Boston come so close to a baseball riot. Fans glared at the press box. They shouted insults at the writers. They raised their fists in threatening gestures. It was an unprecedented display of anger, and it seemed to refuse to subside. The earmarks of a mob riot were all there. An hour after the game ended, people were still lingering around the exit from the press box, jeering at the writers as they came out.

What was remarkable about the performance of the fans was that they were in revolt *against* the writers for the *sake*

of Williams. Fans can behave this way, openly and aggres-
sively, for other ball players, but they hadn't been doing it
for Ted.

Yet here they had undeniably turned towards the man,
pushing aside all his trespasses against them—his pigeon-
shooting, his spitting performances, his refusals to doff his
cap in their direction after hitting a homer, his blasts
against the government for its handling of the Korean situation, his rap against the Marine Corps, his charges about
"gutless" draft boards (as well as "gutless" politicians and
"gutless" newspapermen).

The public was expressing its affection for Williams, the
nonconformist. Here was a man who flaunted the frustra-
tions that get the little man down. Here was a 39-year-old
athlete hitting almost .400, defying age in a young man's
game, and getting away with it. The fans may have wanted
to show it before, but now they were demonstrating publicly
that they wanted to see Williams win.

His comeback in 1957, after he had been stricken by a
respiratory condition, as well as his batting average and
his apparent effort to do the job in the field—these things
stirred the fans. And when the results of the Most Valuable
Player award voting were announced after the season, the
stir became a bolt. It was rally 'round The Kid, boys.

Williams had finished second to Mickey Mantle in the
MVP voting. One writer of the 24 eligible to cast ballots
placed Ted in ninth place, and another put him tenth (or
last). There is no justice, the fans shouted. The season produced no outstanding player who could match Williams'
performance. Mantle, handicapped by leg trouble, showing
some uncertainty in the field, and not dominating the batting rolls as he had the season before, had not been a stand-
out. Williams has been shafted by an enemy press, people
argued.

Ted Williams backers emerged suddenly from everywhere and spoke their piece. The more the writers moved to avoid a finger of suspicion as the culprits who had placed Ted ninth and tenth on their ballot, the bolder fans grew. The turnabout was—and remains—startling. It is, suddenly, editorial suicide to needle Williams in print.

"The guy amazes me with his popularity," John Gillooly of the Boston *Record* says. "If I write one knock about him, even kiddingly, letters pile into the office telling me I'm a meathead, just like Williams says I am. The letters approach the point of violence. He must have ten fans for him for every one fan against him."

"Those are gamblers' odds," says Tom Dowd, the Red Sox traveling secretary. "In my contacts with the fans, I'd have to boost that ratio to 25 to one in favor of Williams. Everybody loves the guy. First, he's a slugger, and people can't resist a slugger. Then, he has charm, even physical charm. Here's one thing I think you have to concede. If Jayne Mansfield were headlining a nightclub show and Ted walked in, all heads would turn to look at him for an instant. Then they'd turn back to Jayne. But they'd look!"

There is so much evidence of Williams' popularity today that much of it has stunned the city of Boston. Just recently, a fellow sent the following letter, which was published, to the editor of a Boston newspaper: "Ted Williams is not a team man. He plays solely for the glory of Mr. Williams. Want to blast me for that? My telephone number is WA. 3-9881. (Signed.) Al Brown."

Mr. Brown received some phone calls, about 150, and 85 per cent of them blasted him. They told him how wrong he was, how right Williams was, and that they would not suffer such insults in print as had been piled on their hero's head. Mr. Brown was so smothered by words of protest that he never got a chance to argue back.

This was only a sampling of the newfound vigor of Williams' followers. There were many others, coming from all sections of New England and running right through the 1957 season and into this year. Newspaper editors were amazed by it. They first felt the new grip of the man on the public fancy during a three-week newspaper strike in Boston. The offices of the six daily Boston papers were manned by skeleton staffs during the strike—made up, for the most part, of editors. Among their other duties during the strike, they had to handle the telephone calls. This was in August, and the results of Red Sox games were important to many people in Boston. But when they called the newspaper offices, they asked in this order: (1) What did Williams do today? (2) What was the score?

The editors realized quickly enough that if they were going to continue to answer the phone calls, they had better check Williams' batting average daily. People, even when starved for news, wanted to know about Williams first.

Early this year, the tabloid Boston *American* ran a series of articles on "The Case For Ted Williams." The articles carried through three weeks, 15 stories in all. That was a lot of copy for a newspaper, but the editors felt they were justified in letting the series run long. The serial—1,200 words to the story for an overall off-season total of 18,000 words—had been prompted by letters from fans who objected to some of the slurs against their favorite athlete, and said it was about time a defense of the man was presented to the public.

Within ten days, another Boston paper began a comic-strip serial on Williams' life. This series, by cartoonist Vic Johnson, ran for seven full weeks, 49 strips in all.

And Williams fans still clamored for more. High school girls wrote letters asking what books they could read about Ted because they were writing theses for their senior-year English courses, and they had chosen Williams as their subject. Ted may be a more popular thesis candidate in New England high schools today than Elvis Presley.

A politician waged a city council campaign for a proposition that he felt had to win public approval. He wanted
to change the name of Kenmore Square (the junction of two
of Boston's main roads) to Williams Square. When Ted made
his annual appearance at the Sportsman's Show in Boston,
where he puts on fly-casting exhibitions for handsome fees,
all attendance records tumbled. Over 150,000 customers
came through the turnstiles to see their baseball hero toy
with a rod and reel. Artists began showing up this winter
with portraits of Williams for sale—and they sold.

Tim Horgan, a columnist for the Boston *Traveler,* wrote
recently: "It's getting so a citizen can't voice the minority,
or dim, view of Teddy without getting shot on the spot.
Drastic issues might be involved now, like freedom of
speech, pursuit of happiness and the right to hassle, and
that would amount to a fierce overlay.

"Teddy may be 100 per cent strong, clean and pure. He
may also be a bum. He may be terribly misunderstood,
maligned and everything else, except underpaid. He may
also court his knocks. It's a cinch he is, was and always will
be surrounded by controversy. That's wholesome enough if
nobody comes in armed. Teddy can incite any emotion from
anger and anguish to zeal and zounds!

"The trouble seems to be that one vital piece has gone
out of the affair, and that's what's turning it into a peril.
It's been forgotten that Teddy is still only human. Please,
girls, when the old gorge rises, just pause, ponder and laugh
a little bit, too."

Horgan was answering the swelling Williams rooting
section, a brigade that wanted to be heard and didn't want
to hear knocks against their boy. These are the people who
have killed off Boston's Murderers' Row, who have made
Ted Williams popular. Where did they come from?

They have grown over the years, people who have found
that Williams, in his independence, in his individuality and

in his talent, spoke and played for them. They are the fans who worshipped Rocky Marciano because he could punch. They are the fellows who hate to have to wear a necktie and find a champion of their little cause in the open-collar persistence of Williams. They are the fellows who have nursed private dislikes for their draft board and were happy when Ted spoke out against them. They are ex-servicemen who liked the way Williams spanked the Marine Corps. In his outbursts, in his once wanting to be a fireman, in his rebellion against conventions, Williams has had the common touch. He reaches people where they live.

There was, too, the unpublicized element—the way Ted made meeting him an unforgettable event for people. There was a day last summer, for example, when he and a friend, after touring Cape Cod, were on their way back to Boston for a game that night. The friend asked Ted to do him a favor and stop off at Carney Hospital, in the suburbs of the city and on the way to the ballpark, to visit the friend's mother.

"So long as you get me to the park by six," Williams said.

When Ted walked in, Carney Hospital went into an uproar. Nursing sisters scurried to the third floor to take a peek at the famed Red Sox slugger who was visiting there. Ambulatory patients jammed the hallways. A nun asked Ted if he would "just put your head in the door" to say hello to a patient who was a baseball fan and was in need of a boost.

Within 15 minutes, Ted was back in the car and on his way to Fenway Park. He had visited with some 25 bedridden patients, he had promised the nuns that he would be back for a lengthy visit one day (and you have to believe he will, if you know the man) when he didn't have to hurry away to play ball. The word of another visit by the baseball star spread rapidly through the hospital, and doctors later reported that it had been a tonic to their patients.

This, too, is how Ted Williams became popular. Nothing had been planned for the hospital visit, but the personal and voluntary touch of the man had made an indelible impression. It must be assumed that the people who met him that day spoke about Ted and his pleasant visit to their family and friends, and in this way Williams fandom becomes compounded, among people who may or may not care about baseball, into an army of enthusiasts.

Will it last? Or will popularity spoil Ted Williams? I doubt that the man's current support can be beaten down—except by Williams himself. And you have to assume that he is too smart, too alert to lose what he has built up over the years—the popularity he disdains publicly but appreciates privately. He has too many friends now, big people and little people, who have shown him what friendship and loyalty mean, for him to foul out.

There is his association with the now-famous Jimmy Fund Hospital in Boston, a part of the Children's Medical Center, devoted to the solution of the problem of cancer, and his friendship with the hospital's distinguished director, Dr. Sidney Farber, a great name in medical research. Before the baseball season opens, Ted and Dr. Farber will get together to map out plans for the season—all done without publicity—when Williams will visit children for the hosptial.

"I've seen Ted with our children," Dr. Farber says, "and he is better for them than a new collie dog. He comes in quietly to visit. He comes without publicity. And I have to respect the man for it. This is a contribution he makes to society. When you put together all the things Ted has done, quietly and earnestly, for other people, it's then that you find a wonderful human being who has done much good.

When he became part of the Jimmy Fund, he didn't lend his name to it. He gave his heart."

Then Dr. Farber talks about baseball and Williams. "My two teenage boys watch Ted at Fenway Park, and we have some serious talks around the dinner table about baseball and Ted. Here's what I tell my boys. There is a man running 100 yards in ten seconds and he steps on a little pebble, falls down and breaks his neck. The same man, walking 100 yards at his leisure, would never even have noticed that pebble. There is that tremendous strain to strive to do so well in Ted. That intenseness, that fight toward perfection. I can't understand why people sometimes boo him. Here is a man with greatness as an athlete. If he bats .400, which is considered as near to perfection as a player can get, it means also that he has failed 600 times. I think we should remember the 400 times he hit safely and not dwell on the rest.

"What I see in Ted when he visits the hospital is the instant transformation in the children. This is quite apart from his batting average. This is his capacity to attract complete, worshipful attention in a completely natural way. And to carry this capacity gracefully. I respect the man."

Then there is Ted's friendship with the Most Reverend Richard J. Cushing, archbishop of the Archdiocese of Boston. "We're good friends," the archbishop says. "I feel he likes me, and I think a great deal of him. In my opinion, he is not only a great athlete but also a great competitor. He is a Hall of Fame candidate. He is fighting and winning the greatest battle of them all—the fight against himself. He has had battles all the way. I've seen him grow. I think he's winning this battle.

"I don't know anything about his background. But if he had received the preparation, if he had had the higher education, if he had had the social contacts, this fellow would have been an outstanding man in any field. Some men have to fight the battle of intemperance. Not Ted. Some have to fight against smoking. Not Ted. I have great admiration for his accomplishments in his war against himself. He has had to conquer an innate shyness, impatience and a tendency to be irritable. In my opinion—and you must understand that this is my opinion—he has been an immense help with the morale of unfortunates. You see so often where he has helped children. I know where he has lifted the hopes and spirits of older people, too."

There is Ted's hut-mate from the Korean War, Lieutenant Colonel Patrick Harrison, now stationed with the Marine Air Wing at Norfolk, Virginia. "If a few of those writers who have smeared Ted could only know him, they would write differently," Colonel Harrison says. "If they did, they'd have the same respect and admiration for him that I have. They'd know he was as powerful and as human a man as there is in this world. I don't know if anyone ever called him more names than I used to. I was just a weekend baseball fan and I used to say what a poor sport he was. I hoped he would fall on his butt every time he chased a fly ball. I didn't think any athlete was as unsportsmanlike as he was.

"Then I got to know him. I roomed with him in Korea. Didn't someone once say he wasn't a team player? Well, I could tell more about his teamwork in the Marine Corps, where there was 'no tomorrow.' I remember Ted in pain that only a doctor could explain, suffering intensely in his determination to remain part of the Marine team. Sure, he pretends he is an antagonist of the Marines. But he never missed an assignment in Korea, never missed a flight no matter what the weather. When the chips were down, he was there."

The friendships of Ted Williams extend everywhere. There are the bellhops who received Ted's share of World Series tickets. And the photographer who asked him to visit a sick child, and Ted agreed, with one proviso: "Don't bring

your camera." And the newspaperman who ran into financial straits, and Ted offered to pay the school tuition for his
two children. And the fan who needed and received financial
help from him. And the big-name baseball player who suffered a heavy financial loss, but survived the bad times
through Ted's help. And the blind fisherman who has free
use of Williams' name on any of the fishing line he produces
(a commercial company in any field would pay in five figures
for the same privilege). These people are all on Ted's side,
and they are bringing him new friends all the time. They
are part of the swelling sentiment that is surrounding Williams—a sentiment which reached its peak in 1957, became
militant after the MVP vote, and is now the topping on a
great career.

That's how Ted Williams became popular.

Hub Fans Bid Kid Adieu

JOHN UPDIKE

1960

After struggling through his worst season ever in 1959 (hitting just .254), Williams refused to quit. He came back in 1960 to end his career with a .316 batting average and 29 home runs, including the one he hit in his last time at bat.

John Updike's classic account of that final game is a lyrical tribute to Williams' artistry. According to the poet and essayist Donald Hall, whose own tribute to Williams appears later in this collection, Updike's essay marks the beginning of the "High Belletristic Tradition" of baseball writing, which "represents the fan's view from the stands, glorified by good prose."

Fenway Park, in Boston, is a lyric little bandbox of a ballpark. Everything is painted green and seems in curiously sharp focus, like the inside of an old-fashioned peeping-type Easter egg. It was built in 1912 and rebuilt in 1934, and offers, as do most Boston artifacts, a compromise between Man's Euclidean determinations and Nature's beguiling irregularities. Its right field is one of the deepest in the American League, while its left field is the shortest; the high left-field wall, three hundred and fifteen feet from home plate along the foul line, virtually thrusts its surface at right-handed hitters.

On the afternoon of Wednesday, September 28th, 1960, as I took a seat behind third base, a uniformed groundkeeper was treading the top of this wall, picking batting-practice home runs out of the screen, like a mushroom gatherer seen in Wordsworthian perspective on the verge of a cliff. The day was overcast, chill, and uninspirational. The Boston team was the worst in twenty-seven seasons. A jangling medley of incompetent youth and aging competence, the Red Sox were finishing in seventh place only because the Kansas City Athletics had locked them out of the cellar. They were scheduled to play the Baltimore Orioles, a much nimbler blend of May and December, who had been dumped from pennant contention a week before by the insatiable Yankees. I, and 10,453 others, had shown up primarily because this was the Red Sox's last home game of the season, and therefore the last time in all eternity that their regular left fielder, known to the headlines as TED, KID, SPLINTER, THUMPER, TW, and, most cloyingly, MISTER WONDERFUL, would play in Boston. "WHAT WILL WE DO WITHOUT TED? HUB FANS ASK" ran the headline on a newspaper being read by a bulb-nosed cigar smoker a few rows away. Williams' retirement had been announced, doubted (he had been threatening retirement for years), confirmed by Tom Yawkey, the Red Sox owner, and at last widely accepted as the sad but probable truth. He was forty-two and had redeemed his abysmal season of 1959 with a—considering his advanced age—fine one. He had been giving away his gloves and bats and had grudgingly consented to a sentimental ceremony today. This was not necessarily his last game; the Red Sox were scheduled to travel to New York and wind up the season with three games there.

I arrived early. The Orioles were hitting fungoes on the field. The day before, they had spitefully smothered the Red Sox, 17-4, and neither their faces nor their drab gray visiting-team uniforms seemed very gracious. I wondered who had invited them to the party. Between our heads and the lowering clouds a frenzied organ was thundering through, with an appositeness perhaps accidental, "You *maaaade* me love you, I didn't wanna do it, I didn't wanna do it . . ."

The affair between Boston and Ted Williams was no mere summer romance; it was a marriage composed of spats, mutual disappointments, and, towards the end, a mellowing hoard of shared memories. It fell into three stages, which may be termed Youth, Maturity, and Age; or Thesis, Antithesis, and Synthesis; or Jason, Achilles, and Nestor.

First, there was the by now legendary epoch* when the

---

*This piece was written with no research materials save an outdated record book and the Boston newspapers of the day; and Williams' early career preceded the dawning of my *Schlagballewusstein* (Baseball-consciousness). Also for reasons of perspective was my account of his beginnings skimped. Williams first attracted the notice of a major-league scout—Bill Essick of the Yankees—when he was a fifteen-year-old pitcher with the San Diego American Legion Post team. As a pitcher-outfielder for San Diego's Herbert Hoover High School, Williams recorded averages of .586 and .403. Essick balked at signing Williams for the $1,000 his mother asked; he was signed instead, for $150 a month, by the local Pacific Coast League franchise, the newly created San Diego Padres. In his two seasons with this team, Williams hit merely .271 and .291, but his style and slugging (23 home runs the second year) caught the eye of, among others, Casey Stengel, then with the Boston Braves, and Eddie Collins, the Red Sox general manager. Collins bought him from the Padres for $25,000 in cash and $25,000 in players. Williams was then nineteen. Collins' fond confidence in the boy's potential matched Williams' own. Williams reported to the Red Sox training camp in Sarasota in 1938 and, after showing more volubility than skill, was shipped down to the Minneapolis Millers, the top Sox farm team. It should be said, perhaps, that the parent club was equipped with an excellent, if mature, outfield, mostly purchased from Connie Mack's dismantled A's. Upon leaving Sarasota, Williams is supposed to have told the regular outfield of Joe Vosmik, Doc Cramer, and Ben Chapman that he would be back and would make more money than the three of them put together. At Minneapolis he hit .366, batted in 142 runs, scored 130, and hit 43 home runs. He also loafed in the field, jabbered at the fans, and smashed a water cooler with his fist. In 1939 he came north with the Red Sox. On the way, in Atlanta, he dropped a foul fly, accidentally kicked it away in trying to pick it up, picked it up, and threw it out of the park. It would be nice if, his first time up in Fenway Park, he had hit a home run. Actually, in his first Massachusetts appearance, the first inning of an exhibition game against Holy Cross at Worcester, he *did* hit a home run, a grand slam. The Red Sox season opened in Yankee Stadium. Facing

young bridegroom came out of the West and announced "All
I want out of life is that when I walk down the street folks
will say 'There goes the greatest hitter who ever lived.' "
The dowagers of local journalism attempted to give ele-
mentary deportment lessons to this child who spake as a
god, and to their horror were themselves rebuked. Thus
began the long exchange of backbiting, bat-flipping, booing,
and spitting that has distinguished Williams' public relations.* The spitting incidents of 1957 and 1958 and the
similar dockside courtesies that Williams has now and then
extended to the grandstand should be judged against this
background: the left-field stands at Fenway for twenty years
have held a large number of customers who have bought
their way in primarily for the privilege of showering abuse
on Williams. Greatness necessarily attracts debunkers, but
in Williams' case the hostility has been systematic and un-
appeasable. His basic offense against the fans has been to
wish that they weren't there. Seeking a perfectionist's vac-

Red Ruffing, Williams struck out and, the next time up, doubled for his first major-
league hit. In the Fenway Park opener, against Philadelphia, he had a single in
five trips. His first home run came on April 23, in that same series with the A's.
Williams was then twenty, and played *right* field. In his rookie season he hit .327;
in 1940, .344.

*See *Ted Williams,* by Ed Linn (Sport Magazine Library), Chapter 6, "Williams
vs. the Press." It is Linn's suggestion that Williams walked into a circulation war
among the seven Boston newspapers, who in their competitive zeal headlined
incidents that the New York papers, say, would have minimized, just as they
minimized the less genial side of the moody and aloof DiMaggio and smoothed
Babe Ruth into a folk hero. It is also Linn's thought, and an interesting one, that
Williams thrived on even adverse publicity, and needed a hostile press to elicit,
contrariwise, his defiant best. The statistics (especially of the 1958 season, when
he snapped a slump by spitting in all directions, and inadvertently conked an
elderly female fan with a tossed bat) seem to corroborate this. Certainly Williams
could have had a truce for the asking, and his industrious perpetuation of the
war, down to his last day in uniform, implies its usefulness to him. The actual
and intimate anatomy of the matter resides in locker rooms and hotel corridors
fading from memory. When my admiring account was printed, I received a letter
from a sports reporter who hated Williams with a bitter and explicit immediacy.
And even Linn's hagiology permits some glimpses of Williams' locker-room manners that are not pleasant.

uum, he has quixotically desired to sever the game from the ground of paid spectatorship and publicity that supports it. Hence his refusal to tip his cap* to the crowd or turn the other cheek to newsmen. It has been a costly theory—it has probably cost him, among other evidences of good will, two Most Valuable Player awards, which are voted by reporters**—but he has held to it. While his critics, oral and literary, remained beyond the reach of his discipline, the opposing pitchers were accessible, and he spanked them to the tune of .406 in 1941.*** He slumped to .356 in 1942 and went off to war.

In 1946, Williams returned from three years as a Marine pilot to the second of his baseball avatars, that of Achilles, the hero of incomparable prowess and beauty who nevertheless was to be found sulking in his tent while the Trojans (mostly Yankees) fought through to the ships. Yawkey, a

---

*But he did tip his cap, high off his head, in at least his first season, as cartoons from that period verify. He also was extravagantly cordial to taxi-drivers and stray children. See Linn, Chapter 4, "The Kid Comes to Boston": "There has never been a ballplayer—anywhere, anytime—more popular than Ted Williams in his first season in Boston." To this epoch belongs Williams' prankish use of the Fenway scoreboard lights for rifle practice, his celebrated preference for the life of a fireman, and his determined designation of himself as "The Kid."

**In 1947 Joe DiMaggio and in 1957 Mickey Mantle, with seasons inferior to Williams', won the MVP award because sportswriters, who vote on ballots with ten places, had vengefully placed Williams ninth, tenth, or nowhere at all. The 1941 award to DiMaggio, even though this was Williams' .406 year, is more understandable, since this was also the *annus miraculorum* when DiMaggio hit safely in 56 consecutive games.

***The sweet saga of this beautiful decimal must be sung once more. Williams, after hitting above .400 all season, had cooled to .39955 with one doubleheader left to play, in Philadelphia. Joe Cronin, then managing the Red Sox, offered to bench him to safeguard his average, which was exactly .400 when rounded to the third decimal place. Williams said (I forget where I read this) that he did not want to become the .400 hitter with just his toe over the line. He played the first game and singled, homered, singled, and singled. With less to gain than to lose, he elected to play the second game and got two more hits, including a double that dented a loudspeaker horn on the top of the right-field wall, giving him six-for-eight on the day and a season's average that, in the forty years between Rogers Hornsby's .403 (1925) and the present, stands as unique.

timber and mining maharajah, had surrounded his central jewel with many gems of slightly lesser water, such as Bobby Doerr, Dom DiMaggio, Rudy York, Birdie Tebbets, and Johnny Pesky. Throughout the late forties, the Red Sox were the best paper team in baseball, yet they had little three-dimensional to show for it, and if this was a tragedy, Williams was Hamlet. A succinct review of the indictment—and a fair sample of appreciative sports-page prose—appeared the very day of Williams' valedictory, in a column by Huck Finnegan in the Boston *American* (no sentimentalist, Huck):

> Williams' career, in contrast [to Babe Ruth's], has been a series of failures except for his averages. He flopped in the only World Series he ever played in (1946) when he batted only .200. He flopped in the playoff game with Cleveland in 1948. He flopped in the final game of the 1949 season with the pennant hinging on the outcome (Yanks 5, Sox 3). He flopped in 1950 when he returned to the lineup after a two-month absence and ruined the morale of a club that seemed pennant-bound under Steve O'Neill. It has always been Williams' records first, the team second, and the Sox non-winning record is proof enough of that.

There are answers to all this, of course. The fatal weakness of the great Sox slugging teams was not-quite-good-enough pitching rather than Williams' failure to hit a home run every time he came to bat. Again, Williams' depressing effect on his teammates has never been proved. Despite ample coaching to the contrary, most insisted that they *liked* him. He has been generous with advice to any player who asked for it. In an increasingly combative baseball atmosphere, he continued to duck beanballs docilely. With umpires he was gracious to a fault. This courtesy itself annoyed his critics, whom there was no pleasing. And against the ten crucial games (the seven World Series games with the St. Louis Cardinals, the 1948 playoff with the Cleveland Indians, and the two-game series with the Yankees at the end of the 1949 season, when one victory would have given the Red Sox the pennant) that make up the Achilles' heel of Williams' record, a mass of statistics can be set showing that day in and day out he was no slouch in the clutch.* The correspondence columns of the Boston papers now and then suffer a sharp flurry of arithmetic on this score; indeed, for Williams to have distributed all his hits so they did nobody else any good would constitute a feat of placement unparalleled in the annals of selfishness.

Whatever residue of truth remains of the Finnegan charge those of us who love Williams must transmute as best we can, in our own personal crucibles. My personal memories of Williams began when I was a boy in Pennsylvania, with two last-place teams in Philadelphia to keep me company. For me, "W'ms, lf" was a figment of the box scores who always seemed to be going 3-for-5. He radiated, from afar, the hard blue glow of high purpose. I remember listening over the radio to the All-Star Game of 1946, in which Williams hit two singles and two home runs, the second one off a Rip Sewell "blooper" pitch; it was like hitting a balloon out of the park. I remember watching one of his home runs from the bleachers of Shibe Park; it went over the first baseman's head and rose methodically along a straight line and was still rising when it cleared the fence. The trajectory seemed qualitatively different from anything anyone else

---

*For example: In 1948, the Sox came from behind to tie the Indians by winning three straight: in those games Williams went two for two, two for two, and two for four. In 1949, the Sox overtook the Yankees by winning nine in a row; in that streak, Williams won four games with home runs.

might hit. For me, Williams is the classic ballplayer of the game on a hot August weekday, before a small crowd, when the only thing at stake is the tissue-thin difference between a thing done well and a thing done ill. Baseball is a game of the long season, of relentless and gradual averaging-out. Irrelevance—since the reference point of most individual contests is remote and statistical—always threatens its interest, which can be maintained not by the occasional heroics that sportwriters feed upon but by players who always *care;* who care, that is to say, about themselves and their art. Insofar as the clutch hitter is not a sportswriter's myth, he is a vulgarity, like a writer who writes only for money. It may be that, compared to such managers' dreams as the manifestly classy Joe DiMaggio and the always helpful Stan Musial, Williams was an icy star. But of all team sports, baseball, with its graceful intermittences of action, its immense and tranquil field sparsely settled with poised men in white, its dispassionate mathematics, seems to be best suited to accommodate, and be ornamented by, a loner. It is an essentially lonely game. No other player visible to my generation concentrated within himself so much of the sport's poignance, so assiduously refined his natural skills, so constantly brought to the plate that intensity of competence that crowds the throat with joy.

By the time I went to college, near Boston, the lesser stars Yawkey had assembled around Williams had faded, and his rigorous pride of craftsmanship had become itself a kind of heroism. This brittle and temperamental player developed an unexpected quality of persistence. He was always coming back—back from Korea, back from a broken collarbone, a shattered elbow, a bruised heel, back from drastic bouts of flu and ptomaine poisoning. Hardly a season went by without some enfeebling mishap, yet he always came back, and always looked like himself. The delicate mechanism of timing and power seemed sealed, shockproof, in some case deep within his frame.* In addition to injuries, there was a heavily publicized divorce, and the usual storms with the press, and the Williams Shift—the maneuver, custom-built by Lou Boudreau of the Cleveland Indians, whereby three infielders were concentrated on the right side of the infield.** Williams could easily have learned to punch singles through the vacancy on his left and fattened his average hugely. This was what Ty Cobb, the Einstein of average, told him to do. But the game had changed since Cobb; Williams believed that his value to the club and to the league was as a slugger, so he went on pulling the ball, trying to blast it through three men, and paid the price of perhaps fifteen points of lifetime average. Like Ruth before him, he bought the occasional home run at the cost of many directed singles—a calculated sacrifice certainly not, in the case of a hitter as average-minded as Williams, entirely selfish.

After a prime so harassed and hobbled, Williams was granted by the relenting fates a golden twilight. He became at the end of his career perhaps the best *old* hitter of the

---

*Two reasons for his durability may be adduced. A non-smoker, non-drinker, habitual walker, and year-round outdoorsman, Williams spared his body the vicissitudes of the seasonal athlete. And his hitting was in large part a mental process; the amount of cerebration he devoted to such details as pitchers' patterns, prevailing winds, and the muscular mechanics of swinging a bat would seem ridiculous, if it had not paid off. His intellectuality, as it were, perhaps explains the quickness with which he adjusted, after the war, to the changed conditions— the night games, the addition of the slider to the standard pitching repertoire, the new cry for the long ball. His reaction to the Williams Shift, then, cannot be dismissed as unconsidered.

**Invented, or perpetrated (as a joke?) by Boudreau on July 14, 1946, between games of a doubleheader. In the first game of the doubleheader, Williams had hit three homers and batted in eight runs. The shift was not used when men were on base and, had Williams bunted or hit late against it immediately, it might not have spread, in all its variations, throughout the league. The Cardinals used it in the lamented World Series of that year. Toward the end, in 1959 and 1960, rather sadly, it had faded from use, or degenerated to the mere clockwise twitching of the infield customary against pull hitters.

century. The dividing line falls between the 1956 and the 1957 seasons. In September of the first year, he and Mickey Mantle were contending for the batting championship. Both were hitting around .350, and there was no one else near them. The season ended with a three-game series between the Yankees and the Sox, and, living in New York then, I went up to the Stadium. Williams was slightly shy of the four hundred at-bats needed to qualify; the fear was expressed that the Yankee pitchers would walk him to protect Mantle. Instead, they pitched to him. It was wise. He looked terrible at the plate, tired and discouraged and unconvincing. He never looked very good to me in the Stadium.* The final outcome in 1956 was Mantle .353, Williams .345.

The next year, I moved from New York to New England, and it made all the difference. For in September of 1957, in the same situation, the story was reversed. Mantle finally hit .365; it was the best season of his career. But Williams, though sick and old, had run away from him. A bout of flu had laid him low in September. He emerged from his cave in the Hotel Somerset haggard but irresistible; he hit four successive pinch-hit home runs. "I feel terrible," he confessed, "but every time I take a swing at the ball it goes out of the park." He ended the season with thirty-eight home runs and an average of .388, the highest in either league since his own .406, and, coming from a decrepit man of thirty-nine, an even more supernal figure. With eight or so of the "leg hits" that a younger man would have beaten out, it would have been .400. And the next year, Williams, who in 1949 and 1953 had lost batting championships by decimal whiskers to George Kell and Mickey Vernon, sneaked be-

*Shortly after his retirement, Williams, in *Life,* wrote gloomily of the Stadium, "There's the bigness of it. There are those high stands and all those people smoking—and, of course, the shadows. . . . It takes at least one series to get accustomed to the Stadium and even then you're not sure." Yet his lifetime batting average there is .340, only four points under his median average.

hind his teammate Pete Runnels and filched his sixth title, a bargain at .328.

In 1959, it seemed all over. The dinosaur thrashed around in the .200 swamp for the first half of the season, and was even benched ("rested," Manager Mike Higgins tactfully said). Old foes like the late Bill Cunningham began to offer batting tips. Cunningham thought Williams was jiggling his elbows;* in truth, Williams' neck was so stiff he could hardly turn his head to look at the pitcher. When he swung, it looked like a Calder mobile with one thread cut; it reminded you that since 1954 Williams' shoulders had been wired together. A solicitous pall settled over the sports pages. In the two decades since Williams had come to Boston, his status had imperceptibly shifted from that of a naughty prodigy to that of a municipal monument. As his shadow in the record books lengthened, the Red Sox teams around him declined, and the entire American League seemed to be losing life and color to the National. The inconsistency of the new super-stars—Mantle, Colavito, and Kaline—served to make Williams appear all the more singular. And off the field, his private philanthropy—in particular, his zealous chairmanship of the Jimmy Fund, a charity for children with cancer—gave him a civic presence matched only by that of Richard Cardinal Cushing. In religion, Williams appears to have been a humanist, and a selective one at that, but he and the abrasive-voiced Cardinal, when their good works intersect and they appear in the public eye together, make a handsome pair of seraphim.

*It was Cunningham who, when Williams first appeared in a Red Sox uniform at the 1938 spring training camp, wrote with melodious prescience: "The Sox seem to think Williams is just cocky enough and gabby enough to make a great and colorful outfielder, possibly the Babe Herman type. Me? I don't like the way he stands at the plate. He bends his front knee inward and moves his foot just before he takes a swing. That's exactly what I do just before I drive a golf ball and knowing what happens to the golf balls I drive, I don't believe this kid will ever hit half a singer midget's weight in a bathing suit."

Humiliated by his '59 season, Williams determined, once more, to come back. I, as a specimen Williams partisan, was both glad and fearful. All baseball fans believe in miracles; the question is, how *many* do you believe in? He looked like a ghost in spring training. Manager Jurges warned us ahead of time that if Williams didn't come through he would be benched, just like anybody else. As it turned out, it was Jurges who was benched. Williams entered the 1960 season needing eight home runs to have a lifetime total of 500; after one time at bat in Washington, he needed seven. For a stretch, he was hitting a home run every second game that he played. He passed Lou Gehrig's lifetime total, and finished with 521, thirteen behind Jimmy Foxx, who alone stands between Williams and Babe Ruth's unapproachable 714. The summer was a statistician's picnic. His two-thousandth walk came and went, his eighteen-hundredth run batted in, his sixteenth All-Star Game. At one point, he hit a home run off a pitcher, Don Lee, off whose father, Thornton Lee, he had hit a home run a generation before. The only comparable season for a forty-two-year-old man was Ty Cobb's in 1928. Cobb batted .323 and hit one homer. Williams batted .316 but hit twenty-nine homers.

In sum, though generally conceded to be the greatest hitter of his era, he did not establish himself as "the greatest hitter who ever lived." Cobb, for average, and Ruth, for power, remain supreme. Cobb, Rogers Hornsby, Joe Jackson, and Lefty O'Doul, among players since 1900, have higher lifetime averages than Williams' .344. Unlike Foxx, Gehrig, Hack Wilson, Hank Greenberg, and Ralph Kiner, Williams never came close to matching Babe Ruth's season home-run total of sixty.* In the list of major-league batting records, not one is held by Williams. He is second in walks drawn, third in home runs, fifth in lifetime averge, sixth in

*Written before Roger Maris' fluky, phenomenal sixty-one.

•

runs batted in, eighth in runs scored and in total bases, fourteenth in doubles, and thirtieth in hits.* But if we allow him merely average seasons for the four-plus seasons he lost to two wars, and add another season for the months he lost to injuries, we get a man who in all the power totals would be second, and not a very distant second, to Ruth. And if we further allow that these years would have been not merely average but prime years, if we allow for all the months when Williams was playing in sub-par condition, if we permit his early and later years in baseball to be some sort of index of what the middle years could have been, if we give him a right-field fence that is not, like Fenway's, one of the most distant in the league, and if—the least excusable "if"—we imagine him condescending to outsmart the Williams Shift, we can defensibly assemble, like a colossus induced from the sizable fragments that do remain, a statistical figure not incommensurate with his grandiose ambition. From the statistics that are on the books, a good case can be made that in the *combination* of power and average Williams is first; nobody else ranks so high in both categories. Finally, there is the witness of the eyes; men whose memories go back to Shoeless Joe Jackson—another unlucky natural—rank him and Williams together as the best-looking hitters they have seen. It was for our last look that ten thousand of us had come.

Two girls, one of them with pert buckteeth and eyes as black as vest buttons, the other with white skin and flesh-colored hair, like an underdeveloped photograph of a redhead, came and sat on my right. On my other side was one of those frowning chestless young-old men who can frequently be seen, often wearing sailor hats, attending ball

*Again, as of 1960. Since then, Musial and Willie Mays may have surpassed him in some statistical areas.

games alone. He did not once open his program but instead tapped it, rolled up, on his knee as he gave the game his disconsolate attention. A young lady, with freckles and a depressed, dainty nose that by an optical illusion seemed to thrust her lips forward for a kiss, sauntered down into the box seat right behind the roof of the Oriole dugout. She wore a blue coat with a Northeastern University emblem sewed to it. The girls beside me took it into their heads that this was Williams' daughter. She looked too old to me, and why would she be sitting behind the visitor's dugout? On the other hand, from the way she sat there, staring at the sky and French-inhaling, she clearly was *somebody*. Other fans came and eclipsed her from view. The crowd looked less like a weekday ballpark crowd than like the folks you might find in Yellowstone National Park, or emerging from automobiles at the top of scenic Mount Mansfield. There were a lot of competitively well-dressed couples of tourist age, and not a few babes in arms. A row of five seats in front of me was abruptly filled with a woman and four children, the youngest of them two years old, if that. Someday, presumably, he could tell his grandchildren that he saw Williams play. Along with these tots and second-honeymooners, there were Harvard freshmen, giving off that peculiar nervous glow created when a sufficient quantity of insouciance is saturated with enough insecurity; thick-necked Army officers with brass on their shoulders and steel in their stares; pepperings of priests; perfumed bouquets of Roxbury Fabian fans; shiny salesmen from Albany and Fall River; and those gray, hoarse men—taxi drivers, slaughterers, and bartenders—who will continue to click through the turnstiles long after everyone else has deserted to television and tramporamas. Behind me, two young male voices blossomed, cracking a joke about God's five proofs that Thomas Aquinas exists—typical Boston College levity.

The batting cage was trundled away. The Orioles fluttered to the sidelines. Diagonally across the field, by the Red Sox dugout, a cluster of men in overcoats were festering like maggots. I could see a splinter of white uniform, and Williams' head, held at a self-deprecating and evasive tilt. Williams' conversational stance is that of a six-foot-three-inch man under a six-foot ceiling. He moved away to the patter of flashbulbs, and began playing catch with a young Negro outfielder named Willie Tasby. His arm, never very powerful, had grown lax with the years, and his throwing motion was a kind of muscular drawl. To catch the ball, he flicked his glove hand onto his left shoulder (he batted left but threw right, as every schoolboy ought to know) and let the ball plop into it comically. This catch session with Tasby was the only time all afternoon I saw him grin.

A tight little flock of human sparrows who, from the lambent and pampered pink of their faces, could only have been Boston politicians moved toward the plate. The loudspeakers mammothly coughed as someone huffed on the microphone. The ceremonies began. Curt Gowdy, the Red Sox radio and television announcer, who sounds like everybody's brother-in-law, delivered a brief sermon, taking the two words "pride" and "champion" as his text. It began. "Twenty-one years ago, a skinny kid from San Diego, California . . ." and ended, "I don't think we'll ever see another like him." Robert Tibolt, chairman of the board of the Greater Boston Chamber of Commerce, presented Williams with a big Paul Revere silver bowl. Harry Carlson, a member of the sports committee of the Boston Chamber, gave him a plaque, whose inscription he did not read in its entirety, out of deference to Williams' distaste for this sort of fuss. Mayor Collins, seated in a wheelchair, presented the Jimmy Fund with a thousand-dollar check.

Then the occasion himself stooped to the microphone, and his voice sounded, after the others, very Californian; it seemed to be coming, excellently amplified, from a great distance, adolescently young and as smooth as a butternut. His thanks for the gifts had not died from our ears before he glided, as if helplessly, into, "In spite of all the terrible things that have been said about me by the knights of the keyboard up there . . ." He glanced up at the press rows suspended behind home plate. The crowd tittered, appalled. A frightful vision flashed upon me, of the press gallery pelting Williams with erasers, of Williams clambering up the foul screen to slug journalists, of a riot, of Mayor Collins being crushed. ". . . And they *were* terrible things," Williams insisted, with level melancholy, into the mike. "I'd like to forget them, but I can't." He paused, swallowed his memories, and went on, "I want to say that my years in Boston have been the greatest thing in my life." The crowd, like an immense sail going limp in a change of wind, sighed with relief. Taking all the parts himself, Williams then acted out a vivacious little morality drama in which an imaginary tempter came to him at the beginning of his career and said, "Ted, you can play anywhere you like." Leaping nimbly into the role of his younger self (who in biographical actuality had yearned to be a Yankee), Williams gallantly chose Boston over all the other cities, and told us that Tom Yawkey was the greatest owner in baseball and we were the greatest fans. We applauded ourselves lustily. The umpire came out and dusted the plate. The voice of doom announced over the loudspeakers that after Williams' retirement his uniform number, 9, would be permanently retired—the first time the Red Sox had so honored a player. We cheered. The national anthem was played. We cheered. The game began.

Williams was third in the batting order, so he came up in the bottom of the first inning, and Steve Barber, a young pitcher born two months before Williams began playing in the major leagues, offered him four pitches, at all of which he disdained to swing, since none of them were within the strike zone. This demonstrated simultaneously that Williams' eyes were razor-sharp and that Barber's control wasn't. Shortly, the bases were full, with Williams on second. "Oh, I hope he gets held up at third! That would be wonderful," the girl beside me moaned, and sure enough, the man at bat walked and Williams was delivered into our foreground. He struck the pose of Donatello's David, the third-base bag being Goliath's head. Fiddling with his cap, swapping small talk with the Oriole third baseman (who seemed delighted to have him drop in), swinging his arms with a sort of prancing nervousness, he looked fine—flexible, hard, and not unbecomingly substantial through the middle. The long neck, the small head, the knickers whose cuffs were worn down near his ankles—all these clichés of sports cartoon iconography were rendered in the flesh.

With each pitch, Williams danced down the baseline, waving his arms and stirring dust, ponderous but menacing, like an attacking goose. It occurred to about a dozen humorists at once to shout "Steal home! Go, go!" Williams' speed afoot was never legendary. Lou Clinton, a young Sox outfielder, hit a fairly deep fly to center field. Williams tagged up and ran home. As he slid across the plate, the ball, thrown with unusual heft by Jackie Brandt, the Oriole center fielder, hit him on the back.

"Boy, he was really loafing, wasn't he?" one of the collegiate voices behind me said.

"It's cold," the other voice explained. "He doesn't play well when it's cold. He likes heat. He's a hedonist."

The run that Williams scored was the second and last of the inning. Gus Triandos, of the Orioles, quickly evened the score by plunking a home run over the handy left-field wall. Williams, who had had this wall at his back for twenty years,* played the ball flawlessly. He didn't budge. He just stood still, in the center of the little patch of grass that his patient footsteps had worn brown, and limp with lack of interest, watched the ball pass overhead. It was not a very interesting game. Mike Higgins, the Red Sox manager, with nothing to lose, had restricted his major-league players to the left-field line—along with Williams, Frank Malzone, a first-rate third baseman, played the game—and had peopled the rest of the terrain with unpredictable youngsters fresh, or not so fresh, off the farms. Other than Williams' recurrent appearances at the plate, the *maladresse* of the Sox infield was the sole focus of suspense; the second baseman turned every grounder into a juggling act, while the shortstop did a breathtaking impersonation of an open window. With this sort of assistance, the Orioles wheeled their way into a 4-2 lead. They had early replaced Barber with another young pitcher, Jack Fisher. Fortunately (as it turned out), Fisher is no cutie; he is willing to burn the ball through the strike zone, and inning after inning this tactic punctured Higgins' string of test balloons.

Whenever Williams appeared at the plate—pounding the dirt from his cleats, gouging a pit in the batter's box with his left foot, wringing resin out of the bat handle with his vehement grip, switching the stick at the pitcher with an electric ferocity—it was like having a familiar Leonardo appear in a shuffle of *Saturday Evening Post* covers. This man, you realized—and here, perhaps, was the difference, greater than the difference in gifts—really desired to hit the ball. In the third inning, he hoisted a high fly to deep center. In the fifth, we thought he had it; he smacked the ball hard and high into the heart of his power zone, but the deep right field in Fenway and the heavy air and a casual

*In his second season (1940) he was switched to left field, to protect his eyes from the right-field sun.

east wind defeated him. The ball died. Al Pilarcik leaned his back against the big "380" painted on the right-field wall and caught it. On another day, in another park, it would have been gone. (After the game, Williams said, "I didn't think I could hit one any harder than that. The conditions weren't good.")

The afternoon grew so glowering that in the sixth inning the arc lights were turned on—always a wan sight in the daytime, like the burning headlights of a funeral procession. Aided by the gloom, Fisher was slicking through the Sox rookies, and Williams did not come to bat in the seventh. He was second up in the eighth. This was almost certainly his last time to come to the plate in Fenway Park, and instead of merely cheering, as we had at his three previous appearances, we stood, all of us, and applauded. I had never before heard pure applause in a ballpark. No calling, no whistling, just an ocean of handclaps, minute after minute, burst after burst, crowding and running together in continuous succession like the pushes of surf at the edge of the sand. It was a sombre and considered tumult. There was not a boo in it. It seemed to renew itself out of a shifting set of memories as the Kid, the Marine, the veteran of feuds and failures and injuries, the friend of children, and the enduring old pro evolved down the bright tunnel of twenty-two summers toward this moment. At last, the umpire signalled for Fisher to pitch; with the other players, he had been frozen in position. Only Williams had moved during the ovation, switching his bat impatiently, ignoring everything except his cherished task. Fisher wound up, and the applause sank into a hush.

Understand that we were a crowd of rational people. We knew that a home run cannot be produced at will; the right pitch must be perfectly met and luck must ride with the ball. Three innings before, we had seen a brave effort fail. The air was soggy, the season was exhausted. Nevertheless, there will always lurk, around the corner in a pocket of our knowledge of the odds, an indefensible hope, and this was one of the times, which you now and then find in sports, when a density of expectation hangs in the air and plucks an event out of the future.

Fisher, after his unsettling wait, was low with the first pitch. He put the second one over, and Williams swung mightily and missed. The crowd grunted, seeing that classic swing, so long and smooth and quick, exposed. Fisher threw the third time, Williams swung again, and there it was. The ball climbed on a diagonal line into the vast volume of air over center field. From my angle, behind third base, the ball seemed less an object in flight than the tip of a towering, motionless construct, like the Eiffel Tower or the Tappan Zee Bridge. It was in the books while it was still in the sky. Brandt ran back to the deepest corner of the outfield grass, the ball descended beyond his reach and struck in the crotch where the bullpen met the wall, bounced chunkily, and vanished.

Like a feather caught in a vortex, Williams ran around the square of bases at the center of our beseeching screaming. He ran as he always ran out home runs—hurriedly, unsmiling, head down, as if our praise were a storm of rain to get out of. He didn't tip his cap. Though we thumped, wept, chanted "We want Ted" for minutes after he hid in the dugout, he did not come back. Our noise for some seconds passed beyond excitement into a kind of immense open anguish, a wailing, a cry to be saved. But immortality is nontransferable. The papers said that the other players, and even the umpires on the field, begged him to come out and acknowledge us in some way, but he refused. Gods do not answer letters.

Every true story has an anticlimax. The men on the field refused to disappear, as would have seemed decent, in the smoke of Williams' miracle. Fisher continued to pitch, and escaped further harm. At the end of the inning, Higgins sent Williams out to his left-field position, then instantly replaced him with Carrol Hardy, so we had a long last look at Williams as he ran out there and then back, his uniform jogging, his eyes steadfast on the ground. It was nice, and we were grateful, but it left a funny note.

One of the scholasticists behind me said, "Let's go. We've seen everything. I don't want to spoil it." This seemed a sound aesthetic decision. Williams' last word had been so exquisitely chosen, such a perfect fusion of expectation, intention, and execution, that already it felt a little unreal in my head, and I wanted to get out before the castle collapsed. But the game, though played at by clumsy midgets under the feeble flow of the arc lights, began to tug at my attention, and I loitered in the runway until it was over. Williams' homer had, quite incidentally, made the score 4-3. In the bottom of the ninth inning, with one out, Marlin Coughtry, the second-base juggler, singled. Vic Wertz, pinch-hitting, doubled off the leftfield wall, Coughtry advancing to third. Pumpsie Green walked, to load the bases. Willie Tasby hit a double-play ball to the third baseman, but in making the pivot throw Billy Klaus, an ex–Red Sox infielder, reverted to form and threw the ball past the first baseman and into the Red Sox dugout. The Sox won, 5-4. On the radio as I drove home I heard that Williams, his own man to the end, had decided not to accompany the team to New York. He had met the little death that awaits athletes. He had quit.

The Kid's Last Game

ED LINN

1961

Ed Linn, a longtime and astute observer of Ted Williams, takes us inside the locker room and dugout to give us a close-up look at Williams on his last day as a player. While Updike describes the final game from the perspective of a spectator (albeit one with a poet's perception), Linn provides an insider's point of view as a working journalist on assignment for *Sport*. He writes from the trenches, venturing into the Red Sox locker room that for so many years had been the battleground between Williams and the press. And Linn makes it clear that no quarter was given, not even on that final day. Ted Williams remained true to himself to the very end.

Linn's essay provides a balanced retrospective, both of the press wars and of the man he calls "the most remarkable and colorful and full-blooded human being to come upon the athletic scene since Babe Ruth."

Wednesday, September 26, was a cold and dreary day in Boston, a curious bit of staging on the part of those gods who always set the scene most carefully for Ted Williams. It was to be the last game Ted would ever play in Boston. Not until the game was over would Williams let it be known that it was the last game he would play anywhere.

Ted came into the locker room at 10:50, very early for him. He was dressed in dark brown slacks, a yellow sport shirt and a light tan pullover sweater, tastily brocaded in the same color. Ted went immediately to his locker, pulled off the sweater, then strolled into the trainer's room.

Despite all the triumphs and the honors, it had been a difficult year for him. As trainer Jack Fadden put it, "It hasn't been a labor of love for Ted this year; it's just been labor." On two separate occasions, he had come very close to giving it all up.

The spring-training torture had been made no easier for Ted by manager Billy Jurges. Jurges believed that the only way for a man Ted's age to stay in condition was to reach a peak at the beginning of the season and hold it by playing just as often as possible. "The most we can expect from Williams," Jurges had said, at the time of Ted's signing, "is 100 games. The least is pinch-hitting." Ted played in 113 games.

Throughout the training season, however, Ted seemed to be having trouble with his timing. Recalling his .254 average of the previous season, the experts wrote him off for perhaps the 15th time in his career. But on his first time at bat in the opening game, Ted hit a 500-foot home run, possibly the longest of his career, off Camilo Pascual, probably the best pitcher in the league. The next day, in the Fenway Park opener, he hit a second homer, this one off Jim Coates. Ted pulled a leg muscle running out that homer, though, and when a man's muscles go while he is doing nothing more than jogging around the bases, the end is clearly in sight.

It took him almost a month to get back in condition, but the mysterious virus infection that hits him annually, a holdover from his service in Korea, laid him low again almost immediately. Since the doctors have never been able to diagnose this chronic illness, the only way they can treat him is to shoot a variety of drugs and antibiotics into him, in the hope that one of them takes hold. Ted, miserable and drugged when he finally got back in uniform, failed in a couple of pinch-hitting attempts and was just about ready to quit. Against the Yankees, Ralph Terry struck him out two straight times. The third time up, the count went to 3–2 when Williams unloaded on a waist-high fast ball and sent it into the bullpen in right-center, 400 feet away.

The blast triggered the greatest home-run spurt of Ted's career. Seven days later, he hit his 500th home run. He had started only 15 1960 games and he had hit eight 1960 homers. When he hit his 506th (and 11th of the year), he had homered once in every 6.67 times at bat.

Cold weather always bothered Ted, even in his early years, and so when he strained his shoulder late in August, he was just about ready to announce his retirement again. He had found it difficult to loosen up even in fairly warm weather, and to complicate matters he had found it necessary—back in the middle of 1959—to cut out the calisthenics routine he had always gone through in the clubhouse. The exercising had left him almost too weary to play ball.

Ted started every game so stiff that he was forced to exaggerate an old passion for swinging at balls only in the strike zone. In his first time at bat, he would look for an inside pitch between the waist and knees, the only pitch he could swing at naturally. In the main, however, Ted was more than willing to take the base on balls his first time up.

He stayed on for two reasons. Mike Higgins, who had replaced Jurges as Sox manager, told him bluntly, "You're paid to play ball, so go out and play." The strength behind those words rested in the fact that both Williams and Higgins knew very well that owner Tom Yawkey would continue to pay Ted whether he played or not.

In addition, the Red Sox had two series remaining with the Yankees and Orioles, who were still locked together in the pennant race. Ted did not think it fair to eliminate himself as a factor in the two-team battle. He announced his retirement just after the Yankees clinched the pennant.

Four days earlier, Ted had been called to a special meeting with Yawkey, Higgins, Dick O'Connell (who was soon to be named business manager) and publicity director Jack Malaney. This was to offer Ted the job of general manager, a position that had been discussed occasionally in the past.

Ted refused to accept the title until he proved he could do the job. He agreed, however, to work in the front office in 1961, assisting Higgins with player personnel, and O'Connell with business matters.

The coverage of Ted's last game was at a minimum. It was thought for a while that *Life* magazine wanted to send a crew down to cover the game, but it developed that they only wanted to arrange for Ted to represent them at the World Series. Dave Garroway's "Today" program tried to set up a telephone interview the morning of the game, but they couldn't get in touch with Ted. The Red Sox, alone among big-league clubs, have offered little help to anyone on the public relations front—and never any help at all where Ted Williams was concerned. Ted didn't live at the Kenmore Hotel with the rest of the unattached players. He lived about 100 yards down Commonwealth Avenue, at the Somerset. All calls and messages for him were diverted to the manager's office.

The ceremonies that were to mark his departure were rather limited, too. The Boston Chamber of Commerce had arranged to present him with a silver bowl, and the mayor's office and governor's office had quickly muscled into the picture. By Wednesday morning, however, the governor's office—which had apparently anticipated something more spectacular—begged off. The governor's spokesman suggested the presentation of a scroll at Ted's hotel, a suggestion which Ted simply ignored.

The only civilian in the clubhouse when Ted entered was the man from *Sport,* and he was talking to Del Baker, who was about to retire, too, after 50 years in the game. Ted looked over, scowled, seemed about to say something but changed his mind.

Our man was well aware what Ted was about to say. The Red Sox have a long-standing rule—also unique in baseball—that no reporter may enter the dressing room before the game, or for the first 15 minutes after the game. It was a point of honor with Ted to pick out any civilian who wasn't specifically with a ball player and to tell him, as loudly as possible: "You're not supposed to be in here, you know."

Sure enough, when our man started toward Ted's locker in the far corner of the room, Ted pointed a finger at him and shouted, "You're not supposed to be in here, you know."

"The same warm, glad cry of greeting I always get from you," our man said. "It's your last day. Why don't you live a little?"

Ted started toward the trainer's room again, but wheeled around and came back. "You've got a nerve coming here to interview me after the last one you wrote about me!"

Our man wanted to know what was the matter with the last one.

"You called me 'unbearable,' that's what's the matter."

The full quote, it was pointed out, was that he "was sometimes unbearable but never dull," which holds a different connotation entirely.

"You've been after me for twelve years, that flogging magazine," he said, in his typically well-modulated shout. "Twelve years. I missed an appointment for some kind of luncheon. I forgot what happened . . . it doesn't matter anyway . . . but I forgot some appointment twelve years ago and *Sport* magazine hasn't let up on me since."

Our man, lamentably eager to disassociate himself from this little magazine, made it clear that while he had done most of *Sport*'s Williams articles in the past few years he was not a member of the staff. "And," our man pointed out, "I have been accused of turning you into a combination of Paul Bunyan and Santa Claus."

"Well, when you get back there tell them what . . ." (he searched for the appropriate word, the *mot juste* as they say in the dugouts) ". . . what *flog-heads* they are. Tell them that for me."

Our man sought to check the correct spelling of the adjectives with him but got back only a scowl. Ted turned around to fish something out of a cloth bag at the side of his locker. "Why don't you just write your story without me?" he said. "What do you have to talk to me for?" And then, in a suddenly weary voice: "What can I tell you now that I haven't told you before?"

"Why don't you let me tell you what the story is supposed to be?" our man said. "Then you can say yes or no." It was an unfortunate way to put the question since it invited the answer it brought.

"I can tell you before you tell me," Ted shouted. "No! No, no, no."

Our man had the impression Williams was trying to tell him something. He was right. "Look," Williams said. "If I tell you I don't want to talk to you, why don't you just take my word for it?"

The clubhouse boy had come over with a glossy photo to be signed, and Ted sat down on his stool, turned his back and signed it.

Although we are reluctant to bring *Sport* into the context of the story itself, Ted's abiding hatred toward us tells much about him and his even longer feud with Boston sportswriters. Twelve years ago, just as Ted said, an article appeared on these pages to which he took violent exception. (The fact that he is so well aware that it *was* twelve years ago suggests that he still has the magazine around somewhere, so that he can fan the flames whenever he feels them dying.) What Ted objected to in that article was an interview with his mother in San Diego. Ted objects to any peering into his private life. When he holes himself up in his hotel, when he sets a barrier around the clubhouse, when he disappears into the Florida Keys at the end of the season, he is deliberately removing himself from a world which he takes to be dangerous and hostile. His constant fighting with the newspapermen who cover him most closely is part of the same pattern. What do newspapermen represent except the people who are supposed to pierce personal barriers? Who investigate, who pry, *who find out*?

Ted's mother has been a Salvation Army worker in San Diego all her life. She is a local character, known—not without affection—as "Salvation May." Ted himself was dedicated to the Salvation Army when he was a baby. His generosity, his unfailing instinct to come to the aid of any underdog, is in direct line with the teachings of the Army, which is quite probably the purest charitable organization in the world. Even as a boy, Ted regularly gave his 30-cent luncheon allowance to classmates he considered more needy than himself, a considerable sacrifice since the Williams family had to struggle to make ends meet.

When Ted signed with San Diego at the age of seventeen, he was a tall, skinny kid (six-three, 146 pounds). He gave most of his $150-a-month salary toward keeping up the family house and he tried to build up his weight by gorging himself on the road where the club picked up the check. One day Ted was coming into the clubhouse when Bill Lane, the owner of the Padres, motioned him over. In his deep, foghorn voice, Lane said, "Well, kid, you're leading the list. You've got the others beat."

Ted, pleased that his ability was being noted so promptly, smiled and asked, "Yeah, what list?"

"The dining room list," Lane said. "Hasn't anyone told you that your meal allowance is supposed to be five dollars a day?"

Nobody had. "Okay, Bill," Ted said, finally. "Take anything over five dollars off my salary."

Bill did, too.

Even before *Sport* went into details about his background, the Boston press had discovered his weak point and hit him hard and—it must be added—most unfairly. During Ted's second season with the Sox, one reporter had the ill grace to comment, in regard to a purely personal dispute, "But what can you expect of a youth so abnormal that he didn't go home in the off season to see his own mother?"

When Williams' World War II draft status was changed from 1A to 3A after he claimed his mother as a dependent, one Boston paper sent a private investigator to San Diego to check on her standard of living; another paper sent reporters out onto the street to ask casual passersby to pass judgment on Ted's patriotism.

Reporters were sent galloping out into the street to conduct a public opinion poll once again when Williams was caught fishing in the Everglades while his wife was giving birth to a premature baby.

A press association later sent a story out of San Diego that Ted had sold the furniture out from under his mother— although a simple phone call could have established that it wasn't true. Ted had bought the house and the furniture for his mother. His brother—who had been in frequent trouble with the law—had sold it. The Boston papers picked up that story and gave it a big play, despite the fact that every sports editor in the city had enough background material on Ted's family to know—even without checking—that it couldn't possibly be true. It was, Ted's friends believed, their way of punishing him for not being "cooperative."

Ted had become so accustomed to looking upon any reference to his family as an unfriendly act that when *Sport* wrote about his mother, he bristled—even though her final quote was "Don't say anything about Teddy except the highest and the best. He's a wonderful son." And when he searched for some reason why the magazine would do such a thing to him, he pounced upon that broken appointment, which everybody except himself had long forgotten.

After Ted had signed the photograph the day of his last game, he sat on his stool, his right knee jumping nervously, his right hand alternately buttoning and unbuttoning the top button of his sport shirt.

When he stripped down to his shorts, there was no doubt he was forty-two. The man once called the Splendid Splinter—certainly one of the most atrocious nicknames ever committed upon an immortal—was thick around the middle. A soft roll of loose fat, drooping around the waist, brought on a vivid picture of Archie Moore.

Williams is a tall, handsome man. If they ever make that movie of his life that keeps being rumored around, the guy who plays Bret Maverick would be perfect for the part. But ball players age quickly. Twenty years under the sun had baked Ted's face and left it lined and leathery. Sitting there, Ted Williams had the appearance of an old Marine sergeant who had been to the battles and back.

Sal Maglie, who had the end locker on the other side of the shower room door, suddenly caught Ted's attention. "You're a National Leaguer, Sal," Ted said, projecting his voice to the room at large. "I got a hundred dollars that the Yankees win the World Series. The Yankees will win it in four or five games."

"I'm an American Leaguer now," Sal said, quietly.

"A hundred dollars," Ted said. "A friendly bet."

"You want a friendly bet? I'll bet you a friendly dollar."

"Fifty dollars," Ted said.

"All right," Sal said. "Fifty dollars." And then, projecting his own voice, he said, "I like the Pirates, anyway."

Williams went back to his mail, as the others dressed and went out onto the field.

At length, Ted picked up his spikes, wandered into the trainer's room again, and lifting himself onto the table, carefully began to put a shine on them. A photographer gave him a ball to sign.

Ted gazed at it with distaste, then looked up at the photographer with loathing. "Are you crazy?" he snapped.

The photographer backed away, pocketed the ball and began to adjust his camera sights on Ted. "You don't belong in here," Ted shouted. And turning to the clubhouse boy, he barked, "Get him out of here."

The locker room had emptied before Ted began to dress. For Ted did not go out to take batting practice or fielding practice. He made every entrance onto the field a dramatic event. He did not leave the locker room for the dugout until 12:55, only 35 minutes before the game was scheduled to start. By then, most of the writers had already gone up to Tom Yawkey's office to hear Jackie Jensen announce that he was returning to baseball.

As Ted came quickly up the stairs and into the dugout, he almost bumped into his close friend and fishing companion, Bud Leavitt, sports editor of the Bangor *Daily News*. "Hi, Bud," Ted said, as if he were surprised Leavitt was there. "You drive up?"

A semicircle of cameramen closed in on Williams, like a bear trap, on the playing field just up above. Ted hurled a few choice oaths at them, and as an oath-hurler Ted never bats below .400. He guided Leavitt against the side of the dugout, just above the steps, so that he could continue the conversation without providing a shooting angle for the photographers. The photographers continued to shoot him in profile, though, until Ted took Leavitt by the elbow and walked him the length of the dugout. "Let's sit down," he said, as he left, "so we won't be bothered by all these blasted cameramen."

If there had been any doubt back in the locker room that Ted had decided to bow out with typical hardness, it had been completely dispelled by those first few minutes in the dugout. On his last day in Fenway Park, Ted Williams seemed resolved to remain true to his own image of himself, to permit no sentimentality or hint of sentimentality to crack that mirror through which he looks at the world and allows the world to look upon him.

And yet, in watching this strange and troubled man— the most remarkable and colorful and full-blooded human being to come upon the athletic scene since Babe Ruth— you had the feeling that he was overplaying his role, that he had struggled through the night against the impulse to make his peace, to express his gratitude, to accept the great affection that the city had been showering upon him for years. In watching him, you had the clear impression that in resisting this desire he was overreacting and becoming more profane, more impossible and—yes—more unbearable than ever.

Inside Ted Williams there has always been a struggle of two opposing forces, almost two different persons. (We are fighting the use of the word schizophrenia). The point we are making is best illustrated through Williams' long refusal to tip his hat in acknowledgment of the cheering crowds. It has always been his contention that the people who cheered him when he hit a home run were the same people who booed him when he struck out—which, incidentally, is probably not true at all. More to our point, Ted has always insisted that although he would rather be cheered than booed, he really didn't care what the fans thought of him, one way or the other.

Obviously, though, if he really didn't care he wouldn't have bothered to make such a show of not caring. He simply would have touched his finger to his cap in that automatic, thoughtless gesture of most players and forgotten about it. Ted, in short, has always had it both ways. He gets the cheers and he pretends they mean nothing to him. He is like a rich man's nephew who treats his uncle with disrespect to prove he is not interested in his money, while all the time he is secretly dreaming that the uncle will reward such independence by leaving him most of the fortune.

Ted has it even better than that. The fans of Boston have always wooed him ardently. They always cheered him all the louder in the hope that he would reward them, at last, with that essentially meaningless tip of the hat.

This clash within Williams came to the surface as he sat and talked with Leavitt, alone and undisturbed. For, within a matter of minutes, the lack of attention began to oppress him; his voice began to rise, to pull everybody's attention back to him. The cameramen, getting the message, drifted toward him again, not in a tight pack this time but in a loose and straggling line.

With Ted talking so loudly, it was apparent that he and Leavitt were discussing how to get together, after the World Series, for their annual postseason fishing expedition. The assigment to cover the Series for *Life* had apparently upset their schedule.

"After New York," Ted said, "I'll be going right to Pittsburgh." He expressed his hope that the Yankees would wrap it all up in Yankee Stadium, so that he could join Leavitt in Bangor at the beginning of the following week. "But, dammit," he said, "if the Series goes more than five games, I'll have to go back to Pittsburgh again."

Leavitt reminded Ted of an appearance he had apparently agreed to make in Bangor. "All right," Ted said. "But no speeches or anything."

A young, redheaded woman in her late twenties leaned over from her box seat alongside the dugout and asked Ted if he would autograph her scorecard.

"I can't sign it, dear," Ted said. "League rules. Where are you going to be after the game?"

"You told me that once before," she said, unhappily.

"Well, where are you going to be?" Ted shouted, in the impatient way one would shout at an irritating child.

"Right here," she said.

"All right."

"But I waited before and you never came."

He ignored her.

Joe Cronin, president of the American League, came down the dugout aisle, followed by his assistant, Joe McKenney. Through Cronin's office, the local nine o'clock news-feature program which follows the "Today" program in Boston had scheduled a filmed interview with Ted. The camera had already been set up on the home-plate side of the dugout, just in front of the box seats. Cronin talked to Ted briefly and went back to reassure the announcer that Ted would be right there. McKenney remained behind to make sure Ted didn't forget. At last Ted jumped up and shouted, "Where is it, Joe, dammit?"

When Ted followed McKenney out, it was the first time he had stuck his head onto the field all day. There were still not too many fans in the stands, although far more than would have been there on any other day to watch a seventh-place team on a cold and threatening Wednesday afternoon. At this first sight of Ted Williams, they let out a mighty roar.

As he waited alongside interviewer Jack Chase, Ted bit

his lower lip, and looked blankly into space, both characteristic mannerisms. At a signal from the cameraman, Chase asked Ted how he felt about entering "the last lap."

All at once Ted was smiling. "I want to tell you, Jack, I honestly feel good about it," he said, speaking in that quick charming way of his. "You can't get blood out of a turnip, you know. I've gone as far as I can and I'm sure I wouldn't want to try it any more."

"Have we gone as far as we can with the Jimmy Fund?" he was asked.

Ted was smiling more broadly. "Oh, no. We could never go far enough with the Jimmy Fund."

Chase reminded Ted that he was scheduled to become a batting coach.

"Can you take a .250 hitter and make a .300 hitter out of him?"

"There has always been a saying in baseball that you can't make a hitter," Ted answered. "But I think you can *improve* a hitter. More than you can improve a fielder. More mistakes are made in hitting than in any other part of the game."

At this point Williams was literally encircled by photographers, amateur and pro. The pros were taking pictures from the front and from the sides. Behind them, in the stands, dozens of fans had their cameras trained on Ted, too, although they could hardly have been getting anything except the number 9 on his back.

Ted was asked if he were going to travel around the Red Sox farm system in 1961 to instruct the young hitters.

"All I know is that I'm going to spring training," he said. "Other than that, I don't know anything."

The interview closed with the usual fulsome praise of Williams, the inevitable apotheosis that leaves him with a hangdog, embarrassed look upon his features. "I appreciate the kind words," he said. "It's all been fun. Everything I've done in New England from playing left field and getting booed, to the Jimmy Fund."

The Jimmy Fund is the money-raising arm of the Children's Cancer Hospital in Boston, which has become the world center for research into cancer and for the treatment of its young victims. Ted has been deeply involved with the hospital since its inception in 1947, serving the last four years as general chairman of the fund committee. He is an active chairman, not an honorary one. Scarcely a day goes by, when Ted is in Boston, that he doesn't make one or two stops for the Jimmy Fund somewhere in New England. He went out on the missions even on days when he was too sick to play ball. (This is the same man, let us emphasize, who refuses to attend functions at which he himself is to be honored.) He has personally raised something close to $4,000,000 and has helped to build a modern, model hospital not far from Fenway Park.

But he has done far more than that. From the first, Williams took upon himself the agonizing task of trying to bring some cheer into the lives of these dying children and, perhaps even more difficult, of comforting their parents. He has, in those years, permitted himself to become attached to thousands of these children, knowing full well that they were going to die, one by one. He has become so attached to some of them that he has chartered special planes to bring him to their deathbeds.

Whenever one of these children asks to see him, whatever the time, he comes. His only stipulation is that there must be no publicity, no reporters, no cameramen.

We once suggested to Ted that he must get some basic return from all this work he puts into the Jimmy Fund. Ted considered the matter very carefully before he answered. "Look," he said finally, "it embarrasses me to be praised for anything like this. The embarrassing thing is that I don't feel I've done anything compared to the people at the hospital who are doing the important work. It makes me happy to think I've done a little good; I suppose that's what I get out of it."

"Anyway," he added thoughtfully, "it's only a freak of fate, isn't it, that one of those kids isn't going to grow up to be an athlete and I wasn't the one who had the cancer."

At the finish of the filmed interview he had to push his way through the cameramen between him and the dugout. "Oh———," he said.

But when one of them asked him to pose with Cronin, Ted switched personalities again and asked, with complete amiability, "Where is he?"

Cronin was in the dugout. Ted met Joe at the bottom of the steps and threw an arm around him. They grinned at each other while the pictures were being taken, talking softly and unintelligibly. After a minute, Ted reached over to the hook just behind him and grabbed his glove. The cameramen were still yelling for another shot as he started up the dugout steps. Joe, grinning broadly, grabbed him by the shoulder and yanked him back down. While Cronin was wrestling Ted around and whacking him on the back, the cameras clicked. "I got to warm up, dammit," Ted was saying. He made a pawing gesture at the cameramen, as if to say, "I'd like to belt you buzzards." This, from all evidence, was the picture that went around the country that night, because strangely enough, it looked as if he were waving a kind of sad good-bye.

When he finally broke away and raced up to the field, he called back over his shoulder, "See you later, Joe." The cheers arose from the stands once again.

The Orioles were taking infield practice by then, and the Red Sox were warming up along the sideline. Ted began to play catch with Pumpsie Green. As he did—sure enough—the cameramen lined up just inside the foul line

THE TED WILLIAMS READER

for some more shots, none of which will ever be used. "Why don't you cockroaches get off my back?" Ted said, giving them his No. 1 sneer. "Let me breathe, will you?"

The bell rang before he had a chance to throw two dozen balls. Almost all the players went back to the locker room. Remaining on the bench were only Ted Williams, buttoned up in his jacket, and Vic Wertz. One of the members of the ground crew came over with a picture of Williams. He asked Ted if he would autograph it. "Sure," Ted said. "For you guys, anything."

Vic Wertz was having his picture taken with another crew member. Wertz had his arm around the guy and both of them were laughing. "How about you, Ted?" the cameraman asked. "One with the crewmen?"

Ted posed willingly with the man he had just signed for, with the result that the whole herd of cameramen came charging over again. Ted leaped to his feet. "Twenty-two years of this bull————," he cried.

The redhead was leaning over the low barrier again, but now three other young women were alongside her. One of them seemed to be crying, apparently at the prospect of Ted's retirement. An old photographer, in a long, weather-beaten coat, asked Ted for a special pose. "Get lost," Ted said. "I've seen enough of you, you old goat."

Curt Gowdy, the Red Sox broadcaster, had come into the dugout to pass on some information about the pregame ceremonies. Ted shouted, "The devil with all you miserable cameramen." The women continued to stare, in fascination, held either by the thrill of having this last long look at Ted Williams or by the opportunity to learn a few new words.

A Baltimore writer came into the dugout, and Ted settled down beside him. He wanted to know whether the writer could check on the "King of Swat" crown that had been presented to him in his last visit to Baltimore. Ted wasn't sure whether he had taken it back to Boston with him or whether the organization still had it.

"You know," he told the writer, "Brown's a better pitcher now than he's ever been. Oh, he's a great pitcher. Never get a fat pitch from him. When he does, it comes in with something extra on it. Every time a little different. He knows what he's doing."

Ted is a student of such things. He is supposed to be a natural hitter, blessed with a superhuman pair of eyes. We are not about to dispute this. What we want to say is that when Ted first came to the majors, the book on him was that he would chase bad balls. "All young sluggers do," according to Del Baker, who was managing Detroit when Ted came up. "Ted developed a strike zone of his own, though, by the second year."

When Ted took his physical for the Naval reserve in World War II, his eyes tested at 20/10 and were so exceptional in every regard that while he was attending air gunnery school he broke all previous Marine records for hitting the target sleeve. But Ted has a point of his own here. "My eyesight," he says, "is now 20/15. Half the major leaguers have eyes as good as that. It isn't eyesight that makes a hitter; it's practice. *Con-sci-en-tious* practice. I say that Williams has hit more balls than any guy living, except maybe Ty Cobb. I don't say it to brag; I just state it as a fact. From the time I was 11 years old, I've taken every possible opportunity to swing at a ball. I've swung and I've swung and I've swung."

Ted always studied every little movement a pitcher made. He always remained on the bench before the game to watch them warming up. From his first day to his last, he hustled around to get all possible information on a new pitcher.

It has always been his theory that we are all creatures

of habit, himself included. Pitchers, he believes, fall into observable patterns. A certain set of movements foretells a certain pitch. In a particular situation, or on a particular count, they go to a particular pitch. There were certain pitchers, Ted discovered, who would inevitably go to their big pitch, the pitch they wanted him to swing at, on the 2-2 count.

And so Ted would frequently ask a teammate, "What was the pitch he struck you out on?" or "What did he throw you on the 2-2 pitch?"

When a young player confessed he didn't know what the pitch had been, Ted would grow incredulous. "You don't know the pitch he struck you out on? I'm not talking about last week or last month. I'm not even talking about yesterday. Today! Just now! I'm talking about the pitch he struck you out on just now!"

Returning to his seat on the bench, he'd slump back in disgust and mutter, "What a rockhead. The guy's taking the bread and butter out of his mouth and he don't even care how."

In a very short time, the player would have an answer ready for Williams. Ted always got the young hitters thinking about their craft. He always tried to instruct them, to build up their confidence. "When you want to know who the best hitter in the league is," he'd tell the rookies, "just look into the mirror."

Among opposing players, Williams was always immensely popular. Yes, even among opposing pitchers. All pitchers love to say, "Nobody digs in against *me*." Only Ted Williams was given the right to dig in without getting flipped. Around the American League, there seemed to be a general understanding that Williams had too much class to be knocked down.

Waiting in the dugout for the ceremonies to get under

way, Ted picked up a bat and wandered up and down the aisle taking vicious practice swings.

The photographers immediately swooped in on him. One nice guy was taking cameras from the people in the stands and getting shots of Ted for them.

As Ted put the bat down, one of them said, "One more shot. Teddy, as a favor."

"I'm all done doing any favors for you guys," Williams said, "I don't have to put up with you any more, and you don't have to put up with me."

An old woman, leaning over the box seats, was wailing, "Don't leave us, Ted. Don't leave us."

"Oh hell," Ted said, turning away in disgust.

The redhead asked him plaintively, "Why don't you act nice?"

Ted strolled slowly toward her, grinning broadly. "Come on, dear," he drawled, "with that High Street accent you got there."

Turning back, he stopped in front of the man from *Sport,* pointed over his shoulder at the cameramen and asked, "You getting it all? You getting what you came for?"

"If you can't make it as a batting coach," our man said, "I understand you're going to try it as a cameraman."

"What does *Sport* magazine think I'm going to do?" Ted asked. "That's what I want to know. What does *Sport* magazine think I'm going to be?"

Speaking for himself, our man told him, he had not the slightest doubt that Ted was going to be the new general manager.

"*Sport* magazine," Ted said, making the name sound like an oath. "Always honest. Never prejudiced."

At this point he was called onto the field. Taking off his jacket, he strode out of the dugout. The cheers that greeted him came from 10,454 throats.

Curt Gowdy, handling the introductions, began: "As we all know, this is the final home game for—in my opinion and most of yours—the greatest hitter who ever lived. Ted Williams."

There was tremendous applause.

"Twenty years ago," Gowdy continued, "a skinny kid from San Diego came to the Red Sox camp . . ."

Ted first came to the Red Sox training camp at Sarasota in the spring of 1938. General manager Eddie Collins, having heard that Ted was a creature of wild and wayward impulse, had instructed second baseman Bobby Doerr to pick him up and deliver him, shining and undamaged.

It was unthinkable, of course, that Ted Williams would make a routine entrance. Just before Doerr was set to leave home, the worst flood of the decade hit California and washed out all the roads and telephone lines. When Williams and Doerr finally arrived in Sarasota, ten days late, there was a fine, almost imperceptible drizzle. Williams, still practically waterlogged from the California floods, held out a palm, looked skyward, shivered and said in a voice that flushed the flamingos from their nests, "So this is Florida, is it? Do they always keep this state under a foot of water?"

Williams suited up for a morning workout out in the field, jawed good-naturedly with the fans and got an unexpected chance to hit when a newsreel company moved in to take some batting-cage shots.

The magic of Ted Williams in a batter's box manifested itself that first day in camp. The tall, thin rookie stepped into the box, set himself in his wide stance, let his bat drop across the far corner of the plate, wiggled his hips and shoulders and jiggled up and down as if he were trying to tamp himself into the box. He moved his bat back and forth a few times, then brought it back into position and twisted his hands in opposite directions as if he were wringing the neck of the bat. He was set for the pitch.

And somehow, as if by some common impulse, all sideline activity stopped that day in 1938. Everybody was watching Ted Williams.

"Controversial, sure," Gowdy said, in bringing his remarks about Ted to a close, "but colorful."

The chairman of the Boston Chamber of Commerce presented Ted a shining, silver Paul Revere bowl "on behalf of the business community of Boston." Ted seemed to force his smile as he accepted it.

A representative of the sports committee of the Chamber of Commerce then presented him with a plaque "on behalf of visits to kids' and veterans' hospitals."

Mayor John Collins, from his wheelchair, announced that "on behalf of all citizens" he was proclaiming this day "Ted Williams Day." The mayor didn't know how right he was.

As Mayor Collins spoke of Ted's virtues ("nature's best, nature's nobleman"), the muscle of Ted's upper left jaw was jumping, constantly and rhythmically. The mayor's contribution to Ted Williams Day was a $1,000 donation to the Jimmy Fund from some special city fund.

Gowdy brought the proceedings to a close by proclaiming, "Pride is what made him great. He's a champion, a thoroughbred, a champion of sports." Curt then asked for "a round of applause, an ovation for No. 9 on his last game in his Boston." Needless to say, he got it.

Ted waited, pawed at the ground with one foot. Smilingly, he thanked the mayor for the money. "Despite the fact of the disagreeable things that have been said of me—and I can't help thinking about it—by the Knights of the Keyboard out there [he jerked his head toward the press box], baseball has been the most wonderful thing in my life.

If I were starting over again and someone asked me where is the one place I would like to play, I would want it to be in Boston, with the greatest owner in baseball and the greatest fans in America. Thank you."

He walked across the infield to the dugout, where the players were standing, applauding along with the fans. Ted winked and went on in.

In the press box, some of the writers were upset by his gratuitous rap at them. "I think it was bush," one of them said. "Whatever he thinks, this wasn't the time to say it."

Others made a joke of it. "Now that he's knighted me," one of them was saying, "I wonder if he's going to address me as Sir."

In the last half of the first inning, Williams stepped in against Steve Barber with Tasby on first and one out. When Barber was born—February 22, 1939—Ted had already taken the American Association apart, as it has never been taken apart since, by batting .366, hitting 43 home runs and knocking in 142 runs.

Against a left-hander, Williams was standing almost flush along the inside line of the batter's box, his feet wide, his stance slightly closed. He took a curve inside, then a fast ball low. The fans began to boo. The third pitch was also low. With a 3-0 count, Ted jumped in front of the plate with the pitch, like a high-school kid looking for a walk. It was ball four, high.

He got to third the easy way. Jim Pagliaroni was hit by a pitch, and everybody moved up on a wild pitch. When Frank Malzone walked, Jack Fisher came in to replace Barber. Lou Clinton greeted Jack with a rising liner to dead center. Jackie Brandt started in, slipped as he tried to reverse himself, but recovered in time to scramble back and make the catch. His throw to the plate was beautiful to behold, a low one-bouncer that came to Gus Triandos chest high. But Ted, sliding hard, was in under the ball easily.

Leading off the third inning against the right-handed Fisher, Ted moved back just a little in the box. Fisher is even younger than Barber, a week younger. When Fisher was being born—March 4, 1939—Ted was reporting to Sarasota again, widely proclaimed as the superplayer of the future, the Red Sox's answer to Joe DiMaggio.

Ted hit Fisher's 1-1 pitch straightway, high and deep. Brandt had plenty of room to go back and make the catch, but still, as Williams returned to the bench, he got another tremendous hand.

Up in the press box, publicity man Jack Malaney was announcing that uniform No. 9 was being retired "after today's game." This brought on some snide remarks about Ted wearing his undershirt at Yankee Stadium for the final three games of the season. Like Mayor Collins, Malaney was righter than he knew. The uniform was indeed going to be retired after the game.

Williams came to bat again in the fifth inning, with two out and the Sox trailing, 3–2. And this time he unloaded a tremendous drive to right center. As the ball jumped off the bat, the cry "He did it!" arose from the stands. Right fielder Al Pilarcik ran back as far as he could, pressed his back against the bullpen fence, well out from the 380-foot sign, and stood there, motionless, his hands at his sides.

Although it was a heavy day, there was absolutely no wind. The flag hung limply from the pole, stirring very occasionally and very fairly.

At the last minute, Pilarcik brought up his hands and caught the ball chest high, close to 400 feet from the plate. A moan of disappointment settled over the field, followed by a rising hum of excited conversation and then, as Ted came back toward the first-base line to get his glove from Pumpsie Green, a standing ovation.

"Damn," Ted said, when he returned to the bench at the end of the inning. "I hit the living hell out of that one. I really stung it. If that one didn't go out, nothing is going out today!"

In the top of the eighth, with the Sox behind 4–2, Mike Fornieles came to the mound for the 70th time of the season, breaking the league record set by another Red Sox relief star, Ellis Kinder. Kinder set this mark in 1953, the year Williams returned from Korea.

As Fornieles was warming up, three teenagers jumped out of the grandstand and ran toward Ted. They paused only briefly, however, and continued across the field to the waiting arms of the park police.

Ted was scheduled to bat second in the last of the eighth, undoubtedly his last time at bat. The cheering began as soon as Willie Tasby came out of the dugout and strode to the plate, as if he was anxious to get out of there and make way for the main event. Ted, coming out almost directly behind Tasby, went to the on-deck circle. He was down on one knee and just beginning to swing the heavy, lead-filled practice bat as Tasby hit the first pitch to short for an easy out.

The cheering seemed to come to its peak as Ted stepped into the box and took his stance. Everybody in the park had come to his feet to give Ted a standing ovation.

Umpire Eddie Hurley called time. Fisher stepped off the rubber and Triandos stood erect. Ted remained in the box, waiting, as if he were oblivious to it all. The standing ovation lasted at least two minutes, and even then Fisher threw into the continuing applause. Only as the ball approached the plate did the cheering stop. It came in low, ball one. The spectators remained on their feet, but very suddenly the park had gone very quiet.

If there was pressure on Ted, there was pressure on Fisher, too. The Orioles were practically tied for second place, so he couldn't afford to be charitable. He might have been able to get Ted to go after a bad pitch, and yet he hardly wanted to go down in history as the fresh kid who had walked Ted Williams on his last time at bat in Boston.

The second pitch was neck high, a slider with, it seemed, just a little off it. Ted gave it a tremendous swing, but he was just a little out in front of the ball. The swing itself brought a roar from the fans, though, since it was such a clear announcement that Ted was going for the home run or nothing.

With a 1–1 count, Fisher wanted to throw a fast ball, low and away. He got it up too much and in too much, a fast ball waist high on the outside corner. From the moment Ted swung, there was not the slightest doubt about it. The ball cut through the heavy air, a high line drive heading straightaway to center field toward the corner of the special bullpen the Red Sox built for Williams back in 1941.

Jackie Brandt went back almost to the barrier, then turned and watched the ball bounce off the canopy above the bullpen bench, skip up against the wire fence which rises in front of the bleachers and bounce back into the bullpen.

It did not seem possible that 10,000 people could make that much noise.

Ted raced around the bases at a pretty good clip. Triandos had started toward the mound with the new ball, and Fisher had come down to meet him. As Ted neared home plate, Triandos turned to face him, a big smile on his face. Ted grinned back.

Ted didn't exactly offer his hand to Pagliaroni after he crossed the plate, but the young catcher reached out anyway and made a grab for it. He seemed to catch Ted around the wrist. Williams ran back into the dugout and ducked through the runway door to get himself a drink of water.

The fans were on their feet again, deafening the air with their cheers. A good four or five minutes passed before anybody worried about getting the game under way again.

When Ted ducked back into the dugout, he put on his jacket and sat down at the very edge of the bench alongside Mike Higgins and Del Baker. The players, still on their feet anyway, crowded around him, urging him to go out and acknowledge the cheers.

The fans were now chanting. "We want Ted . . . we want Ted . . . we want Ted." Umpire Johnny Rice, at first base, motioned for Ted to come out. Manager Mike Higgins urged him to go on out. Ted just sat there, his head down, a smile of happiness on his face.

"We wanted him to go out," Vic Wertz said later, "because we felt so good for him. And we could see he was thrilled, too. For me, I have to say it's my top thrill in baseball."

But another player said, "I had the impression—maybe I shouldn't say this because it's just an impression—that he got just as much a kick out of refusing to go out and tip his hat to the crowd as he did out of the homer. What I mean is he wanted to go out with the home run, all right, but he also wanted the home run so he could sit there while they yelled for him and tell them all where to go."

Mike Higgins had already told Carroll Hardy to replace Ted in left field. As Clinton came to bat, with two men out, Higgins said, "Williams, left field." Ted grabbed his glove angrily and went to the top step. When Clinton struck out, Ted was the first man out of the dugout. He sprinted out to left field, ignoring the cheers of the fans, who had not expected to see him again. But Higgins had sent Hardy right out behind him. Ted saw Carroll, and ran back in, one final time. The entire audience was on its feet once again, in wild applause.

Since it is doubtful that Higgins felt Williams was in any great need of more applause that day, it is perfectly obvious that he was giving Ted one last chance to think about the tip of the hat or the wave of the hand as he covered the distance between left field and the dugout.

Ted made the trip as always, his head down, his stride unbroken. He stepped on first base as he crossed the line, ducked down into the dugout, growled once at Higgins and headed through the alleyway and into the locker room.

He stopped only to tell an usher standing just inside the dugout, "I guess I forgot to tip my hat."

To the end, the mirror remained intact.

After the game, photographers were permitted to go right into the clubhouse, but writers were held to the 15-minute rule. One writer tried to ride in with the photographers, but Williams leveled that finger at him and said, "You're not supposed to be here."

Somehow or other, the news was let out that Ted would not be going to New York, although there seems to be some doubt as to whether it was Williams or Higgins who made the announcement. The official Boston line is that it had been understood all along that Ted would not be going to New York unless the pennant race was still on. The fact of the matter is that Williams made the decision himself, and he did not make it until after he hit the home run. It would have been foolish to have gone to New York or anywhere else, of course. Anything he did after the Boston finale would have been an anticlimax.

One of the waiting newspapermen, a pessimist by nature, expressed the fear that by the time they were let in, Ted would be dressed and gone.

"Are you kidding?" a member of the anti-Williams clique said. "This is what he lives for. If the game had gone 18 innings, he'd been in there waiting for us."

He was indeed waiting at his locker, with a towel wrapped around his middle. The writers approached him, for the most part, in groups. Generally speaking, the writers who could be called friends reached him first, and to these men Ted was not only amiable but gracious and modest.

Was he going for the home run?

"I was gunning for the big one," he said, with a grin. "I let everything I had go. I really wanted that one."

Did he know it was out as soon as it left his bat?

"I knew I had really given it a ride."

What were his immediate plans?

"I've got some business to clean up here," he said. "Then I'll be covering the World Series for *Life*. After that, I'm going back to Florida to see how much damage the hurricane did to my house."

The other players seemed even more affected by the drama of the farewell homer than Ted. Pete Runnels, practically dispossessed from his locker alongside Ted's by the shifts of reporters, wandered around the room shaking his head in disbelief, "How about that?" he kept repeating. "How about that? How about that?"

As for Ted, he seemed to be in something of a daze. After the first wave of writers had left, he wandered back and forth between his locker and the trainer's room. Back and forth, back and forth. Once he came back with a bottle of beer, turned it up to his lips and downed it with obvious pleasure. For Ted, this is almost unheard of. He has always been a milk and ice-cream man, and he devours them both in huge quantities. His usual order after a ball game is two quarts of milk.

Williams remained in the locker room, making himself available, until there were no more than a half-dozen other players remaining. Many of the writers did not go over to him at all. From them, there were no questions, no congratulations, no good wishes for the future. For all Ted's color, for all the drama and copy he had supplied over 22 years, they were glad to see him finally retire.

When Ted finally began to get dressed, our man went

over and said, "Ted, you must have known when Higgins sent you back out that he was giving you a final chance to think about tipping the hat or making some gesture of farewell. Which meant that Higgins himself would have liked you to do it. While you were running back, didn't you have any feeling that it might be nice to go out with a show of good feeling?"

"I felt nothing," he said.

"No sentimentality? No gratitude? No sadness?"

"I said *nothing*," Ted said. "Nothing, nothing nothing!"

As our man was toting up the nothings, Ted snarled, "And when you get back there tell them for me that they're full of . . ." There followed a burst of vituperation which we cannot even begin to approximate, and then the old, sad plaint about those twelve years of merciless persecution.

Fenway Park has an enclosed parking area so that the players can get to their cars without beating their way through the autograph hunters. When Ted was dressed, though, the clubhouse boy called to the front office in what was apparently a prearranged plan to bring Williams' car around to a bleacher exit.

At 4:40, 45 minutes after the end of the game and a good hour after Ted had left the dugout, he was ready to leave. "Fitzie," he called out, and the clubhouse boy came around to lead the way. The cameramen came around, too.

The locker-room door opens onto a long corridor, which leads to another door, which in turn opens onto the back walks and understructure of the park. It is this outer door which is always guarded.

Waiting in the alleyway, just outside the clubhouse door, however, was a redheaded, beatnik-looking man, complete with the regimental beard and the beachcomber pants. He handed Ted a ball and mentioned a name that apparently meant something to him. Ted took the ball and signed it.

"How come you're not able to get in?" he said, "If they

let the damn newspapermen in, they ought to let you in."
Walking away, trailed by the platoon of cameramen, he
called out to the empty air, "If they let the newspapermen
in, they should have let him in. If they let the newspapermen in, they should let everybody in."

He walked on through the backways of the park, past
the ramps and pillars, at a brisk clip, with Fitzie bustling
along quickly to stay up ahead. Alongside of Williams, the
cameramen were scrambling to get their positions and snap
their pictures. Williams kept his eyes straight ahead, never
pausing for one moment. "Hold it for just a minute, Ted,"
one of them said.

"I've been here for 22 years," Ted said, walking on.
"Plenty of time for you to get your shot."

"This is the last time," the cameraman said. "Cooperate
just this one last time."

"I've cooperated with you," Ted said. "I've cooperated too
much."

Fitzie had the bleacher entrance open, and as Ted passed
quickly through, a powder-blue Cadillac pulled up to the
curb. A man in shirtsleeves was behind the wheel. He looked
like Dick O'Connell, whose appointment as business manager had been announced the previous night.

Fitzie ran ahead to open the far door of the car for Ted.
Three young women had been approaching the exit as Ted
darted through, and one of them screamed, "It's him!" One
of the others just let out a scream, as if Ted had been somebody of real worth, like Elvis or Fabian. The third woman
remained mute. Looking at her, you had to wonder whether
she would ever speak again.

Fitzie slammed the door, and the car pulled away. "It
was him," the first woman screamed. "Was it *really* him?
Was it *him?*"

Her knees seemed to give way. Her girlfriends had to

support her. "I can't catch my breath," she said. "I can hear my heart pounding." And then, in something like terror: "I CAN'T BREATHE."

Attracted by the screams, or by some invisible, inexplicable grapevine, a horde of boys and men came racing up the street. Ted's car turned the corner just across from the bleacher exit, but it was held up momentarily by a red light and a bus. The front line of pursuers had just come abreast of the car when the driver swung around the bus and pulled away.

There are those, however, who never get the word. Down the street, still surrounding the almost empty parking area, were still perhaps 100 loyal fans waiting to say their last farewell to Ted Williams.

In Boston that night, the talk was all of Williams. Only 10,454 were at the scene, but the word all over the city was: "I knew he'd end it with a home run . . ." and "I was going to go to the game, but—"

In future years, we can be sure, the men who saw Ted hit that mighty shot will number into the hundreds of thousands. The wind will grow strong and mean, and the distance will grow longer. Many of the reports of the game, in fact, had the ball going into the centerfield bleachers.

The seeds of the legend have already been sown. George Carens, an elderly columnist who is more beloved by Ted than by his colleagues, wrote:

"Ted was calm and gracious as he praised the occupants of the Fenway press penthouse at home plate before the game began. Afterwards he greeted all writers in a comradely way, down through his most persistent critics. In a word, Ted showed he can take it, and whenever the spirit moves him he will fit beautifully into the Fenway PR setup."

Which shows that people hear what they want to hear and see what they want to see.

In New York the next day, Phil Rizzuto informed his television audience that Ted had finally relented and tipped his hat after the home run.

And the *Sporting News* headline on its Boston story was:

SPLINTER TIPS CAP
TO HUB FANS AFTER
FAREWELL HOMER

A New York Sunday paper went so far as to say that Ted had made "a tender and touching farewell speech" from home plate at the end of the game.

All the reports said that Ted had, in effect, called his shot because it was known that he was shooting for a home run. Who wants to bet that, in future years, there will not be a story or two insisting that he *did* point?

The legend will inevitably grow, and in a way it is a shame. A man should be allowed to die the way he lived. He should be allowed to depart as he came. Ted Williams chose his course early, and his course was to turn his face from the world around him. When he walked out of the park, he kept his eyes to the front and he never looked back.

The epitaph for Ted Williams remains unchanged. He was sometimes unbearable but he was never dull. Baseball will not be the same without him. Boston won't be quite the same either. Old Boston is acrawl with greening statues of old heroes and old patriots, but Ted has left a monument of his own—again on his own terms—in the Children's Cancer Hospital.

He left his own monument in the record books too. For two decades he made the Red Sox exciting in the sheer anticipation of his next time at bat.

He opened his last season with perhaps the longest home run of his career and he closed it with perhaps the most dramatic. It was typical and it was right that the Williams era in Boston should end not with a whimper. It was entirely proper that it should end with a bang.

So, the old order passeth and an era of austerity has settled upon the Red Sox franchise.

And now Boston knows how England felt when it lost India.

"Saint" Goes Marching In

BUD COLLINS

1966

Bud Collins, who would later gain fame as a television tennis analyst, provides on-the-spot coverage for the Boston *Globe* of the announcement, on January 20, 1966, of Williams' election (by the highest percentage of votes ever) to the Hall of Fame. His whimsical portrayal of the "precanonization" ritual underscores the irony of the scene: "St. Ted" smiling a blessing over the fraternity of journalists who had antagonized him for so many years, but who, in the end, bestowed upon him baseball immortality.

At 10:01 A.M. (EST) Thursday, in a crowded room at Fenway Park, the precanonization of St. Ted began.

It was then that St. Ted—born humbly Theodore Samuel Williams in San Diego in 1918—learned that he will be enshrined in the Cooperstown, N.Y., tabernacle called the Baseball Hall of Fame. He is being elevated to a position alongside St. Babe, St. Ty, St. Big Train, St. DiMag, St. Abner Doublehead, and all the others who have ascended to glory from the diamond.

This was a beautiful moment, thrilling, the heavenly glow of television lights and flash cameras illuminating the scene. Newspapermen, who wouldn't congregate this early for an interview with Lady Godiva, were shoving against each other, straining to see.

The ceremony drew more people than will buy tickets to watch the Red Sox on opening day. There were 67 reporters, cameramen, commentators and canonization followers in the place.

Reporters were trying to get their heads clear so that they could remember every detail. They wanted to get it down so they could tell their grandchildren about it. Some day in the future when the kids whine, "Tell us about baseball again, Grampy. Was that something the football players did to relax on their two months off?"

There was Hy Hurwitz, a journalist who has presided over these things before and could be depended on to do it with dignity and not fall apart, or be blinded by the lights. At 10:01 he produced the large manila envelope and deftly ripped it open. From it he took a sheet of paper, and began to speak.

• GOOD WORKS RECOGNIZED

Several people thought that Hurwitz should have said: "In the category for hitting and acting, this year's award goes to . . ."

But Hurwitz isn't theatrical. He merely intoned: "Elected to the Hall was Ted Williams with 282 votes. That's a record—93.3 percent of the votes. No one else was elected."

Nineteen years of good works with a bat had been recognized.

There were rumors that Williams was to be sanctified. That is why he and the press appeared at Fenway Thursday. Still, it was not certain. While the world fidgeted and wondered, three men were protecting the secret—Hurwitz, and John Mullin and Walter Donahue of the *Globe*.

Mullin and Donahue are keepers of a frightening beast,

a burping, hissing, wheezing Honeywell 200 computer chained in a top secret second floor room of the *Globe* building.

Into that room Wednesday Hurwitz brought the ballots for foolproof tabulation. Mullin and Donahue fed the machine 2,523 cards representing something or other. Donahue pushed a button and shielded his eyes. Mullin and Hurwitz hit the deck. There was a gnashing of gears and a belch. Out popped a card saying: "No. 1 is John Coleman, Philadelphia."

Coleman was a pitcher who lost 48 games in 1883.

"Coleman—in the Hall of Fame?" screamed Mullin. He kicked the machine. "Get with it!"

After that everything was all right. In 88 seconds the computer had the votes counted, and Williams was in.

There is some unfinished business, of course. The ritual at Cooperstown must be carefully planned, the relics collected—bats, gloves, garments, a vial of the saintly spittle.

St. Ted was not vengeful. He smiled a blessing over the journalists, and said that most of them were good men. "I know the majority of you were for me," he said. "Only the minority gave me the (unfavorable) treatment."

But on this day he was the patron saint of the majority and the minority in the press box. And it was a wonderful feeling for those who left Fenway in a state of forgiveness.

The Batter

JIMMY CANNON

1966

This commentary on Williams' election to the Hall of Fame by one of the most influential sportswriters is indicative of the price Williams paid for his stubborn refusal to curry favor from journalists. While he acknowledges the justice of the election of "the greatest batter of his time," Cannon can find nothing else to praise. For Cannon, a noted Joe DiMaggio loyalist, the solitary act of hitting was an appropriate expression of Williams' reclusive and defensive personality. According to most sources, however, Williams was less of a "loner" than Cannon's remarks suggest and was well liked by most of his teammates.

Ironically, in spite of the reservations expressed here about Williams' all-around ability, when Cannon named his all-time All-Star team in his syndicated column of June 3, 1969, his outfield consisted of Joe DiMaggio, Willie Mays, and Ted Williams.

The innocent often confuse greatness with nobility in sports. The obscure generally allow their own desire to design an image of the renowned. But crows can't be angels no matter how high they fly. Ted Williams belongs in the Hall of Fame only because he was the greatest batter of his time in the sport.

Some ball journalists declined to vote for him because

they considered him rude—and abusive. They proved Williams was correct when he vilified them as slanderous and prejudiced incompetents. There wasn't anyone on the ballot who could be taken as a serious competitor for Williams, who hit .406 in '41.

The bat appeared to grant Williams the solitude his nature demanded. Always when I watched him hit, I felt that he considered that to be the only important act in baseball. The rest, his attitude suggested, was merely a series of intermissions between times at bat. The bat also gave Williams a majestic security. Doubt seemed to disfigure all else that Williams accomplished on a ball field.

As a hitter, Williams could depend on himself alone. It then became a tournament between him and the pitcher. He was able to escape from the community of the team. It is why, I imagine, he also enjoys fishing. This is a sport a man performs all by himself. He was a flier both in the Second World War and Korea.

It was logical that he become a pilot. The air arm is the only branch of the service where a man can still hold onto some of his independence. There is no lonelier place than the sky, and Williams was always a recluse even among the multitudes.

In left field, his stance always was one of indifference. It was as though he were leaning against an invisible fence. There was never that tension that tightens the bodies of other outfielders, that clenched posture which indicates the anticipation of excitement. The pursuit of a baseball couldn't have moved Williams much, although he did smash himself up going into a wall for a fly ball in an All-Star game.

The defensive part of the game had to bore him. That was what delayed him coming to bat. He was an average fielder, but not as awkward as a lot of biased reporters contend. He was the only .400 hitter who didn't run fast.

Never did Williams seem to be one of nine. He was a man imprisoned in his own identity, which he refused to share with the others in the common cause of the team. But when he was the hitter he was Ted Williams, not one of the Red Sox. Then he was separated from his unwanted accomplices, his talent a private possession, poised and oddly gentle.

The conspiracy was clear to him then. The nine players on the other team were all against him. Their intentions were obvious. They admitted they were allied against him. In other places, the foes were sometimes hard to detect, but Williams never stopped looking for them. He was a suspicious man. He searched for them everywhere.

It was as though he wished the unpopularity on himself. It was too bad. The reward for being the greatest hitter of his generation was snide bickering, which made him sound like a petulant boy.

As a fielder, Williams became part of a majority arrayed against a hitter. Anyone on his side could defeat the batter. It was an accident when the ball was hit to him. He couldn't control the direction of the fly, or the grounder.

He had to wait helplessly for it to happen. What counted with Williams was the man alone, defying all of them in the ballpark, using his skills against nine specific opponents. He was great at that and he gave me the impression the feats on a ball field were valueless to him unless they were accomplished against big odds.

Maybe that's why he demanded trouble. It was as though the other players were wrong when they accepted homage from the buffs or the sportswriters. He seemed to try to reverse the tradition of applause. Abuse became a genuine accolade reserved only for the truly great. He would never touch the peak of his cap in the ball player's old gesture of gratitude when the buffs were screaming his name, stomping in a glad jig which was their tribute to him. Once he was fined for making obscene gestures at the people in the stands. Another time he hit a woman with a bat which he threw in a fit of harmful disgust.

Umpires found him an agreeable man. They were involved with the act of his hitting, and so they were spared his scorn. He seldom criticized pitchers and talked about most of them with respect, bound to them by a glorious animosity. Long ago Williams decided a lot of people were his enemies and used the bat to fend us off. But unless you lied to yourself, you had to praise Ted Williams as a hitter. That's as far as I intend to go.

Ball journalists had to fawn on him to hold his acquaintanceship. He rejected his responsibility of greatness although he was the most generous tipper in baseball with clubhouse help and he is still dedicated to raising funds in the interests of cancerous children.

Such as Joe DiMaggio, and Bob Feller, who were great when he was, were subjected to the same pressures. They declined to use their greatness to intimidate those who refused to be subservient to their whims. But it was right to put him in the Hall of Fame. It is not a tomb to commemorate the charm of ball players, but a monument to their skills.

Strictly Personal

ARTHUR DALEY

1969

On the occasion of Williams' surprise return to baseball in 1969 (as manager of the Washington Senators), a fellow New York columnist paints a portrait that is strikingly different from that of Jimmy Cannon. The only opinion Daley shares with Cannon is that Williams was "the finest hitter of his generation."

T he portrait of Ted Williams as painted by his detractors among the baseball writers pictured him as something of an ogre. They have said he was rude, crude and uncivil. He brushed them off and bawled them out. Since Boston fans never tired reading about Williams, the uncooperative hero often placed the task of chronicling him in depth somewhere between the difficult and the impossible.

But no one ever could get me to put the rap on him. At all times I found him wonderful, a guy who even went out of his way to help me. Maybe I was lucky to strike such a rapport with him. But now that the finest hitter of his generation has returned to baseball as the surprise manager of the Washington Senators, it seems proper enough to offer a strictly personal appraisal of this many-faceted man.

On the first day of spring training in 1954, Ted took a tumble in the outfield grass at Sarasota in Florida and fractured his collarbone. Not until late at night did word of his injury reach St. Pete where I was staying. It was imperative that I talk to Ted because this might be the biggest story of the preseason exercises. But how? I knew he'd go into total hiding and the long trip the next morning—we drove to Sarasota by ferry in those days—could be wasted. I would have to pin him down first with a phone call before breakfast.

• *NO HOPE*

"I'm sorry, sir," said the operator at the Red Sox hotel. "But there is no direct telephone to Mr. Williams's room. All I can do is give him the message that you called. But I'd better warn you that Mr. Williams never returns calls. It might take an hour to get word to him."

Five minutes later my phone rang.

"Hello, Arthur," said a cheerful voice. "This is Ted. How are you?"

Here was a fellow whose career had just been jeopardized by a disabling crackup and he was asking me how I felt! We talked for an hour and he babbled out more information than I could possibly use. Gratefully I canceled my contemplated ferry ride because it no longer was necessary. Me not like Williams? No, siree!

He could be a strange one at times, though, and one incident a few years later amused me vastly. I walked over to the batting cage at Sarasota and leaned against it, watching that exquisite Williams swing. He cut at the ball, looked up, saw me and frowned.

"I thought you're a friend of mine," he said, coiling for another swing.

"I thought so, too," I said. He sent a ball screaming over the fence.

"What's the idea then of that column you wrote about me last winter?" He said. "I see your stuff. You can't get away with anything with me." He cracked a line drive to center, still frowning.

"You big fathead," I said. "You can't even read. I didn't knock you. For the most part that was a highly complimentary column."

"It was?" he said in a small boy's voice, taking a final swing. He walked out of the cage and started to laugh.

"Hello," he said, sticking out his hand. Only Williams would be so unembarrassed as to drop his hello into the middle of a conversation.

For a quarter of a century I'd heard about Ted's phenomenal eyesight, so acute that examining Navy doctors claimed that they came across it only once in 100,000 cases. It was said of him that he could identify a duck on the wing long before most people even can spot the duck. Two years ago this unique eyesight really was brought to my attention in a vivid personal way.

● *WITHOUT BINOCULARS*

For about a half-dozen years the Red Sox had been hiding out in the Arizona desert each spring, but in 1967 they returned to Florida in a new base at Winter Haven. I drove there with Jack Hand and Jerry Izenberg. I parked the car on a plateau behind the left-field fence and we were a couple of hundred yards from the batting cage at the far, far end of the enclosure.

The field spread out before us but we were so far away that we couldn't even make out the numbers on the players' backs. They were half-sized figures, not even Carl Yastrzemski being identifiable. When we drew much closer I finally noticed the big guy at the batting cage was a civilian.

•

Eventually it dawned on me that it was Williams, chatting with Milt Richman, the historian. The greeting was warm and after a while Ted wandered off to hit fungoes.

"Ted has the damndest eyesight ever," said Richman in total awe. "As soon as you stepped out of the car, Ted said, 'There's Arthur Daley. I like him.' Gosh, I could barely see the car. But he recognized the first guy to step out of the car, you."

Other writers may write about Williams how they choose. But my personal experiences with him are such that I can't complain. Why should I?

THE KID COMES BACK

ROBERT LIPSYTE

1969

Like many other honest writers, Robert Lipsyte does not ignore the perplexing contradictions of Ted Williams' personality, nor does he allow them to negate the fullness of the man who endured, and survived, the "media meat-grinder" to emerge as a genuine American hero.

Lipsyte ends his *New York Times* column with one of the classic lines of the Williams "literature."

Ted Williams stands on ripple-soled baseball shoes, turning easily at the hips as he talks, a suggestion of belly overhanging the wide red-leather uniform belt. It is not the paunch of a middle-aged man melting out of shape; it is the hard gut of a man who has had his steaks and even now, at 50, could trim it off, tighten the screws if he had to, come back and pull the wall down with his square, strong fingers. His big arms are crossed over a broad chest that curves up into a long, thick neck. Atop the neck, like a ball on a column, is a small head with a large, hawkish nose and narrow hazel eyes that seem as if they could change color with his mood.

His voice is deep and smooth and there is a snag of

laughter in it now as he describes his first serious mistake as a major league manager. It occurred in Washington in the Senators' third game of the season, against the Yankees. Jim Hannan was pitching with a seven-run lead in the sixth inning.

"He was getting weak, we recognized it, he was pitching high," says Williams, "then he walked the man, we get an out, then a squeak hit, now the bases are loaded. We decided to leave him in. Fernandez is up. Fernandez hasn't gotten a foul all day. Not a foul. Then, voom!" Williams laughs, liking the sound of the word "voom." He repeats it and turns away, leaving the batting cage to tape an interview for television.

• " . . . HARD BLUE GLOW . . . "

In the years after the war, the consistently publicized baseball heroes were five outfielders. The two most recent, Mickey Mantle and Willie Mays, were offered as one-dimensional characters, Mantle dogged by fears of an early death and crippling leg injuries, Mays as a kind of shrewd innocent delighted with his own skill. Stan Musial, the solid, dependable family man, was away from the Eastern media meat-grinder and Joe DiMaggio, an antelope of breathtaking skills, was cruelly ground up, especially in retrospect when he married and was divorced from Marilyn Monroe.

This left Williams, a player who "radiated, from afar, the hard blue glow of high purpose," in John Updike's memorable story of his last game. Williams, the skinny weakling from a broken home in San Diego, came East with a bat and a willingness to channel all his time and energy and intelligence into trying to become the greatest hitter who ever lived. Many people think he was, and yet, ironically, in this game of statistics, he left few batting records behind him.

● *THE STORIES SEEMED POSSIBLE*

Five years a Marine flyer, several times divorced, Williams was always consistent. He had to overpower the Boudreau Shift, not outfox it. When asked by an interviewer, Joan Flynn Dreyspool, if he had ever read Hemingway's "The Old Man and the Sea," he had to say, "I never could 'uv sat in that boat as long as the old man did. First of all, it wouldn't take me that long to catch the fish—if I caught it. Why, I got that 1,235-pound black marlin in 28 minutes."

Before his last game in 1960, he publicly sneered at the Boston sportswriters who had heckled him throughout his career and then he refused to tip his cap as he rounded the bases after the home run in his last time at bat. In his retirement, he fished from the Florida Keys, an arid, corrosive land where men traditionally come to terms with themselves, go mad or rot. He occasionally appeared for Sears, his employer, and in 1966, when he was inducted into the Hall of Fame, he said: "I hope that Satchel Paige and Josh Gibson somehow will be inducted here as symbols of the great Negro players who are not here because they were not given a chance."

The stories about Williams always seemed possible, the towering rages, the secret trips to help handicapped boys, the incredible charm that appealed to men and women. Tuesday, when the Senators played the Yankees here, a man describing a recent television talk-show appearance by Williams said he "acted like a second-rate John Wayne." But it is Wayne, the movie actor, who is the second-rate Ted Williams.

Islamorada, Miramichi, Bangor, and Winter Haven

THOMAS BOSWELL

1982

An avid student of the science of hitting during his playing days, following his retirement Ted Williams applied his accumulated wisdom as a hitting instructor for the Red Sox.

In this stylish profile of Williams at the 1978 spring training camp, Thomas Boswell portrays the "professor emeritus of hitting" as a man who may have mellowed somewhat over the years, but who, at the age of sixty, has lost none of his passion for the two great loves of his life—hitting and fishing. He remains, in Boswell's words, "an American original."

For five years Ted Williams was away from the hunt that he loves best. He had tried to satisfy himself with the fly cast at dawn, the down-turning flick of the wrist and the splash. In winter he lives in the Florida Keys, trolling for bonefish near Islamorada. In summer the spiky air of Canada calls him to Miramichi to pursue the Atlantic salmon, greatest of game fish. And in the fall the woods of Maine are lovely, dark, and deep. What better, for a man without promises to keep than to set out early from Bangor with gun on arm.

But what of spring?

For Williams the month of March was always one thing: Open season on pitchers. The Splendid Splinter—age sixty—leans against the batting cage again. Once more The Kid is a hunter of pitchers, training his favorite pack of hounds: the hitters.

Here in the spring-training camp of the Boston Red Sox, Batting Coach Williams is at home the way few men are anywhere, the way he is in only one other place—in a fishing boat on a lost lake.

These wild animals of Winter Haven fascinate him. Williams, professor emeritus of hitting, presses his face against the mesh of the batting cage as these brutish critters pass in revue before him. The lynxish Yaz, the ponderous Boomer, the bristling Rice, the fierce Fisk, the wild and untamed Hobson: each is a separate specie of homo homerus (home-run man).

Ostensibly, Williams has been hired "to help the rookies and minor league kids any damn way I can." But Williams has not had this sort of marble to chisel in half a lifetime, not since the late forties and early fifties when Williams, Pesky, Doerr, Stephens, and Co. produced 1,027 runs in one year.

As soon as a Bosox regular becomes restless and discontent, Williams approaches, delighted to take the thorn from a swing.

"Come on, Fisk, you idiot," stormed Carlton Fisk, lashing in the cage.

"In the spring you always feel betwixt and between," commiserated Williams. "The darn pitchers are ahead of us.

"Your hands aren't cocked in close enough. They're too high and far away," said Williams, grabbing Fisk and wrestling him into the proper position. "How can you feel quick and explosive if you're not compact? Am I right? Am I right?"

"I missed baseball," said Williams, who had been out of the sport since managing the Washington Senators in 1969–71 and Texas in 1972. "This is the uniform I should never have taken off," Williams added, meaning the Boston red, white, and blue. "You're always a fan of this game after you've played it. You enjoy being around it, listening to the young guys in the clubhouse. This is my chance to be up close to the game for a few weeks. I'll leave when the rookies are shipped out. But it's enough to give me an interest in the game again."

The Red Sox players are glad to have him as up close as he wants to get. Home-run king Jim Rice has carried The Book (Williams' *My Turn at Bat*) with him everywhere since he broke into the league. Dwight ("Dewey") Evans calls Williams "a genius and a great guy."

When Williams played a challenge tennis match against Carl Yastrzemski, 240-pound George ("Boomer") Scott volunteered to be a ball boy.

"Ted's never been this sweet-tempered for this long at a stretch in his life," joked one front-office man.

"He's mellowed a lot," said Coach Johnny Pesky, a longtime friend. "But his enthusiasm for the game hasn't. He brings that sharp mind to everything. It isn't just the rookies who are in awe of him. A lot of us have always been."

Williams is just as prone to feats of skill as ever. "Hear that airplane engine?" Williams will say. "Bet I can spot it before you do." And, of course, he does.

Many a bet was made on how long Williams could resist getting into the batting cage himself. That didn't last long. "I waited for a warm day with nobody around, then took a hundred swings," said Williams.

"I'd have paid to see it," lamented Evans. Only a few did.

"He wore that indoor pitching machine out," marveled

rookie Chuck Rainey. "Nothing but line drives. Nice easy swing.

"Somebody switched the machine to curves. He took one, then said, 'Oh, breaking balls, huh,' and he lined them all over the place. It's like riding a bicycle to him. He'll never forget."

Two stupid questions follow Williams everywhere—one joking, one serious. Will he make a comeback as DH? Will he manage again?

Such constant petty prodding has driven Williams back to his fishing boat before. But he tolerates fools more generously than he once did.

"No comebacks," he said. "I wouldn't want to tamper with the mystique of my last at bat [when he homered]."

Once, Williams might have snapped, "What the hell's a mystique?"

Manager Don Zimmer, who calls himself, "just a .235 hitter with a metal plate in his head," can be thankful that Williams has finally convinced all comers that he is not after Zimmer's job.

"I have absolutely no interest in managing anywhere again," said Williams. "I'll come back as the season goes along to see a hitter who's struggling. But I won't do it too often. I want my summers the way they are."

Williams silently snaps his wrist in the imaginary two-part motion of a perfect fly cast. Miramichi is waiting. "A thousand salmon in one summer," he said. "That's my goal."

Williams still has his old sore spot—vanity.

Comparisons with Rod Carew, who once hit .388, annoy Williams. He will not point out, but his old friends are anxious to, that when Williams hit .388 at age thirty-eight his slugging percentage was 200 points higher than Carew's was in '78, and his on-base percentage 100 points higher.

"Ted doesn't think a comparison between a man who

has less than 100 career homers [Carew] and one who had 521 is any comparison at all," said a Williams friend of twenty years.

Williams' other no-touch area is his separation from his third wife and their two children who live in Vermont, while Williams remains in Islamorada.

"There isn't anybody in the game today who's near Number Nine," said Pesky. "Willie Mays was the last one who had that kind of presence."

Williams is an American original—independent, still fiercely private, a paradoxical conservative renegade. He leaves the Winter Haven clubhouse in garb that would draw stares if he were selling bait on a pier. His toes-up tennis shoes are worthy of comedian Prof. Irwin Cory. His baggy khaki pants are too short and his old baggy sweater too long. In other words, he looks great.

Scott, in his huge rings and necklace of "second basemen's teeth" is demonstrating his stance to the great man and insisting, "I'm one of the greatest hitters who ever lived."

"Well," grinned the amused Williams, "you'd be a hell of a lot greater if you'd open up your front foot so you can clear your hips and get that big rear of yours into the ball."

Scott, who challenges anyone who mentions his weight to a point-blank duel with Louisville sluggers, dropped his jaw and said, "Show me what you mean, man."

Williams and Scott start the eternal wrestling match, Williams not only talking theory but trying to transmit the subjective feel of a proper swing by twisting and shoving and adjusting Scott's body.

"Am I right? Am I right?" badgered the grinning, excited Williams.

"Right on, Number Nine," said the Boomer.

The Necessary Shape
of the Old-Timers' Game
and *Couplet*

DONALD HALL

1985

As a player in a 1982 old-timers' game, Ted Williams becomes an object of reminiscence in this touching essay and accompanying poem. We see him as Hall does, from a distance, both in space (from a center-field bleacher seat) and in time.

Memory and nostalgia are essential elements of baseball's powerful hold on the imagination. An old-timers' game reminds us of the continuity of baseball, both in our history as a nation and in our individual lives. Donald Hall evokes the memory of Ted Williams as he once was, as well as remind us of the persistent survival of the child in both player and spectator.

Hall's melancholy poem, which recounts Williams' shoestring catch of a fly ball in the old-timers' game, concludes with an apt allusion to Achilles, the sulking but almost invulnerable warrior.

● *THE NECESSARY SHAPE OF THE OLD TIMERS' GAME*

For some of us, events like the Cracker Jack Old-Timers' Baseball Classic are obligatory, ineluctable, and essential. They complete the great game of baseball, extending the diamond's spectrum into vibrations of the ultimate shade.

Maybe some of us are crazy. We prefer an old-timers'

game to game one of an ordinary World Series (though probably not to game six, 1975, Boston Red Sox and Cincinatti Reds). Certainly we prefer it to the ordinary All Star game, that annual convention of the mere masters of the moment, when superb athletes at the peak of their form take a day away from pennant races, do a little extra BP, show off a little, and send us yawning to bed.

For some of us, an event in which Luke Appling takes Warren Spahn deep—in *1982*—takes precedence over mere excellence. We applaud the magic of restitution. Bar wrinkles, bar waistlines, bar gimp, bar gray hair and bald head: by a ludic spell we no longer inhabit the 1980s; we wipe mist from the mirror and it is thirty, it is forty years ago. . . . Better still, our magic mixes eras, and there are impossible juxtapositions—as if we introduced Don Quixote to Huckleberry Finn: In Cincinnati a few years back, I watched Willie Mays raise a can of corn to Dixie Walker.

In 1982, the Boston Red Sox, who rarely undertake such things, constructed themselves an old-timers' game. I live a mere two hours north of Fenway Park, in New Hampshire, and wound up with seats under the scoreboard in the center-field bleachers. At Fenway Park such a position is no disadvantage: at least by contrast with symmetrical football stadia like Pittsburgh and Cincinnati, where box seats extend two hours north of home plate.

Most of the ball players, that afternoon, looked fit and fine. Maybe Jackie Jensen was a *little* thicker around the middle, but he moved like the old halfback he was. Earl Wilson had a *little* trouble getting the ball up to the plate, but Jim Lonborg didn't. There was Mel Parnell, there was Frank Malzone, Bobby Doerr, Tommy Harper, Walt Dropo, Rick Ferrell (eldest at seventy-seven), Dick Radatz, Jimmy Piersall, Billy Goodman, Rico Petrocelli . . .

Most of all, there was Ted Williams. It was mostly the

return of number 9 that filled Fenway Park that day. Forty years ago I discussed Ted Williams with my New Hampshire farmer grandfather (who remembered Babe Ruth pitching for the Sox) while he and I hayed together, hot afternoons of World War II. Even then, we remembered past greatness—.406 in 1941—and we daydreamed about his triumphant return.

In 1982, old number 9 had aged a bit—stiff, portly, gray—yet he retained in his age that languid arrogant athlete's grace which I recalled: the Splendid Splinter, the Kid, Teddy Baseball, who retired in 1960 and hit a home run for his last at-bat. In 1982, at the old-timers' game, he hit his best in BP, a ball that bounced into the right-field stands. During the three-inning workout, he flied to right off Lonborg in the first, then struck out on a high pitch, 3-2, in the third.

The old fellow knew that we wanted him to lose one into the grandstand; trying to oblige us, he struck out swinging mightily rather than take a walk. It was satisfying to see him swing again, even if he missed. The Williams swing was slower but its shape remained intact: a great flat circle looping around itself, coiling the body up in its follow-through.

An old-timers' game is not only magical restitution but also essential shape.

The game of baseball starts in the first light of dawn, as small children swing bats in schoolyards and vacant lots. (These days I spend happy baseball days umpiring grammar school softball games, boys and girls together, on the playing field outside the Danbury, New Hampshire, Primary School; these contests are contentious, polite, and nobody wins by more than ten runs.) Later comes Little League, later junior high . . . By late morning, in high school, the true athletes begin to detach themselves in the bright light.

For some there is then college, for some rookie league and class A, and for a very few the high noon of the major leagues.

For symmetry and shape we require the crepuscular evening baseball of the old-timers' game, where the children of fifty years ago, and the bright heroic twenty-eight-year-olds of our maturity, gather to celebrate in shadow the rituals of noon.

Only a week after playing with the boys of twilight, at Fenway Park in 1982, the stylish body of Jackie Jensen collapsed in death, a sudden heart attack. That afternoon we had watched him thrive . . .

And in the first inning, we watched as a batter lifted a fly toward Ted Williams in left field, a loping, curving ball, easy to catch but that would drop in front of him if he did not hasten. Slow to start, he stumbled-ran forward; at the last moment, he extended his right hand down toward his ankle and snapped the ball from the air. It was a catch no one would have noticed forty years before, but now it summoned all of us out of our seats, applauding, and weeping as we applauded.

Of course, on the field, in twilight as at noon, the requisite manner was not weeping but teasing. It was Curt Gowdy who said it: "Good field no hit."

• *COUPLET*

Old-Timers' Day,
Fenway Park, 1 May 1982

When the tall puffy
figure wearing number
nine starts
late for the fly ball,
laboring forward
like a lame truckhorse
startled by a gartersnake,
—this old fellow
whose body we remember
as sleek and nervous
as a filly's—

and barely catches it
in his glove's
tip, we rise
and applaud weeping:
On a green field
we observe the ruin
of even the bravest
body, as Odysseus
wept to glimpse
among shades the shadow
of Achilles.

Williams: The Slugging Professor

IRA BERKOW

1985

Several writers, including Arthur Daley, have called Williams the finest natural hitter since Shoeless Joe Jackson. The title of Ira Berkow's *New York Times* column, together with the honorary degree of "professor emeritus of hitting" bestowed by Thomas Boswell in a preceding article, underscore an essential point about Ted Williams: whatever natural talent he had was augmented by his systematic and intense study of every aspect of hitting.

Always eager to share as well as acquire knowledge about hitting—as many players, including those from opposing teams, have attested over the years—Williams published his theories in *The Science of Hitting*, which Berkow calls "the authoritative text" on the subject. Berkow's column makes it clear that at age sixty-seven Williams retains the primary attribute of a good teacher—passion for his subject matter. The "professor" remains an outspoken and enthusiastic teacher—and an historian—of the craft of hitting a baseball.

Winter Haven, Fla., March 22—In his open-air classroom here among the swaying palms and noisy bats, Professor Theodore Samuel Williams was expounding on the virtues of getting your belly button out in front of the ball.

"It's that little magic move at the plate," he was saying recently, beside the batting cage on a field behind Chain

O'Lakes Stadium. He wore a Red Sox uniform and a blue windbreaker with little red stockings embossed at the heart and stood on ripple-soled baseball shoes. It was late morning, cool but sunny as he spoke to a couple of young players. "Hips ahead of hands," he said in a deep, ardent baritone, "hips ahead of hands."

And the one-time Splendid Splinter—he is a Splinter no longer—demonstrated with an imaginary bat and an exaggerated thrust of his abdomen. "We're talking about optimum performance, and the optimum is to hit the ball into your pull field with authority. And getting your body into the ball before it reaches the plate—so you're not swinging with all arms—that's the classic swing. But a lot of batters just can't learn it, or won't."

Dr. Williams—and if he isn't a bona fide Ph.D. in slugging, who is?—is author of the authoritative textbook *The Science of Hitting*. He also is the last professor or hitter or anyone else to bat .400 in the major leagues (he hit .406 in 1941) and had a scholarly career average of .344. This spring, he is serving the Red Sox as batting instructor with minor league players.

Ted Williams on hitting is Lindbergh on flying, Picasso on painting and Little Richard on Tutti Frutti.

Professor Williams is now 67 years old and drives around the Red Sox complex in a golf cart, stopping now at this field, now at that. And though he says he's "running out of gas," it hardly seems so to the casual visitor, and there are many who come just to see him in the leathery flesh. He arrives before 9 A.M. at the training site and spends a long, full day under the Florida sun observing the young players.

He knows that there are as many theories on hitting as there are stars in the sky. "Like I've heard somewhere they tell a batter to keep his head *down*," he said. "No way you can open your body and carry through with your head down that way." He says that he may not be right for all the players, but he urges them to "listen—you can always throw away what you don't want, and keep what works for you."

And, like the good teacher, he *listens*, too. An image returns of him in the clubhouse, sitting on a storage trunk and nodding in understanding while a minor-leaguer quietly talks to him.

In the batting cage now was the third baseman Steve Lyons, a 6-foot-3-inch, 190-pound, left-handed batter who bears a physical resemblance to the young Ted Williams. Lyons, after four seasons in the minor leagues, has a chance to make the parent club.

Williams watched him swing. "He's improvin' good," said Williams, "improvin' good. Has good power and good contact."

Last season, Lyons's batting average jumped to .268 in Triple A ball, 22 points higher than the previous year in Double A. He credits some of that improvement to Williams.

"He's not quick to criticize or change you immediately," Lyons said. "He watches, and then when he talks, people listen. He tries to be positive in his approach. He'll say, 'You've got a good swing, but there's not enough action into the ball. Cock your bat back farther.' "

When Williams was young, he sought advice. Before his rookie year with the Red Sox in 1939, he met Rogers Hornsby and asked, "What do I have to do to be a good hitter?" Hornsby said, "Get a good ball to hit."

"That's not as easy as it sounds," said Williams. "If the pitcher throws a good pitch, low and outside or high and inside—in the strike zone but not in the batter's groove—you let it go with less than two strikes. With two strikes, you move up a little bit on the knob of the bat. But too many hitters aren't hitters from the head up, and never become as good as they can be."

Sometimes the best advice is no advice at all. "When I

was comin' up," said Williams, "Lefty O'Doul said to me, 'Don't let anybody change you.' And when I saw Carl Yastrzemski, I thought pretty much the same thing. He had a big swing, and I thought he should cut down his swing just a little. But I never came right out and said it. I'd say, 'Gotta be quicker, a little quicker.' And I think it took him longer than it should've to get his average up. Look at his record. He batted under three hundred his first two years in the big leagues. Then he hit .321. Same guy, same swing, same everything. But he got a little quicker, got a little quicker."

It was Paul Waner who told Williams about getting the belly button out in front of the ball. "And I saw the best hitters doing it. Cronin did it, and Greenberg did it, and York and DiMaggio," he said. Of current-day players, Pete Rose and Rod Carew hit that way. "Reggie Jackson doesn't but he's so strong that he can get away with that arm action. Now, Al Oliver isn't the classic hitter—a swishy, inside-out hitter—but he's gonna get 3,000 hits because he makes such good contact.

"Guys like Mantle and Mays—great, classic hitters—could have been even better if they had thought more at the plate. They struck out too much—and they'll tell you that, too. You got to concede a little to the pitcher, even the greatest hitters have to. Look at DiMaggio, he struck out only a half or a third as many times as he walked. It meant he was looking for his pitch—he was in control, not the pitcher."

Williams no longer teaches by example, and said that the last time he stood in the batter's box was in last year's old-timers' game in Fenway Park.

"I hit two little ground balls to the pitcher, he said. "I was so anxious up there, I couldn't *wait* for the ball, and hit them at the end of the bat."

Was he embarrassed? "Was I?" said the professor. "I didn't want to run to first base."

Ted Williams

JOHN UPDIKE

1986

Twenty-six years after the appearance of his essay on Ted Williams' final game, John Updike contributed this profile to a special fortieth anniversary issue of *Sport* dedicated to "The 40 Who Changed Sports."

He appears in television commercials now, but seems sheepish saying the lines, a leathery-faced old gent whose eyes look a bit menacing even as they strive to twinkle. For a long time, as Joe DiMaggio urbanely peddled coffee machines on the little round-cornered screen, Ted Williams was conspicuous for his absence from the public eye, save when he peeped out of the dugout while managing the overlookable Senators/Rangers of 1969–72. When he appeared in an old-timers' game at Fenway Park in 1984, he made a valiant shoestring catch but could hardly get his bat on the ball, though he was given an extra, out-of-turn "ups." His recent interviews are eerily good natured, as he blesses the newest version of the Red Sox or the newest unsuccessful attempt—by Rod Carew, George Brett, Wade Boggs—to supplant him as the last .400 hitter.

It is now 45 years, five years longer than the life of *Sport* magazine, since the cocky, lanky kid from San Diego closed out the season with an average of .406. That statistic has emerged from the shadows of 1941 (when Jolting Joe hit in 56 straight games and the Japanese attacked Pearl Harbor) to become Williams' most famous feat, the tarnish-proof polish on the silver of his reputation; but it really is the 15 postwar years of his career, harassed though they were by injuries, sportswriters, boos, disappointments on the field and marital misadventures off it, the Korean War and the Williams Shift, that established him as a steady wonder, the best hitter of his era and a kind of link between the highly technological players of today and the rough-hewn statistical giants (Cobb and Hornsby, Sisler and Ruth, Napoleon Lajoie and Shoeless Joe Jackson) of a virtually mythological time whose living witnesses are increasingly few.

By 1986 more than a generation of baseball fans and players has grown up who never saw Williams play—never saw him *hit,* one should say, for though he was a dutiful outfielder with a strong arm when young, and a baserunner who went through the motions and stole as much as four bases a season, he always looked as if his heart was at the plate, which it was. Hitting was his thing, and even when the Red Sox, in the late Forties, had stars at almost every position, the crowd waited through the lineup to see Ted's turn at bat. A tall man with broad shoulders, he towered over the plate, and seemed greedy while there, wringing the bat handle with his fists, switchily moving it back and forth as if showing the pitcher exactly where he wanted the poor ball placed. He had a wide stance with nothing contorted about it, no peekaboo around his shoulder like Stan Musial, no funny work with his feet like so many of today's overcoached fusspots.

His swing was long, much longer than Ruth's (how *did* Ruth hit all those home runs out of that chop?) and beautiful

the way Sam Snead's swing is beautiful, all body parts working together and the ball just an incident in the course of
the arc. *Pop the hips* was his theory, just like a golf pro's,
though the golf ball isn't coming at you at 90 miles an hour
with English on it, out of a mess of billboards. He didn't
seem to swing up, the way some power hitters do, and the
first Williams homer I remember, seen from the stands of
old Shibe Park in Philadelphia, was a line drive that was
still rising as it cleared the rightfield fence. There was something very pure about the way he hit, and though his power
totals and his averages are not the best, nobody ranks so
high in both departments of hitting. To put it another way,
nobody else with over 500 homers (521) has so high an
average (.344). He was the strongest good hitter, or the
finest-tuned slugger, the game has seen and, though temperamental and injury-prone, showed an impressive durability; he won his fifth batting championship in 1957 by
hitting .388, and won his sixth the next year at the age of
40.

He came from California to a dowdy New England me-
tropolis with too many newspapers, and was instant news.
He was, like Ty Cobb, an angry man, hungry for greatness;
but unlike Cobb he had a sweet smile. The smile can be
seen on the old prewar photos, and in televised interviews
now, as the philosophical fisherman from Islamorada fields
an especially tricky question. In all my years of Williams-
watching (listening, usually, to the voice of Curt Gowdy), I
don't recall him contesting an umpire's call, or having words
with a pitcher who had dusted him off. In his enthusiasm
for the fine points of the game, he would swap expertise
with members of the opposite team as well as his own. He
was felt, by some Boston columnists at least, to be insuffi-
ciently competitive, except where his own records were
concerned. He was also hot tempered, rabbit-eared, con-

temptuous of sportswriters and too proud to tip his hat after hitting a home run.

Boston wanted to love The Kid, but he was prickly in its embrace. And the teams he ornamented didn't win all the marbles; the spectacular Sox of 1946 lost the World Series and after that, pennants just slipped away while Williams sulked, spat, threw bats and threatened retirement. In the end, the city loved him all the more because the relationship had proved so complex; "some obstacle," as Freud wrote, "is necessary to swell the tide of libido to its height." No sports figure—not Bobby Orr or Larry Bird or Rocky Marciano—had a greater hold over the fans of New England than Williams. From the generous team-owner Tom Yawkey he received top dollar—what now seems a paltry $125,000 a season—but he was one of the few ballplayers who all by himself brought people to the park. In 1957 the third-place Red Sox drew 1,181,087 and the sportswriter Harold Kaese wrote, "The Red Sox drew 181,087 and Ted Williams drew the other million."

He had talent: a big man with great eyes. He had intensity, and nobody practiced longer or thought harder about the niceties of the little war between pitchers and hitters. But he also had a poignancy, a flair for the dramatic, a magic potential that allows a solitary figure in white knickers to dominate a tiered array of tens of thousands. His career abounds with thunder that remained etched on the air: the last-day six-for-eight that lifted his average in 1941 up from .3995; the home run that same year that won the All-Star Game in Detroit; the home run he hit in 1946 off of a Rip Sewell blooper pitch; the home run with which he went off to Korea (he flew 39 missions, crash-landed a bullet-riddled plane and hit .407 in the two baseball months after he returned) and the one that concluded his career. But behind that thunder stood a multitude of hot days and wearisome nights, games that didn't mean much beyond the moment, to which Williams brought his electric, elegant best. We loved him because he generated excitement; he got us out of our own lives and showed us, in the way he stood up at the plate, what the game was all about.

An Evening with The Kid

IRA BERKOW

1988

Almost fifty years after Williams' rookie season, Ira Berkow observes The Kid as a senior citizen at a Boston fund-raiser for the benefit of the Jimmy Fund campaign against childhood cancer. The brash rookie, the one-time problem child of baseball, has become an elder statesman of baseball, honored by 4,200 guests, including fellow Hall-of-Famers Joe DiMaggio and Bob Feller, writer Stephen King, and Senator John Glenn.

Berkow notes that even as a senior citizen Williams retains "the dream of striving to be the best"; he is still "The Kid."

He was once called The Kid. He also had other nicknames: The Splendid Splinter. The Thumper, Teddy Ballgame. None of them quite apply anymore for Ted Williams, who recently turned 70 years old, except The Kid.

No longer is he a splinter, splendid or otherwise, and he thumps no baseballs as in days of yore, nor plays any ball games, and hasn't for nearly 30 years.

But there is still the en-*thoos*-iasm, as he says the word, the stubbornness, perhaps, the dream of striving to be the best and striving for the best that marked him as a boy, surely, and as a young man, certainly, and as a senior citizen, absolutely.

On Thursday night in the Wang Center here, Theodore Samuel Williams, the last of the .400 hitters, The Kid, returned for kids. It was a benefit in his honor, "An Evening with 9, and Friends," for the Jimmy Fund, a fund-raising arm of the Dana-Farber Cancer Institute, with a special interest in children's cancer.

For 40 years Williams, who, no Red Sox fan need be told, wore the red No. 9 of their team, has been closely associated with the Jimmy Fund. He has visited ailing children, usually without photographers, attended affairs for the fund, and always lent his name to the cause. Never, though, until now, would he consent to be honored at a fund-raiser.

"It took an awful, awful, awful, *awful* lot to get me here," he said before the evening's program. "I just thought there were millions and *millions* of people who've done a lot more for this than I have."

Friends finally prevailed, and Williams arrived even wearing a tie; he rarely submits to such a silly social convention. It was a black string tie held at the neck by a silver oval clasp with an embossed gold salmon, for, as the world knows, Williams is as avid about catching a fish as he was about clubbing a baseball.

For the evening with Williams, 4,200 people filled the ornate old theater and paid a total of $250,000 that went to the Jimmy Fund.

The friends of Williams, introduced one by one and "interviewed" by David Hartman on a stage set like a fishing cabin, included former teammates like Dom DiMaggio and Bobby Doerr, rivals like Joe DiMaggio and Bob Feller; Tommy Lasorda and Reggie Jackson; John Glenn, who was Williams' squadron commander as a fighter pilot in the war in Korea; Tip O'Neill, the former Speaker of the House from Boston; Bud Leavitt, a Maine sportswriter and longtime fishing pal of Williams; and Stephen King, the writer and a New Englander, who represented baseball fandom and Williams fandom.

King spoke of our greatest baseball heroes as having "a resonance that others don't have," such as rock stars or movie stars. Their careers become the stuff of legends. And Williams perhaps resonated more than most not only because of his extraordinary baseball prowess, but because of his dedication and his humanity, even his vulnerability: he might be quick to anger, would hold a grudge, he stubbornly refused to hit to left when teams packed the right side of the field in the notorious "Williams shift."

And there was in Williams that core of boyish delight in playing the game. When he first came up to the Red Sox in the spring of 1939, he informed the veterans with callow forthrightness about left field: "Hey, this job is mine!"

He cared so much about doing so well. Doerr recalled that Williams, the perfectionist, once stepped out of the batter's box and waited for a cloud to go by because the shadow it created was distracting to him.

A film clip at one point showed Williams hitting a homer and nearly galloping with glee around the bases. The audience laughed with appreciation.

Lasorda came out and said: "He was electrifying with a bat in his hands, like a beautiful painting. Enough about Joe DiMaggio." More laughs.

But both Williams and DiMaggio were electrifying at the plate.

"Dom, who was the best hitter you ever saw?" asked Hartman, of the bespectacled DiMaggio known as The Little Professor.

The audience hushed. "Well," said Dom DiMaggio, "the best *right*-handed hitter"—the audience roared at the unexpected but perfect cop-out—"was Joe. But the best left-handed hitter by far was Ted Williams."

Feller recalled how he could never get his famous fast-ball by Williams. Joe DiMaggio, his hair now all white, spoke of his admiration for "the best hitter I ever saw." And Reggie Jackson told of the encouragement Williams gave him as a rookie: "Never let anybody change your swing." Jackson called him "a real nice American natural resource."

Williams' son, John Henry, a young man, brought out a 5-year-old boy named Joey Raymundo, who was wearing a tuxedo. Joey has leukemia and is being treated at the clinic. He presented Williams with a gift from the fund, an oil painting—the frame was as big as the boy—of Williams in baseball action.

Then Williams sat down and pulled out some notes—along with a pair of glasses. "Not a lot of people have seen these," said the man who was known for having remarkable eyesight.

He spoke of how lucky his life had been, and, to a question from Hartman, said, "You're not gonna make this old guy cry."

Finally, Williams looked around at his friends seated nearby on the stage and out to the audience.

"This has been an honor," he said, "and I'm thrilled and a little embarrassed." He paused. "And I wanna thank you."

And despite his resistance, there was a slight catch in his throat and, it seemed, a little moisture in The Kid's eye.

Source List

"Williams Case Grand Lesson," Bill Cunningham. Boston *Post,* August 10, 1939.

"As a Soph," Joe Williams. *New York World–Telegram,* March 16, 1940.

"Ted Williams Blasts Boston," Austen Lake. Boston *Evening American,* August 13, 1940.

"Theodore Goes Mild," M. J. Brandt. *Baseball Magazine,* November 1940.

"Theodore the .400 Thumper," Jack Malaney. *Baseball Magazine,* December 1941.

"Williams' Head Start," Bill Bryson. *Baseball Magazine,* February 1942.

"The 'Why' of Ted Williams," Bob Considine. *Baseball Digest,* November 1946.

"Open Letter to Ted Williams," Grantland Rice. *Sport,* February 1947.

"Two Guys Named Ted Williams," Ed Fitzgerald. *Sport,* April 1948.

"Why We Pick on Ted Williams," Harold Kaese. *Sport,* May 1949.

"Why I Would Trade Ted Williams," Joe Williams. *Sport,* February 1951.

"Ted Undeserving of Fans' Tribute," Dave Egan. Boston *Daily Record,* April 30, 1952.

"Return of the Master," Arthur Daley. *New York Times,* May 13, 1955.

"Handsome Bad Boy of the Boston Red Sox," Al Hirshberg. *Cosmopolitan,* July 1956.

"Ted Is Hope," Robert Creamer. *Sports Illustrated,* March 12, 1956.

"Ted Williams Spits," Red Smith. *New York Herald Tribune,* August 1956.

"Sidetracked Again," Arthur Daley. *New York Times,* November 25, 1957.

"The Ted Williams Miracle," Ed Linn. *Sport,* January 1958.

"How Ted Williams Became Popular," Mike Gillooly. *Sport,* June 1958.

"Hub Fans Bid Kid Adieu," John Updike. *The New Yorker,* October 22, 1960.

"The Kid's Last Game," Ed Linn. *Sport,* February 1961.

" 'Saint' Goes Marching In," Bud Collins. Boston *Globe,* January 21, 1966.

"The Batter," Jimmy Cannon. *New York Journal-American,* January 23, 1966.

"Strictly Personal," Arthur Daley. *New York Times,* February 25, 1969.

"The Kid Comes Back," Robert Lipsyte. *New York Times,* April 17, 1969.

"Islamorada, Miramichi, Bangor, and Winter Haven," Thomas Boswell. *How Life Imitates the World Series,* Doubleday, 1982. A slightly different version appeared as "Williams Returns to the Bats of March," *The Washington Post,* March 21, 1978.

"The Necessary Shape of the Old-Timers' Game," Donald

Hall. *Fathers Playing Catch with Sons,* North Point Press, 1985.

"Couplet," Donald Hall. *Fathers Playing Catch with Sons,* North Point Press, 1985.

"Williams: The Slugging Professor," Ira Berkow. *New York Times,* March 23, 1985.

"Ted Williams," John Updike. *Sport,* December 1986.

"An Evening with The Kid," Ira Berkow. *New York Times,* November 12, 1988.

Permissions

•

About the Editor

Lawrence Baldassaro is Associate Professor of Italian at the University of Wisconsin–Milwaukee. A native of Massachusetts, he is a lifelong Red Sox fan who has written for numerous baseball publications.